Billingshurst's Heritage No. 2
An Historical Miscellany of a West Sussex Village

Compiled by
Geoffrey Lawes

Peacock Press

Rowner Lock restored on the Wey & Arun Canal

Shop and Wealden House, the Causeway, corner of East Street

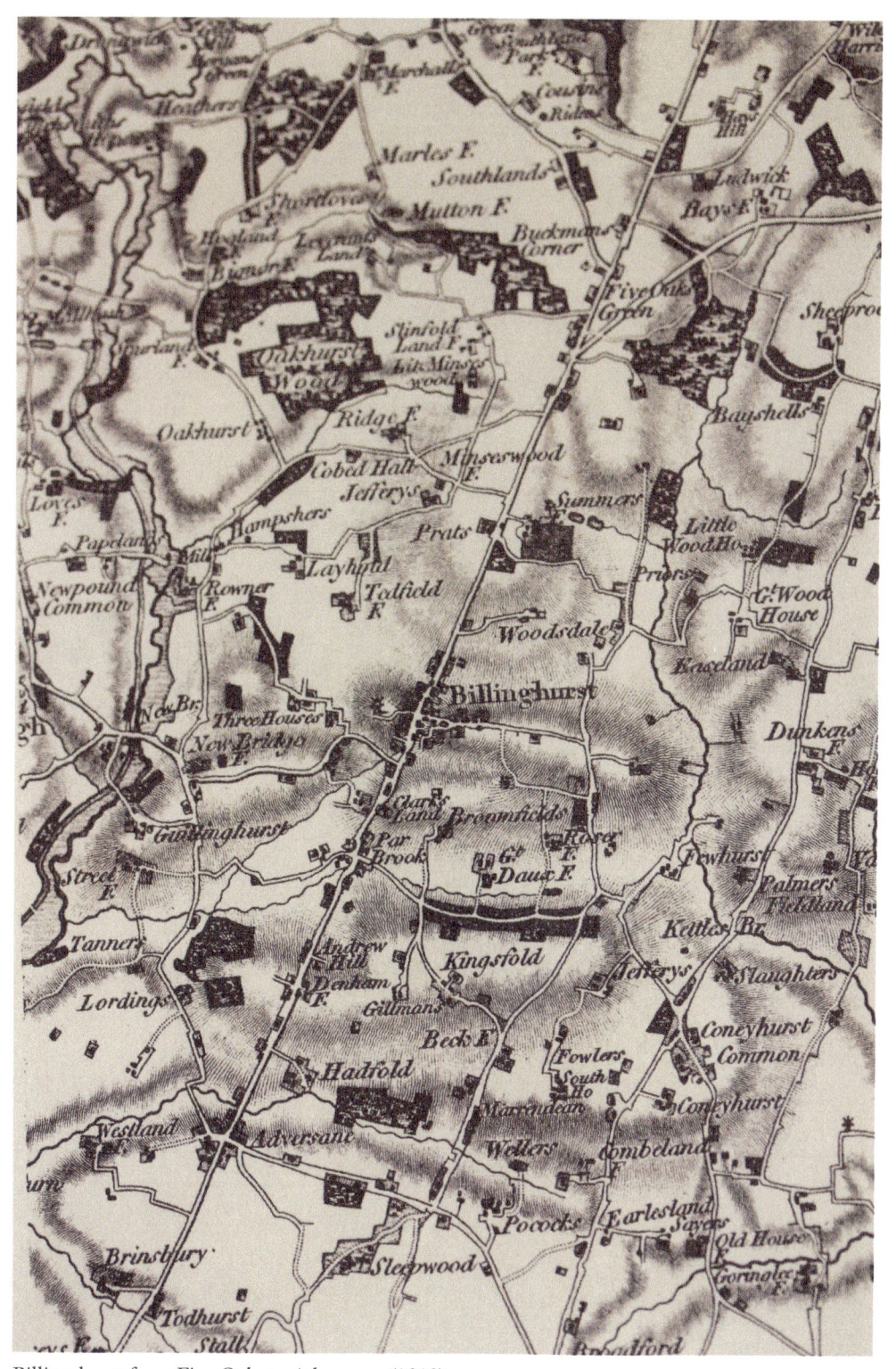

Billingshurst from Five Oaks to Adversane (1819)

Aerial view of Billingshurst 2008

Billingshurst's Heritage No. 2

An Historical Miscellany of a West Sussex Village

**Compiled by
Geoffrey Lawes**

The entry to Jengers Mead

*"God gives all men all earth to love,
But since one's heart is small,
Ordains for each one spot shall prove,
Beloved over all.
Each to his choice, and I rejoice
The lot has fallen to me
In a fair ground –in a fair ground-
Yea, Sussex by the sea!"*
[Rudyard Kipling]

"The lot is fallen unto me in a fair ground: yea, I have a goodly heritage".
[Prayer book, 1662]

Billingshurst's Heritage No. 2
© 2013 Geoffrey Lawes

All rights reserved. No part of this publication may be reproduced, stored in a retrieval system, transmitted in any form or by any means electronic, mechanical, including photocopying, recording or otherwise without prior consent of the copyright holders.

ISBN 978-1-908904-50-8

Published by Peacock Press, 2013
Scout Bottom Farm
Mytholmroyd
Hebden Bridge
HX7 5JS (UK)

Design and artwork
D&P Design and Print
Worcestershire

Printed by Lightning Source, UK

Contents

Village Civics 1
    Inflation and Money Values 1
Local Democracy and Politics 2
    The Parish Council 3
    Statistics 3
    Billingshurst Parish Council 3
    Other Village Bodies 4
    Horsham District Council 4
    West Sussex County Council 5
    Party Politics 6
    Jubilee Fields 7
    Other Facilities 8
    The Utilities 10
    The Western By-pass 11
Natural History 13
The Billingshurst Society 16
Gardening and Horticulture 19
The Billingshurst Horticultural Society 20
Beekeeping in Billingshurst 23
Building Developments in the 70s 24
Kingsfold and Marringdean Road 26
    Early Records of Kingsfold 26
    The Commonwealth and Restoration period 28
    Victorian Times 31
    The Early 20th Century 31
    Ribbon Development 32
    Farm Workers' Income 33
    The Later 20th Century and WW II 34
    Farming and Business 35
    Recent Ownership 37
    Other Older Buildings 37
    Inventories 40
    Later History 43
    Mr Taylor's Account 45
Mr Chitty's deeds – Medieval Farms 48
Ancient Buildings in Billingshurst 49
The Unitarian Chapel 53

Pear Tree Farm and Frank Patterson	54
Notable People with Billingshurst Connections	57
William Cobbett 1763-1835), Billingshurst Visitor	60
The Wey & Arun Canal	62
George Wyndham	64
The Working Years and Decline	64
Restoration	65
Canal Tourist 1869 – a neo Pickwickian Idyll	66
Rowner Watermill	68
The Tedfold Estate and Streele Farm	70
The Railway Network	75
Billingshurst Station	77
Gatwick Airport	78
Station Road Maltings and Whirlwind Limited	79
Printing in Billingshurst	80
Village Memories	81
Things that have changed in Billingshurst that I can remember by	81
Mrs Ireland	81
Ruth Kelleher's Billingshurst Jottings	82
Memories of Mrs ME Marten	83
Memories of Billingshurst – Tom Topper	84
Peter Stockwood Remembers	89
Items of interest	91
Murders in Billingshurst	102
Billingshurst's Institutions	103
The Angling Society	103
The Billingshurst Dramatic Society	105
The Bowling Club	107
The Cricket Club	109
Association Football	114
The Tennis Club	118
The Choral Society	123
Bellringing	125
The Lions charity bookshop	128
The Women's Institute	128
Leisure Centre	130
BBC Situation Comedy – Ever-Decreasing Circles	132

Retail Businesses in Billingshurst **133**
    The Gastronomic Revolution 133
Parbrook **135**
    Cottage Life 137
    Farm work 139
Parish yarns **140**
    Village Humour and other stories 140
    Billy Hoad goes courting in the rain at Billingshurst 1894 140
    Scandalous Behaviour 141
    The Haunting of the King's Arms 141
    Empire Day 141
    Guy Fawkes Night 142
    The Bonfire Hymn 143
The Weald School – a History **144**
    In the Beginning 144
    Early Ideals of the Secondary Modern 145
    Going Comprehensive 147
    A Change of Headteacher 148
    Community Schooling 149
    Economic strictures and troubled times 149
    A new Head, new Initiatives 151
    A Hiccup in Progress 153
    21st Century Schooling 154
    Weald School Alumni 159
Oliver Reed and Josephine Burge **160**
Billingshurst Primary School **161**
The Hamlets - Five Oaks **162**
    The Norman Manors 162
    Origins 163
    17th Century Five Oaks 164
    Later Buildings 165
    19th Century – the new Horsham Road 166
    Well-to-do Incomers 166
    Their Legacy 167
    Other properties 170
    20th Century Developments 171
    Carnivals, Parades and Marches 171
The King comes to Five Oaks **176**
    Memories of Dorothy Pullen 178

More Royal Celebrations	179
The Hamlets- Adversane	**179**
'From Hadfoldshern to Adversane'	180
The Maltings	181
Public Houses	**183**
Kelly's Post Office Directory, 1867	**191**
Kelly's Directory, 1973	**195**
Billingshurst Roads and Estates	**199**
Acknowledgements and Further Reading	**205**
Index	**207**

Foreword

It is fair to say that Geoff Lawes has now truly earned his place among the small select group of village historians. His first book 'Billingshurst's Heritage' was critically acclaimed by his peers and is now into a reprint. I was able to see at first hand the work and dedication that went into that book as he travelled the highways and byways in search of knowledge of the many older buildings in the neighbourhood.

Subsequently, Geoff realised that he had accumulated a great deal of information beyond the self-imposed remit of this first book and, typically, he began to write another. This book is an extension of the earlier one and expands our village history to include the outer reaches of the parish. It also contains a wealth of entertaining anecdotal material for dipping into, consisting as it does of many humorous yarns and other accounts of bygone days as recalled by our village characters and other venerable citizens.

For those that regard Billingshurst as a town - which as it grows it will be hard not to so describe - these books are, and will remain, a wonderful contribution to the canon of the history of village life from which Billingshurst is derived. The book will dispense much knowledge and amusement for all who read it.

John Griffin, friend and neighbour.
December 2013

Billingshurst's Heritage No. 2

Introduction

"A faire field full of folke fonde I there bytwene"

Coronation Parade 1911 – a field full of folk

Of alle manner of men, the mene and riche,
Worchyng and wandryng as the worlde asketh"
[William Langland, 14th Century poet]

In the Billingshurst Society's newsletter a member once lamented, "Except for Wendy Lines' splendid photographic history, Billingshurst's history awaits an author. There is a bulging scrapbook for anyone brave enough to take on the task." Leaving aside any question of courage I have, almost by accident stumbled into this role, as a result of indulging my curiosity about East Street where I live. This exploration morphed into a book which has, thankfully, been well received.

Volume 1 of Billingshurst's Heritage dealt mainly with the church and ancient buildings in East Street and the High Street in the old village centre. Other major areas of the parish were given cursory treatment or neglected altogether. Volume 2 seeks to remedy some of these major omissions and fill gaps in the known history of the village. Some stories may be unfamiliar even to long- time residents as well as those who have joined the community from elsewhere in the comfortable expectation of settling and putting down roots here in Billingshurst.

The earlier volume was arranged on a chronological structure from the earliest times to the present day. Volume 2 takes the form of an historical miscellany of differing topics, often in close relationship with things as they are now, so that the reader can dip into it and use it as a reference book and village guide, hopefully of some value to those new to the Parish. The two village hamlets, Adversane and Five Oaks, are major topics, as are the areas about Marringdean Road, Parbrook and Tedfold. Also described in some detail are the Wey & Arun Canal and the social, cultural and sporting clubs and societies that enrich the lives of Billingshurst people. The history of the Weald School will be of interest to parents of boys and girls nearing the secondary stage of their education. Wherever possible the reminiscences of villagers past and present are quoted verbatim to colour the account with fond details of life in the village as it once was.

In compiling this miscellany I owe a debt of gratitude to those many people named in the 'Acknowledgements' who have contributed their expertise, memories and patient research to the body of knowledge about the village which it has been my pleasure and privilege to collate into two convenient companion volumes. I have enjoyed bearing witness, through my mind's eye to Billingshurst's own 'fair field full of folk' and to offer this snapshot to anyone who chances to read of the tycoons, the rogues, the affluent maltsters, the shopkeepers, the community-minded leaders, the craftsmen and the humble labourers who have graced the fields and streets that we have inherited, a 'brave old world that had such people in it'.

I have attempted throughout to present the story of Billingshurst in a factual and objective fashion, though I am conscious that sometimes my personal prejudices may have coloured such judgements as my wording implies. For this I offer my apologies to anyone I may have offended. Necessarily many worthy folk, many buildings and topics of great interest still remain omitted and unexplored. Detailed discussion of such properties as South House, Kingsfold and Hammonds have to serve as representative examples of equally deserving subjects which of necessity have been passed over or given a mere mention. I hope that colloquial memoires, inventories and other details of farm and village life, in peace and in war, will serve to illustrate the life of the people of Billingshurst in years gone by and as we experience it today.

In my second childhood, as a 'slippered pantaloon', I have once more 'gone willingly' to the School of Billingshurst Studies in the University of West Sussex. 'As You Like It' was my favourite Shakespeare set book for 'School Certificate' in my youth. It has been just as I like it in every moment of making these books, not least in the friendly cooperation I have enjoyed from some two score or more of contributors and advisers.

Geoffrey Lawes, October, 2013

Billingshurst's Heritage No. 2

Village Civics

This historical miscellany of information about the village of Billingshurst begins with a description of the democratic structures that govern our lives. This may appear like a lesson in Civics most appropriate to young people, but it may also prove useful to those who find our multi-layered system of governance obscure and confusing. Basic information about the parish offices may be helpful and subsequent passages also open a window on the various clubs and societies that enhance the social and sporting life of the village.

Inflation and Money Values

From time to time in the text sums of money are stated about such matters as mediaeval fines or Victorian wages. In order to put the reader in mind of the enormous effects of inflation and the varying purchasing power of sterling denominations, the following short table will help an understanding of the approximate value of pounds and old pence at various times through our history.

Date	Value of a £ today	Value of a penny today (240 old pence = £1)
1213	£1 = 475 pounds	1d = £2 (d is an old penny. Two and a half old pennies to one new p).
1313	£1 = 300	1d = £1.25
1413	£1 = 600	1d = £2.50
1513	£1 = 225	1d = 95p
1613	£1 = 110	1d = 46p
1713	£1 = 109	1d = 45p
1813	£1 = 68	1d = 28p
1890	£1 = 75	1d = 31p
1910	£1 = 70	1d = 29p
1920	£1 = 30	1d = 12.5p
1930	£1 = 45	1d = 19p (2d would buy a Mars Bar)
2013	£1 = 1 pound	1p = 1p (purchasing power negligible)

Local Democracy and Politics

In common with the rest of the country a Billingshurst citizen's democratic right to influence those who govern him, make law and to ensure they exercise it properly has been for many years conducted through four layers of elected representatives. The lowest tier for well over a hundred years has been the Parish Council, formally instituted in 1894. For eight centuries before that the affairs of the parish were conducted by the Parish Churchwardens and subordinate officers and the magistrates.

The second tier of local government is the Horsham District Council, established in its present form in 1972/4. Prior to that there were three councils, Horsham Urban and Horsham and Chanctonbury Rural Districts. The third tier is the West Sussex County Council which has existed from the time when Sussex was formally halved in 1888. The top layer which makes national legislation is, of course, parliament, effectively the House of Commons. Billingshurst is part of the Horsham constituency, returning one MP, at the present time the Rt. Hon. Francis Maude, Minister for the Cabinet Office and Paymaster-General. Francis Maude was called to the bar of the Inner Temple in 1977. He was MP for North Warwickshire from 1983 to 1992. After a period in business he became MP for Horsham in 1997 in succession to Sir Peter Hordern. Elections are held for all four bodies at four and five year intervals.

Each layer has particular areas of responsibility for which the duly elected representatives are accountable. Citizens often find this confusing as there is little evident publicity showing which body to contact and who is responsible for what. There have been unsuccessful attempts by Parliament to remove one layer, the County Council, in order to simplify local government. This was achieved in Brighton and Hove which became a Unitary Authority combining District and County functions in 1997. It is arguable that, ever since the end of the 19th century, power to raise taxes and conduct affairs has steadily shifted upwards to the centralised regime of Parliament and out of the hands of local electors.

The Parish Council is said to have only one statutory obligation, the provision of allotments. It has 15 elected members and employs a Parish Clerk and other clerks and assistants. It exercises influence over actions of higher tiers as it is, by law, a statutory consultee, for example on planning matters. Over and above that it has the option of providing amenities of its own choosing for the parishioners for which purposes it raises an annual local tax called the Parish Precept. To this end Billingshurst parish owns substantial land which it administers as sports grounds, recreational areas and gardens, allotments, public open space and as the site of the Community Centre. Its most important function is as a public forum and source of information where local people can seek advice, guidance and a medium through which to make known to authority their needs and grievances. Through its benign influence a complex web of voluntary organisations can flourish, adding to the quality of life of the village people. However it has no powers to make law itself beyond the rules and regulations of its own property.

Billingshurst Parish Council

Phone No: 01403 782555
www.billingshurst.gov.uk
email: council@billingshurst.gov.uk
Location: The Billingshurst Centre, Roman Way
15 elected parish councillors. Parish Meetings held monthly, supported by 7 main Committees and 10 Sub-Committees.
Parish Clerk: Beverley Bell

Chairmen of Council since 1895

Statistics

The village is among the top 15% of least deprived wards in England. 84% of households own a car which contrasts with a national average of 68%. Life expectancy for men in Horsham District is 79 and for women 83, the highest in Sussex. In 2001 the census found that 76% were Christian in religion, 94% were born in the UK and 98% were white. There were 122,088 people living in Horsham District, 2.3 people per hectare. This was a 12.4% increase over 1991 figures. In 2003 records indicate that there were 6.4 burglaries for every 1000 people.

Other Village Bodies. The Community Partnership is a group of public-spirited volunteers who undertake research and development, attract funding grants and organise facilities at the behest of the public and the Parish Council.

The Chamber of Commerce supports the interests of some 80 businesses, shopkeepers and traders. It has staged an annual show called 'Billibiz' to publicise and help make prosperous the commercial life of the village and provides 'networking' opportunities through lunch clubs and other social events.

Horsham District Council, which includes three elected representatives from the Billingshurst ward, has its own specific areas of responsibility. The greatest of these is planning of housing development and the uses of buildings and business premises in accordance with the planning law of the land. This defines any development as "the carrying out of building, engineering, mining or other operations in, on, over or under land or the making of any material change in the use of any building or other land". To this end it has powers to grant or refuse planning permission according to established rules of its own making to those who apply for it and to prosecute anyone who fails to conform. This responsibility includes the particular form of use to which premises are put, alterations to properties and the protection of ancient buildings and communities through the designation of listed buildings and conservation areas. Billingshurst has such a carefully defined conservation area. It is also expected to keep up to date a locally determined twenty-year forward plan for future development, heavily conditioned by the dictates of the government of the day.

Almost equal in importance is responsibility for the collection of waste, the one aspect familiar to most parishioners, and the policing of fly-tipping and other insults to the environment. The District also has responsibility for the actual housing of the public who do not own their own property which it exercises at the moment through an Association called Saxon Weald. Formerly the Council itself built and administered Council Housing. Much of this property has been sold to occupants and many consider that a new tranche of such development should be reintroduced to provide homes for those looking for affordable rental accommodation. At the time of this writing an extensive housing development authorised by the District Council in the 1990s is now maturing and many further piecemeal developments have sprung up. The District Council has recently granted outline planning permission, in the teeth of manifold local protests, for an estate of some 475 houses in the north east quadrant of the parish, with accompanying provision for improvements to the village infrastructure. The plans include an important road which will carry east-west A272 'through traffic' on to the Hilland Farm roundabout, so by-passing the village on three sides.

The District Council is a statutory consultee on many other matters such as hospitals and health, and like the Parish Council is empowered to provide leisure amenities, sports grounds, parks and gardens, and to support the arts through theatre, exhibitions and the Horsham Museum. The District Council is the Collector of Taxes for all forms of local government. It establishes an annual budget for itself to finance its own undertakings, but collects at the same time the Parish Precept, a sum to finance the Sussex Police Authority, and a much larger sum to provide funds to meet the County Council's requirements. This local tax, formerly known as the rates, is called the Community Charge and is levied on property, on a rising scale according to the value of the house. Business premises pay another separate rate.

West Sussex County Council is the top tier of local government which commands the lion's share of the Community Charge. This is largely the result of the County's responsibility for the provision of nursery, primary and secondary education up to the age of 18 for premises, and up to 16 for other educational needs. The general administration of education remains vested in the County, which decides, for example, school admissions, the designated catchment areas of schools and provides transport; but since 1989 control of curricula and school policies, powers of inspection and the use of taxpayers' money, has shifted locally to Governing Bodies and upwards to the Government Department of Education, and Ofsted, the national inspectorate of schools.

The County has other expensive responsibilities. Not the least of these is the disposal and recycling of waste which the District has collected. The County shares with the District the wider elements of strategic planning and has to look after coastal defences, provide for the County Fire Brigade and ensure the maintenance of proper trading standards, emergency services and transport. Even more relevant to most people is their responsibility for providing and maintaining roads and footpaths. The county also oversees the social services and provides public amenities such as the Library Service and the Public Record Office at Chichester. Billingshurst elects one representative to the County Council every four years jointly with Rudgwick.

WSCC Public Library, Mill Way

There are other elected positions in local affairs. Parents elect some of the school governors and all citizens elect a leader of the all-Sussex Police Authority.

Parish Councillors in Billingshurst are, by their own choice, unpaid volunteers. District Councillors are paid a fixed sum and their expenses reimbursed and those in the senior Cabinet positions are entitled to a supplementary allowance. Basic payments were £4665 and the highest payment was of £17,911 in 2013. Similar but more substantial rates apply to the County Councillors. In 2012/13 the basic allowance was £11,030. Cabinet members receive a £19,122 allowance. The Leader was entitled to an extra allowance of £30,744 and that post attracted a total cost of £44,508. All Councillors are entitled to reclaim their expenses.

Party politics do not complicate discussion in the Parish Council. All the representatives are assumed to be independent so there are no group manifestos for action at election time or voting along political party lines. The only drawback is that the voter is often unclear as to what an independent candidate's policy is, if indeed any of them have any specific plans for future implementation. Agreement in committee in the circumstances is sometimes hard to achieve.

At District level politics ostensibly intrude, though at Horsham it has long been conducted on non-ideological lines, with most debate about levels of taxation and the quality of administration, rather than with matters of high political principle. A degree of common ground has existed between the Liberal Democrats and the dominant Conservative majority. Liberal Democrats have had control just once for only four years in the 1990s. Both parties have had the advantage of the wise advice from the Chief Executives and their staff of salaried public servants. The Labour Party has had only small representations on Horsham District Council which was Conservative for most of the early 20th century.

The County Council was for many years in the control of Conservatives and Independents, most of whom usually voted with the Conservatives against a small Labour opposition. During the 1980s the Liberal Democrats developed as the growing opposition group, and in the 1990s they took control for four years. Subsequently their electoral fortunes have ebbed so that by 2013 the official opposition to the Conservative majority became UKIP, the newly emergent United Kingdom Independence Party who held 10 of the 71 elected Council seats.

Jubilee Fields

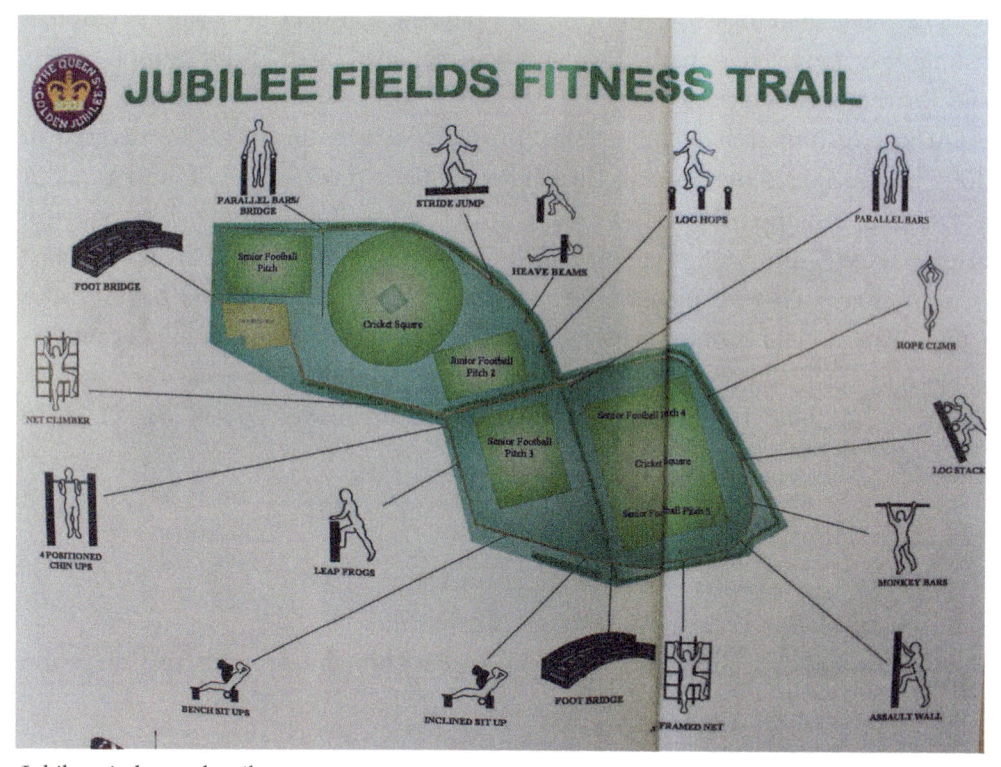

Jubilee pitches and trail

The village playing fields are located immediately west of the western bypass. The main entrance is the first right-hand turn on the A272 road to Wisborough Green.

The Sports Pavilion, Jubilee Fields

The Sports Pavilion Bar – Jubilee Fields

The fields include association football pitches, a cricket field with pavilion, a fishing lake and exercise path. The facility is managed by the Billingshurst Sports and Recreations Association.

An interesting archaeological site, Burnt Row, was thoroughly excavated in 2004 by the Weald School and Brinsbury College, revealing the foundations of a dwelling, renamed Weavers Cottage, a disused well and numerous historical artefacts. As Southern Cottage it had survived until at least 1935. It is now part of a country walk with picnic tables. The land, in 1603, belonged to one John Longhurst and is shown on maps as 'Burntrough'. The last known inhabitant was Edna Hayward who moved into West Street when the cottage was demolished. In the 1920s the cottage had a Coventry pump at the well to send water up to Tedfold Farm.

Other Facilities

Public Library: in the Mill Lane car park, provided by WSCC.
Lawn Tennis Club: Recreation Ground, Lower Station Road.
Bowls Club: off Myrtle Lane self-contained within the grounds of the Weald School.
Cricket Club – Jubilee Fields
Association Football Club – Jubilee Fields
Swimming Pool and Leisure Centre: Off Station Road. Facilities include a gym, pool, sports hall, studio and synthetic pitch.
Billingshurst Family & Children's Centre/Wakoos: Children's Nursery Centre: Off Station Road
Dauxwood Pre-School, Natts Lane
St. Gabriel's Playgroup, East Street
Rainbow Toddlers, Community Centre
British Legion – meet often at various hosts'

Lions Club – Pavilion, Jubilee Fields
Rotary Club – Blacksmith's Arms, Adversane
Women's Institute – St. Mary's Room
Lacemakers – Community Centre
Community Transport Scheme – 01403 787696 Based at the Community Centre
Mini-bus Association - 01403 782695
Scouts and Guides, cubs and Brownies - Scout HQ at Recreation Ground
Trefoil Guild – St, Mary's Room
Choral Society: St. Mary's Church
Meals on Wheels (WRVS) – 01403 265280
Angling Society- AGM in Jubilee Pavilion
Horticultural Society – Women's Hall
Dramatic Society – Women's Hall
Local History Society – Community Centre
Wine and Beer Circle – St Gabriel's Hall
Wednesday Group – St. Mary's Room, East St.
Dog Training Club – The Haven and Rudgwick Village Hall
WEA – 01403 784438
Adult Education – 0845 601 0161
Allotments: Traditional private allotments beside the Bowling Alley, and recent Council sites at Manor Fields
Waste Recycling and Community Tip for the convenient disposal of waste and recyclables– Newbridge Rd. by Jubilee Fields
Registrar, Births, Marriages and Deaths – 01243 642122
Surgery – Roman Way 01403 782931

Community Gardens: Extensive works are ongoing to create attractive gardens and leisure amenities on the site of the old cricket ground and part of the former village football pitch.

The Women's Hall was built at the expense of the Beck Sisters, Ellen and Edith, keen supporters of Mrs Pankhurst and of female emancipation. They added the Mothers' Garden next door in 1926. Here the playground equipment was restored in 2003 at a cost of £25,000 raised by voluntary subscription, bolstered by the Lions Club and the King's Arms.

There are community facilities for public and private hire at The Community Centre, The Women's Hall, St. Gabriel's Hall, St. Mary's Rooms, Trinity Reformed Church

Churches

St. Mary's C of E, East St., St. Gabriel's Catholic, East St., Trinity United Reformed Church, West St., Family Church –Community Centre, Unitarian Chapel off the High Street. Quakers meet at the Blue Idol, Coolham.

Schools

Billingshurst Primary School, 4-11 years, Upper Station Road
The Weald School, Comprehensive Community School, 11 – 18.

Community Recreational Gardens, Upper Station Road

Utilities

Piped water came to Billingshurst in 1911, coal gas from 1907 and mains electricity in 1934. The telephone was introduced, at first with a manual exchange with the few subscribers enjoying a two digit phone number. The automatic telephone exchange off Mill Way, now almost redundant, and a barrier to linkage between two car parks, was built in 1963 and extended in the 70s.

We often overlook the effect of the availability of ample clean piped water coupled with electrical light and power on the possibility of new industries and fresh job opportunities for village people. At last some light industries like The Whirlwind and its water heater successor could flourish and young men and women could find local work other than farm jobs, domestic service or the traditional crafts that had been practised in the village from time immemorial.

Western by-pass

Footbridge over the by-pass to Sports Fields

In 1993 the issue of providing a by-pass at the cost of extra housing which would finance it and other necessary infra-structure projects, mobilised public opinion more than anything before or since. Ten years earlier in 1983 The Billingshurst Society had canvassed opinion, printed numerous letters opposing the idea but finally decided to support it. The Weald School conducted a 10 point survey for a week and Mrs. Paton, Chairman of Governors, reported their findings. On two out of four days 15,600 vehicles travelled through the busiest part of the High Street in a 12 hour period 7 a.m. to 7 p.m. On each weekday more than 2.200 heavy vehicles were in the High Street during the same period. The school also conducted an opinion poll and found 74.4% were in favour of a by-pass despite anxiety about the cost, the likely loss of passing trade, 'concreting over the countryside' and unwanted extra development in the village.

The District Council had tabled a plan for a southern by-pass linking the A272 to the A29 through Daux Wood and crossing the railway line. An overcrowded Parish Council Meeting was followed by another in The Weald School Sports Hall attended by 800 people who unanimously condemned the scheme and favoured a western by-pass with a limited number of about 400 houses. The Council accepted this judgment and proposed three alternative western routes. One was chosen at a 'cost' of over 550 houses to be built in accordance with a design brief which complemented the traditional vernacular architecture of the village.

The road was opened in 1996 to relieve traffic congestion in the village centre along the A29 road from London to Bognor Regis. It is claimed to have reduced North-South through traffic by 40% to 10,000 per day. East-West traffic is estimated at 6200 per day.

Traffic through the High Street gave cause for concern even in the more leisurely days of horse-drawn coaches when vehicle movements were limited to a score of trips of stage coaches, freight wagons and private traps and carriages. The Burial Register notes that in March, 1839 Job Bridger, aged 13 was run over and killed by the Comet Coach and in 1842 Ruth Holden, aged 2, suffered exactly the same fate. Children could then play hop-scotch and cricket in the High Street. In the minutes of the Parish Council of 1909: 'carried unanimously that the attention of the County Council be called to the dangerous speeds at which motor cars pass through Billingshurst'. However by 1939 a writer lamented that he was obliged to drive through at five miles per hour because it was impossible to proceed faster in the continuous queue that stretched from Bognor to London. He called for the urgent building of a by-pass. By 1990, 50 years later, particularly in summer, matters were a great deal worse. The coming of the western by-pass may have reduced 'passing trade', especially for the motor business, but the relief from congestion and exhaust fumes has been warmly welcomed.

The housing development brought with it a number of improvements to the village infrastructure. As well as paying for the by-pass the developers were required to fund such things as Jubilee Sports Fields, the Community Centre, the all-weather pitch at the Weald, enhancements to the High Street and to make financial contributions for the schools and to give a £1M contribution for the new swimming pool.

The A29 follows the ancient Roman Stane Street for many miles. It was known at one time as 'The Devil's Road', supposedly because it was the only engineered road in the neighbourhood and seemed unnaturally straight compared with all other tracks.

Natural History

If we take the long view, the spot on the planet we call Billingshurst has enjoyed or endured a wide variety of climates and its surface has risen and fallen above and below sea level on untold numbers of occasions. Over the last 150 million years, subterranean forces have heaved up the earth's crust into highlands many times and those lofty places have as often been weathered away to be deposited as sediments under seas in the form of sands, chalk, gravels and clay layers. These too have then been folded up, to be eroded once more by water and ice and deposited in new deltas to form new sedimentary strata. To complicate matters further the varying tilt of the earth in relation to the sun and variations in its orbit have caused climatic changes over and above those occasioned by elevation.

The mind-boggling period of time taken for all these changes, occurring worldwide, has enabled the relatively recent emergence of flora and fauna as we now experience them in Billingshurst. As a result of evolution, millions of species of plants and animals that now exist, live alongside us - 21st century *Homo sapiens*. What follows is a brief resume of events and their consequences for wildlife and landscape in our area.

145 Million years ago

Jurassic era –dinosaurs. Sediments laid down in tropical conditions.

135 M

Cretaceous period – our main soils in Sussex were laid down, above the Jurassic strata, under shallow seas, clays, sands and chalk. Horsham stone and Sussex marble were deposited in the clay beds which contains fossils of early carp and freshwater sharks, crocodile and turtles. The climate was sub-tropical. Dinosaurs continued but new groups of mammals and birds emerged. Flowering plants occurred, ferns and horsetail. Ants, gall wasps, early butterflies and moths, marine reptiles, ammonites and multitudes of marine life forms all flourished.

65 M

Tertiary era- dinosaurs were now extinct. This was the age of the mammals. The ancestral horse, dogs, cats and pigs, for example, developed, together with the first primates: ancestors of mankind.

20 M

The Wealden anticline, a great dome, was thrown up by folding upwards under lateral pressure. This loosened arch of rock subsequently was weathered away to leave the chalk escarpments, now known as the North and South Downs, and in Billingshurst clay soils at the surface characteristic of the Lower Weald.

500,000 years ago
The Paleolithic period. Boxgrove man, precursors of Neanderthal man and *Homo sapiens* had arrived in Sussex. Fauna included elephant, rhino, bear, wolf, hyena, mink and vole. Better not go down in the woods today! The climate was mild.

125,000 years ago
First of some 6 or 8 ice ages begin covering glaciated regions north of the Thames.

10,000 years ago
Ice retreating, Tundra conditions with arctic animals, reindeer, polar bears etc. [Many 'Creationist' thinkers believe that God created the earth at some point since this time!]

8,000 years ago
Mesolithic period. The land sinks, waters rise and the 'Continent was isolated'. The British Isles come into being. Our native trees evolved, elm, hazel, birch, pine, alder and lime. Warm wet conditions returned. Mankind has developed as hunter-gatherers, nomadic in life-style and using flint tools.

6,300 years ago
Neolithic first farmers were clearing trees for crops. Fauna now include wild boar, deer, beaver, wolf, and polecat. Ash trees grew. The lynx, reindeer and wild ox died out.

3,500 years ago
Bronze Age. More development on better soils and chalk with some clearance of wood (1500 BC) in valley bottom alluvium such as Billingshurst. Livestock farming begins on favoured sites.

2,700 years ago
Iron Age. Deeper ploughing. Weald forest still largely undisturbed. Native lime trees now (700 BC) extinct.

43 AD

Romans arrive bringing in box bushes, plums, walnuts, mulberries, vines, leeks, garlic, parsley, turnips, cabbages and roses. These were unlikely to have reached Billingshurst.

406 AD

Saxons arrive. Serious work begins around Billingshurst felling the native oaks and farming the fields.

Subsequently: The Normans brought in the rabbit. The black rat brought the plague in the 12th century. It died out in the 1950s like the red squirrel. The brown rat arrived in the 18th century and the grey squirrel in the 19th. The red deer died out then too. Wild polecats disappeared in the 1920s. Ferrets continued as domestic animals for catching rabbits.

Exotic plants from all round the world introduced by plant-hunters have been cultivated in gardens since the 18th century.

E.C.M Haes writes in his *Natural History of Sussex*, 'The Weald Clay is mainly of interest for oak woodland with its carpet of spring flowers, fine display of autumn fungi and great variety of butterflies and moths... It is gumboot country'.

In 1993, Ann Baczkowska, a District Councillor, wrote about Daux and Rosier Woods. "We walk the woods daily and often see Green Woodpeckers, Deer, Fox, Squirrel, Weasels as well as White Admirals and other woodland insects. We are told that the dormouse has been seen there and that the Nightingale is also heard. The woods are largely hazel coppice with oak standards, although other species such as Sweet Chestnut and Holly also grow there. The ground flora is varied and includes Butcher's Broom, Bluebells, Primroses and Wood Anemones, and there are two neglected ponds and a large wet area. We appreciate that Sussex is blessed with many high quality Woodlands, but we feel that Daux and Rosier Woods are of immense local importance as they are the only woods within walking distance of Billingshurst, and as such are enjoyed by many local people as well as wildlife, and are of great landscape value. We would like to see them protected from development." [When this was written the woods were under threat from a proposed southern by-pass.]

Billingshurst's Heritage No. 2

The Billingshurst Society

Aileen Walker and Billingshurst Society Colleagues

In 1975, prompted by anxieties about planning and development issues, a group of like-minded village citizens founded The Billingshurst Society "to provide a forum for discussion on matters concerning the parish and to act as a channel through which members can make known their opinions to the appropriate authorities", meaning the Parish, District and County Councils, the MP, the Police Authority, etc. It campaigned for necessary improvements to lighting, drainage and crossings. It also sponsored such activities as the planting of three hundredweight of daffodil bulbs to help beautify the village and the designing of the village signs. It ran theatre trips, organised walks, held suppers, sponsored 'Made in Billingshurst' exhibitions and the Best Kept Village Competition. Its membership rose to over 800 people.

Mrs. Aileen Walker, who was made MBE in 1998, was the leading light of the Society. She it was who did the pictures for the village signs that Mr. Gordon Simkin designed. She resigned from the Committee in 1988, when a warm appreciation was published in the bi-monthly news letter recognising her contribution to the village, her enthusiasm and knowledge of planning matters. The newsletter kept readers informed on all parish issues as they occurred in the agendas and minutes of the relevant Committees and, though non-political, took on a campaigning stance whenever it judged the majority of the numerous members so wished. In many instances its powerful influence proved persuasive, as about the Southern by-pass, and it welcomed the coming of Budgens Supermarket in 1986. But in the matter of many developments, it was less effectual and was criticised by some as striking an attitude of opposition to nearly every proposed change. When issues of development or conservation were in the balance its stance was generally opposed to expansion. John Richards, a notable local journalist, was a staunch pillar of the Society until he moved away to Boston. He wrote to say how his new community was uninformed by contrast with the useful service to the community that the Billingshurst Society provided. Nevertheless as the membership declined, older officers died or stood down and could not be replaced and meetings were sparsely attended the Society ceased to function in October 2005.

An influential member once wrote in the Society Newsletter: "I suspect that quite a lot of the people who came to 'the country' don't really like it – and won't be happy until Billingshurst looks like Purley...Do we need FEWER car parks, LESS street lighting, FEWER street signs?"

Robin Edgar, styled 'The Bard of Billingshurst' contributed a poem lamenting the passing of the old village character with the coming of the by-pass and housing estates:-

Progress – Well Change?
Sixty years ago 'twas mooted,
Ideas canvassed, schemes all touted,
Meetings called, the options shouted,
'Heated debates' – opponents clouted,
Scepticism, 'senses doubted'...
Finally protesters flouted –
Tarmac ordered, concrete grouted –
Billingshurst's surounderbouted.

Sad, but you are not the first
Small village to be by-pass cursed
Developmentally immersed
Until you think your seams will burst,
Until you can't recall the erst –
while shape of Billingshurst.
Progress now has done its worst,
So Goodbye little village-hurst
And Bonjour Greater Ville-de-hurst.

The Society was indignant about the development of 41 houses at Lakers Meadow, holding that the Butcher's Field should be preserved as open space or used as a car park and also opposed the building of Kingsfold Close. It considered that no playing fields should be built outside the Western by-pass. Its little publications were spiced up with anecdotes, memories and historical accounts to which this book is much indebted.

Gardening and Horticulture

In all likelihood the very first Saxon settlers in Billingshurst built their simple dwellings on the small patches of alluvial and loamier soils they found beside the stream that rose from the Bowling Alley on land around about the present site of Lloyds Bank. The basic clay soils elsewhere would have discouraged tillage. Though they were fertile they were heavy to work in winter, liable to rot seeds in spring and apt to turn solid and crack in summer. Better prospects were available alongside the Roman Road beside the stream and where any New Stone Age Celts might have lived

The early Ordnance Survey maps show how nurseries had developed south of Townland once run by Phillip Puttock and at (Lewkener's) Luckin's Garden on the opposite side of the High Street. To the south between the present sites of the Congregational Church and the Baptist Chapel where Croft Villas stand there were yet more nurseries with good fertile soils kept by John Allman the seedsman. All these plots of fertile soil, cultivated for hundreds of years now lie buried beneath houses, roads and other buildings erected since Victorian times. Elsewhere cottagers have grown their vegetable and tended their flower gardens with pride in their self-sufficiency. Fruit trees, raspberries, blackcurrants, roses and honeysuckle all flourish on the clay. Private enterprise has offered well-maintained allotments east of Little East Street. As late as 1972, High Seat Nurseries were still advertising themselves as Geranium specialists and offering cut flowers, 'particularly Iceland Poppies'. The Billingshurst Allotments Society was formed in 2009 and as a consequence the Parish Council has provided for new public allotments at Manor Fields. The Joyes, and their successors, the Watts, sold seeds and garden sundries for many years from their emporium at Hereford House by the Station. They were major suppliers of agricultural seed corn. Austin's Hardware store still supports Billingshurst gardeners.

Billingshurst's Heritage No. 2

Billingshurst Horticultural Society

In the Flower Show marquee 1969. Suited judges with Joe Kingston and John Sutton

On 6th September 1882 the village schoolchildren were given an extra holiday as there was to be a 'Flower Show' at 'Somers Place', courtesy of Mr. R. Goff. The Royal Sussex Militia Band was in attendance 'at the seat of Mr. Gough' as *The Horsham Advertiser* had it. So began the oldest village club, the Billingshurst Horticultural Society. The emphasis, in Class I, despite the title, was heavily on vegetables, with a few classes for fruit and flowers and a single one for honey. Cheerfully accepting of class distinctions, Class II section read:- 'Prizes to be competed for by Inhabitants, their gardeners or servants, occupying premises of more than £6 per annum'.

Only a few joint shows with Wisborough Green, Loxwood and Kirdford were attempted until the new century. There was one at Barkfold, Kirdford in 1884 and another in Billingshurst in 1887 at Summers. Unfortunately it rained all afternoon, disheartening the organisers, and no more shows graced Billingshurst until 1903. Mr. James Hall Renton then lent Rowfold Grange as the venue and was made President of the Committee. Mr. Joe Luxford was Treasurer and Mr. R. Morris of Five Oaks, Secretary, the latter two both being luminaries of the new democratic Parish Council. They served the Committee for many years. The Show on Wed. Aug 15th had an 'Industrial' section and was deemed a great success according to the Parish Magazine, with children's sports and Bandmaster Wallace and the 2nd V.B. Royal Sussex Band.

The show became an annual event, returning to Summers in 1904 and at Mr. Songhurst's meadow in 1909. The 1910 show was bigger than usual, featuring a floral parade through the village. Mrs Garton describes it in her time: "The Annual Flower Show was a big village event, held in station field, with two or three big marquees. Villagers exhibited produce, craft items, cookery and home-made wine, chutneys, jam, marmalade, rugs and always a village fair to go with it." The Flower Show was always held on a Wednesday. This was 'early closing day' in Billingshurst designed to give shop staff an afternoon off in compensation for working on Saturday mornings. A few businesses still practice what was once a common custom. Mrs. Lines, whose research this account is based on, reports that most early shows were held in the grounds of affluent landowners outside the immediate village. She presumes the parishioners brought their exhibits in wheelbarrows or carts borrowed from employers, or perhaps on trade bikes? Initially a new President was elected each year, and Major General Renton inherited the role together with his uncle's Rowfold estate.

The show ceased in 1916 but a best kept garden competition was held despite the war. After the war allotments came to Billingshurst and at some point the show resumed. By 1924 Mr. Luxford was both Treasurer and Secretary with a 20-strong Committee, including three Wadeys and the famous exhibitor Wally Wicks. There was a separate Ladies Committee too and a separate tent for poultry eggs and ducks! In the 30s the Women's Institute began to play a significant role introducing needlework and other domestic classes.

The Society still named itself 'Horticultural and Industrial' in 1934 when the site was Dr. Puttock's meadow, Alick's Hill. That show featured Skill Competitions and Side Shows, Teas, Ices and Light Refreshments, Messrs. F HARRIS & SONS' Noah's Ark, Roundabouts and Old English Fair. Many of the local gentry were made Vice-Presidents – Comptesse de la Chapelle, Lady Fielding, Miss Beck, Capt. Hall Renton. Other notables on the Committee have familiar Billingshurst names -Ayre, Puttock, Morris, Norris, Cripps , Sherlock and Harold Wadey, a long-time Society eminence. Watts and Sons at the Station handled the entry forms until the business closed down in 1992. The 30s were the Society's golden years, with 1,022 entries in 1936.

Up to 1939 the show was held in one or more marquees at a cost of £17-6s-6d. But during the 'phoney war' of 1940 the East Street School was pressed into service. With the war, by 1941 a threatening reality, the show was arranged but did not take place. Harold Wadey was then Hon. Secretary. The show closed 'for the duration of war' and did not resume until 1948. By then the event cost

£250, double the pre-war bill. A dance was held, there was a visit to Wisley and the word 'Industrial' was lost. In 1950 the chosen day was Saturday for the first time. Races were held, a tug-of-war organised and the Billingshurst Band played. In 1952 came an Exemption Dog Show. The presentation of cups was held on an evening in the Women's or Village Hall. In 1953 there was a special award to celebrate Elizabeth II's Coronation and in 1955 2,250 people attended. The site of the present primary school was one venue in those years and in 1962 it moved to the Recreation Ground, the band did not play and the attendance dropped to 1000. The sports continued in 1965 but there was no longer a fun fair.

The marquee, with its characteristic smell and atmosphere, proved too costly in 1970 and shifted into the Hall of the Weald School where it remained for 27 years until 1997. In 1972 when Mr. Beck and Mr. Kingston were the Honary Officers, the schedules included flowers, fruit and vegetables, floral art, cookery, needlecraft, handwork and painting for children, photography and honey, plus more domestic classes for WI members. In 1997 there was a crisis when Mr. Allan Dugdale, Rural Studies teacher at the Weald and Society Show Secretary, died but Mrs, Dorothy Lake stepped into the breach. In 1998 the show shifted to the new Village Hall, a smaller venue, and the live band and children's entertainer had to cease. The show now loses money and attracts some 600 entries, but other Society activities, visits, lectures, plant sales etc. keep the finances buoyant enough for it to make an annual donation to charity. Some 15 cups and trophies are awarded each year and 4 WI cups together with the Royal Horticultural Society's Banksian Medal, the National body which Billingshurst joined in 1926.

Beekeeping in Billingshurst

Beekeeping has been practised in the village since Saxon times. Honey was the only affordable sweetener available to country people until sugar became cheap enough in the later 19th century to replace it. Villagers and yeomen kept bees in skeps, killing the weightiest colonies with sulphur fumes in September to get at the honey and beeswax, until moveable frame hives were introduced in the 1870s.

Anthony Hammond had a 'beehouse' in the inventory of 1640 valued at about £150 in today's money. Rev. Cecil Brereton, Vicar of Billingshurst, (1886 -1890 and later at Sutton) had a sideline to his Ministering business. This was the rearing of swarms of bees and the raising of queen bees which he advertised for sale in the British Bee Journal for sale all over Britain, to be delivered by post or train. Beecraft was heavily promoted by the clergy and other well-to-do philanthropists in Victorian times. They thought that the poor 'cottagers', as they called them, could eke out their low wages and nourish their children by keeping bees, which required no land, could be collected as unclaimed swarms for nothing and could be kept in skeps that they could make themselves. Victorian thinkers admired 'self-help' and abhorred idleness, and the more politically astute advocating beekeeping as an insurance against revolt, such as the Swing Riots, by the potentially rebellious working classes. William Cobbett wrote: "He must be a stupid countryman indeed who cannot make a beehive and a lazy one if he will not... Scarcely anything is a greater misfortune than shiftlessness".

Thomas W. Cowan, for 40 years President of the British Beekeeping Association, married the rich local brewer Michell's daughter and lived for some 29 years in Horsham, latterly at Comptons Lea. He wrote that 'the importance due to the minor industry of beekeeping in promoting its work among the humbler classes of the community was due to the social position of (the Association's) patrons'. The Gentry and the Clergy, 'people of means', kept bees as an example to their flocks and many people in our district followed their example. Locally today's Billingshurst beekeepers belong to the Wisborough Green Beekeeping branch of the Association. Allan Dugdale, a pillar of the Horticultural Society and Tony Herbert taught the subject at the Weald School and there were formerly beekeeping classes at the village Flower Show. George Wakeford BEM, for services to beekeeping, was the local Beemaster who earned a living by attending to people's hives. He had some 400 colonies under his supervision in his heyday. George wrote a delightful autobiography, *Beemaster*, recently reissued as *Beemaster Revisited*. He died in 1985.

Weald pupils extracting and bottling honey

George Wakeford, Beemaster, showing a novice a queen cell

Building Developments in the 70s

In the 1960s and early 70s a large area of open land comprising farm fields of Broomfield and the parkland and gardens of Cleveland House and Gratwicke were transformed into the mature estates that we know today. Silver Lane is the 'spine road' linking Station Road and East Street. The south end was built first in the early 60s and as development spread north the road was completed on to East Street. Most of the roads in the area lead off it and only Broomfield Cottage and outbuildings of Gratwicke remain of the old mansions. The illustrative map here shows the present network of roads and how they relate to the rural scene before development began.

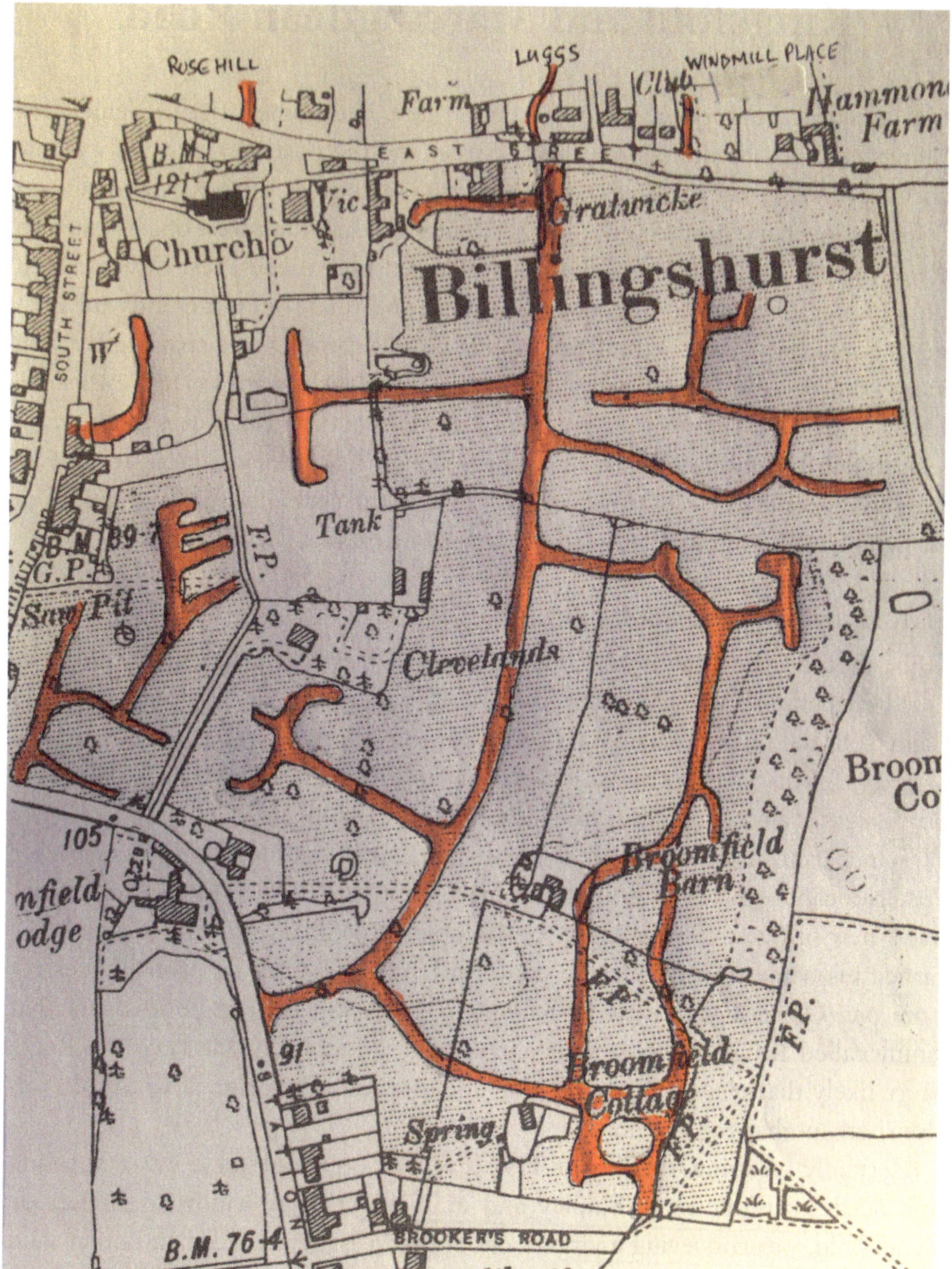
ROSE HILL
LUGGS
WINDMILL PLACE
Farm
Club
Hammond
Farm
EAST STREET
B.M. 121·7
Vic.
Gratwicke
Church
Billingshurst
SOUTH STREET
W
Tank
F.P.
B.M. 89·7
G.P.
Saw Pit
Clevelands
Broom
Co
Broomfield
Barn
105
nfield
odge
F.P.
F.P.
91
Broomfield
Cottage
Spring
B.M. 76·4
BROOKER'S ROAD
Malthouse

Billingshurst's Heritage No. 2

Kingsfold and Marringdean Road

It is tempting to suppose that the factor that determined the settlement of Billingshurst was the junction of Stane Street and the East – West route we now label the A272. However since the eastern arm, East Street, did not extend beyond Coolham for many centuries the High Street was really built west of a T-junction where the road to Petworth joined Stane Street, now called West Street. Much more important than the road east was the second road south, presently the fifth feeder route into Parbrook and Billingshurst. At Parbrook was a crossroads at the end of Natts Lane with a substantial farm track leading westwards on to Newbridge. The ancient road had not yet been named as Marringdean Road. It is said to have been called Billingshurst High Road. By tracing the outline of the history of its farms and people one can capture some sense of the characteristics and doings of the people of Billingshurst. One important estate on that road is Kingsfold.

Early records of Kingsfold

Twice in 1457 the Manor of Pinkhurst proclaimed that a tenement and land called Carpenters, late of William Kyngesfold was open to any heir with a rightful claim. "On the third proclamation came Benedict Browne who received the land –fine 20s." This was confirmed in 1460 in the Pinkhurst Manor Roll. However Carpenters is almost certainly not the land now called Kingsfold.

Which came first? Kingsfold, the place name or Kingsfold, William's surname? Posterity cannot readily resolve the 'chicken and egg' dilemma. Certainly there was a new bridge over the Arun, for example, so William Newbrygge probably earned his name from it. On the contrary Jengers or Gingers probably derives from one Oliver Gynguire who built it in 1370. But we can be less sure that family called Kingsfold took their names from an estate in Marringdean Road. More likely that place was named after the men, and the original Kingsfold was elsewhere, perhaps at Warnham.

Certainly we know that about 1290 a Simon de Kingesfelde was witnessing title deeds to property in Shipley and in 1305 Matilde, widow of Robert de Kyngesfold, was conveying a virgate of land in West Grenestede and other land in Thakeham and Sepele (Shipley) to Simon de Kyngesfold and his wife Lucie. A John de Kyngesfold in the same year sold land in Rusper to another John, son of Symon de Kyngesfold. Symon's son, Rico de Kynggesfold granted land in 1316 to Mattheo de Apslye and Ffelice his wife to pay 2 shillings at two feasts in the year. The Kingsfolds were clearly people of means with ancient title to estates and their surname arose from the place where they first lived.

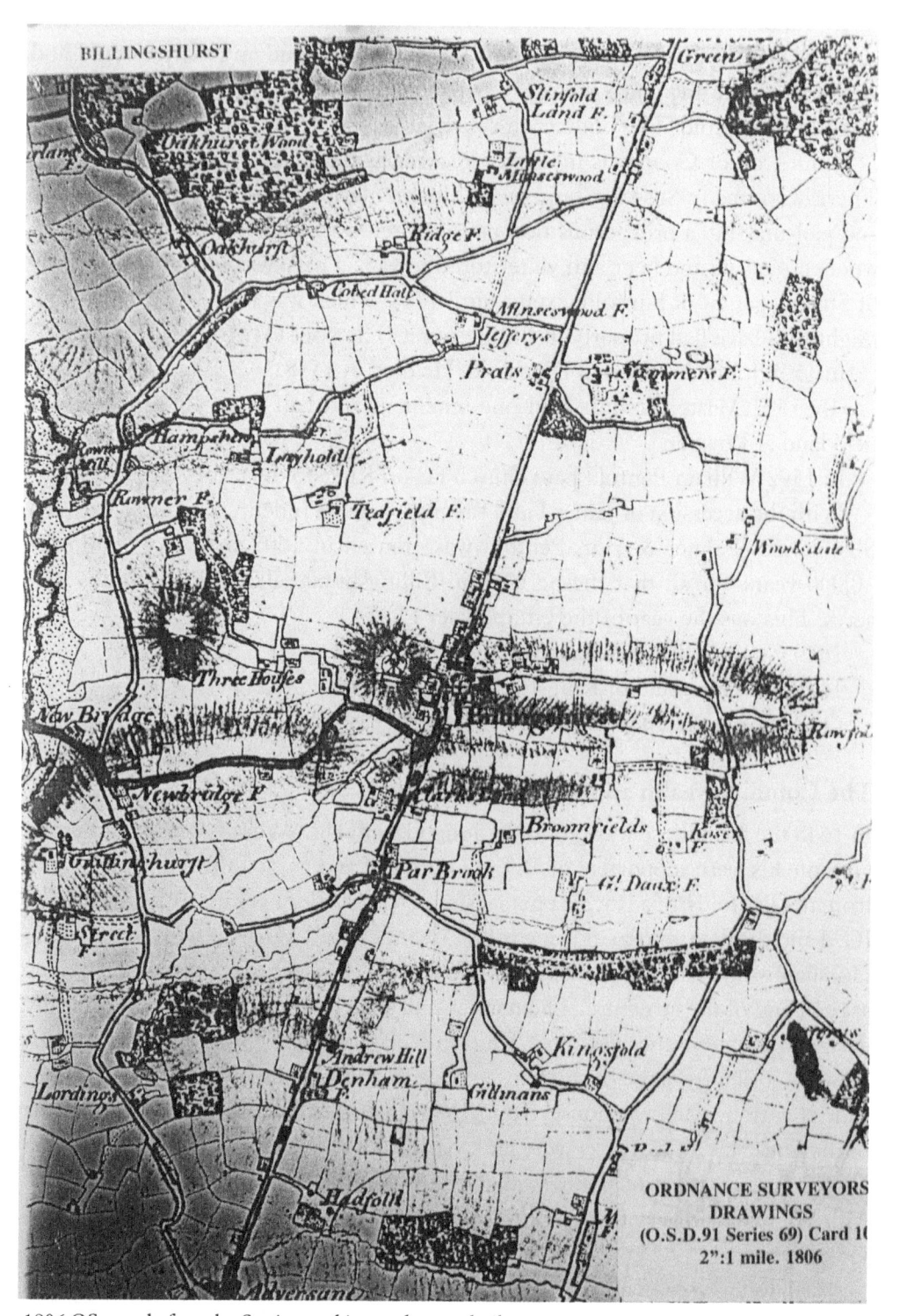

1806 OS map before the Station and its roads were built

In Tudor times in 1527 Richard Bakkes was licensed to let his tenement and land called Kingsfold for 3 years. Fine 4s. Redhoyse Land and Carpenters Land are held by baxe and cowp.(Cooper).

In 1530 Penfold 'The butcher in the dyke' has ownership of Kingsfold land.

John Cop or Cooper is in church records as Churchwarden that same year. There were many Sussex Coopers. The name derives from the trade of barrel and pail-making, a prosperous occupation when water was drawn from wells in wooden buckets and beer and wine stored in vats. There was one Cooper family of Strood, gentry at Slinfold, extant until 1715, which was influential locally and might well have had property in Billingshurst. The poet Cowper belonged to it.

In 1548 John Cooper had Kingsfold. He died in 1558.

By 1577 Master Stydolf held one tenement and half a virgate 4s8d p.a. He held land at Rowner.

In 1592 William Penfold paid church tax on Kingsfold.

With the accession of James I and the Stuarts in an Indenture of lease between Sir Thomas Palmer & Wm Penfold was granted in 1605 to Wm Penfold for 10,000 years 'for all that mesne farm in Billingshurst called Kyngesfold' – 110 acres. This was the year of the Gunpowder Plot.

1630 Cop paid Church Tax for Kingsfold.

1639 John Penfould of Kingsfold was a sidesman.

On 11th March, 1644 John Penfold was deceased.

The Commonwealth and Restoration Period

In 1648 the farmhouse was rebuilt by John Greenfield. We may speculate that the Greenfields were supporters of Oliver Cromwell and gained the land confiscated from the Penfolds, of a Royalist persuasion. Over the door are inscribed the letters IGM and the date, said to indicate John Greenfield and Mary his wife. Locally dug Horsham stone and winklestone was used in its construction. There is a chimney at each end of the structure. The narrow entrance bay with stairs was specifically designed as an entrance vestibule. English Heritage's description reads as follows: 'The Victorian frontage of the house conceals a single pile, two and a half storey, central entrance hallway house, dated 1648. Outshots had been added to the rear of the house by 1725. These were later converted to the second pile as part of the late Victorian alterations. The walls are of unequally coursed sandstone blocks with brick dressings to the windows. These were probably originally plastered to look like stone.'

1652 John Greenfeild of Kingsfold was a churchwarden, and in 1666 also a waywarden, and 1670 an overseer, all offices of the parish vestry. [1666 was the year of the Great Fire of London]. The Greenfield family had emerged as the most notable and wealthiest clan in the locality with extensive property in all parts of the parish for the best part of three centuries.

Aerial view of Kingsfold House

We first hear them in 1504 when Edward Greenfield and his son Walter held "tenement and yardland called Le High Fure" by copyhold. The family were in possession of High Fure and South House for over 300 years until 1811. There is a record of a John Gryndfyld of Daks [Daux] in the early Tudor period and a Thomas Greenfield died there in 1578. In that same year William Greenfield of Daux married Mary Greenfield of South House. In 1610 Edward Grinfeild bought 20 acres of land at Coxbrook from William Lee. Researchers for Sotheby's believed that the land known as Summers was rented by the Greenfields from at least 1530 to 1690. A Richard Greenfield, carpenter, was buying properties in 1593 and one of that name bought Clarksland in 1645. In 1649 master butcher William Greenfield willed Duckmore, Lockyers off East Street and other extensive properties to relatives. He was known to have been at Palmers in 1645. Maurice Greenfield was at Southhouse in 1667 and acting as Churchwarden. A Phillip Greenfield was Churchwarden in 1688 and Overseer of the Poor in 1698. Samuel Greenfield of Greenwich, a waterman, bought premises in Billingshurst in 1702 and was buried at St. Mary's in 1720 aged 48; Maurice Greenfield, late of South House, died in 1752 aged 66.

"While in this life I did remain.
My latter days were grief and pain
Till God was pleased to give relief
None else could ease me in my grief"

There are continuous burials of Greenfields recorded from 1560 to 1675, and yet more later.

Arthur Greenfield lived at Gratwick in Dickens' time in the early 19th century. From about that time their fortunes seem to have faded and they do not feature in the Directories of the period as persons of note. A James Greenfield was a farmer and mealman at Adversane in 1858 and the surname has remained well represented in the district throughout the years. It is now more often found further south around Storrington.

In 1671 Goodman Greenfield was in occupation at Kingsfold.

The following year a new regal coinage was issued. This had farthing and halfpenny coins. Previously those denominations were made by actually halving and quartering small silver coins which were scarce, inconvenient and easily lost. Such was the shortage of small change between 1652 and 1672 that traders took to issuing their own tokens which were offered as change at shops to be afterwards exchanged for goods, serving as an advertisement and giving them credit for those outstanding and any that were lost. Nearly 200 different tokens were issued in Sussex, including a halfpenny one by Mathew Weston of Billingshurst in 1666 and nine in Horsham.

1685 Thomas Greenfield leased land from Katherine Garton (widow of John Garton of Pulborough) – Rowner Farm House and 120 acres.

In 1688 Philip Greenfield was in occupation.

1689 The Pannell Roll shows 'Phil Greenfeild of Kensfold' used the lands.

1712 Philip Greenfield died. Another Phillip succeeded, probably the one paid to repair the workhouse in East St in 1731.

The Penfolds and Coopers were still active in the village, conscientiously hounding the dissenting Quakers, though probably no longer from Kingsfold. We learn from William Albury, a Horsham historian, that at the Petworth Sessions in 1676 information was given by Richard Penfold and Thomas Cooper that: "John Pryor and his wife of Billingshurst and above five persons of sixteen years of age and upwards on Thursday 1st June last were present at an assemblye conventicule or meeting house under cover or pretense of the use of religion in other manner than according to the liturgy and practice of the Church of England Holden and kept in the Barne of the said John Pryor of Billingshurst by a certain person unknown to the said informers who did take upon himself to preach or teach and that the said John Pryor did wittingly and willingly permit and suffer the said building or conventicule in the said Barne contrary to the Act of 22 Charles II to prevent and suppress seditious conventicules.

We doe adjudge the said John Pryor and his wife guilty. In witness thereof: Thomas Henshawe, O. Weekes, William Westbrook."

Pryor was fined £20 and his wife 5 shillings. [Such constraints on freedom of worship were ended by the Toleration Act of 1689, apart from Catholics.]

Kingsfold passed in 1782 to Mr. Jno. Geering as the owner with Wm Towse as the occupier.

Victorian Times

Marringdean Road was not directly linked into Billingshurst as it is now by Upper and Lower Station Roads. These were built to service the Station which did not function until 1859. Originally Natts Lane from Parbrook was the junction to Stane Street, and, of course, there was no railway bridge to limit the access.

In 1858 Mr. J.Meetens is recorded as farming at Kingsfold, and in 1867, Mr. Shilcock.

1878 saw a menage indenture for £4000 from Geo. Carew-Gibson to H &W Farguhar (bankers and lenders of St Jas.) 147 acres Kingsfold Farm House and Garden.

1893 Indenture Oct 20th between W.R.Farguhar and A. Farguhar and Edwin Hunt.

The Early 20th Century

1902 Indenture Jan 29th Edwin Hunt and G.O. Bridgeman. Apl. 18th Indenture G.O.Bridgeman and W.B.Kingsbury. Deed Poll under hand and seal of W.B.Kingsbury.

1903 Power of Attorney to A. Julius, July 8th.

1903 Indenture Sept 9th Emily Kingsbury and T.N.C. Villiers, A. Julius, C.St. J. K.Roche & Cavendish Land Company. It was offered for sale by auction by the trustees, supported by the incentive of excellent development potential along Marringdean Road. "recently enlarged and judiciously restored...with well designed STONE GOTHIC ELEVATIONS, 166 acres with Frontages to both sides of a good Main road of about Three-quarters of a Mile, and affording some capital Sites for the erection of other Residences. There is capital Hunting. The Crawley and Horsham Foxhounds, Warnham Staghounds and Fishing. Water is supplied from...a reservoir pumped up to the house...with...three large storage cisterns and a modern windmill". The gardens and grounds boasted excellent shooting, lawns, a vinery and orchard house and two fish ponds with Jack (pike),Tench, gold and silver fish. Mr. Myram had one of the two cottages and also rented the pasture land for £80 p.a. –"Possession on 3 months' notice".

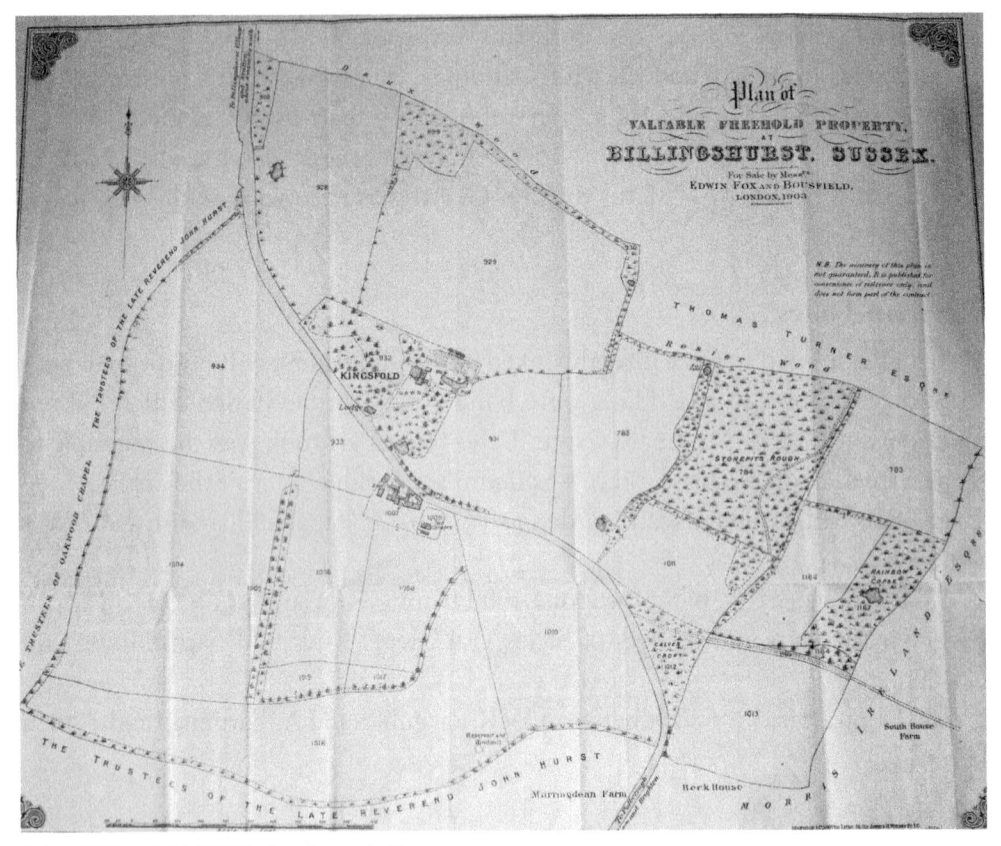

Sale of Kingsfold (1903) Auctioneer's Map

Ribbon Development

There are now in 2013 some 88 properties stretched along the ribbon development, mostly on the western side. Uncontrolled building along roadsides as practised between the world wars was legislated against in 1935 and more rigorously in 1947 when the Town and Country Planning Act circumscribed an Englishman's rights to his own castle and required the Local Authority to make twenty year building development plans for the estimated needs of the future.

The Englishman could no longer build wherever he liked, nor alter his house, add to it nor use it for any purpose he pleased without 'planning permission'. This was to be exercised, after consultation with his neighbours, by his local authority, following national guidelines determined by Parliament. One object of the Act was to protect the countryside so that long, straggling rows of houses were not erected so as to block out views of the rural scenery, to create traffic hazards by innumerable access points onto dangerous roadways, and ever-lengthening service pipes, drains and wires and journeys to shops and amenities as each tentacle slowly accrued. Marringdean Road is the most remarkable instance around Billingshurst and to a lesser extent along both West and East Street and along Stane Street at Parbrook.

The opportunity of development offered by the auctioneers in 1903 was taken up with enthusiasm, mostly by the building of larger, high value properties of distinctive, individual design. In Edwardian times a substantial country cottage could be built for £150/200.

In Dec 1903 Cavendish Land Co. conveyed the property to Sarah A Tucker who passed it in May of the following year to Samuel C Halahan. He became Chairman of the Parish Council for a time.

1904 Mr. Duffield, an estate manager, was regularly importing sheep from Scotland for fattening at Steepwood Farm. He took note of two unused hunting lodges, presumably available at a fair price. They had been imported from Canada in kit form. These he had transported to Billingshurst by rail and resited off Marringdean Road. One called 'The Brier Patch', home of Mr. Ken Longhurst still stands but its neighbour, called The Chalet' on the site of the present 'Long Acre' of the Lines family was demolished some thirty years ago.

Farm workers' Income

The average weekly earnings for a farm labourer in 1909 was 17s 6d (87 pence). It was not much for a man with a wife and children. A typical weekly budget, (quoted by Maud Davis), would be: rent 1s 6d, tea 8d, sugar 6d, bacon 1s 4d, Quaker oats 6d, 2oz tobacco 6d, cheese 9d, lard 9d, suet 2d, baking powder 1d, papers 2d, 1lb soap 3d, oranges 2d, currants 1d, pint of beer 2d, coal 1s 3d, 2 loaves 5d, milk 6d, butter 4d, oil 3d, stockings 6d, rest of baker's bill 3s. Total approximately 13s 6d. An allotment would cost 5s a year, but many villagers had gardens and could keep bees, rabbits and chickens. Another 7d a week might go to the Friendly Society to safeguard against any emergencies. Most items were priced using half pence and farthings. Meat, clothing, fuel, fares, furnishings, any extra 'luxuries' and any savings would necessarily be bought with the unspent balance of 3s 6d. It is not too surprising that children were expected to look for work as soon as they were aged 12. That year people over 70 were able to collect from the Post

Office the very first state pension, means tested and averaging 4 shillings a week. In 1911 Lloyd George introduced his contributory insurance scheme to provide for sickness and unemployment.

In the middle of WW I on Nov 15th 1916 S.C.Halahan sold Kingsfold to Col L.T.C. Twyford and on July 29th 1921 Mrs. Twyford passed the property to Mrs Fanny Clark.

The Later 20th Century and WWII

During WW 2 a prisoner-of-war camp, with pre-fabricated buildings, was established at what is now a housing estate named Kingsfold Close. The 12 acre site was originally called Finlanger Pasture. There is a record of a lease between James Champion and a William Firminger, a bucketmaker with premises in Billingshurst in 1712 and another about a William Firmanger dealing with Daniel Towse, timber hewer, in 1766. William Furlanger's daughter married an Evershed in the mid 17th century. This is most likely the source of that name. It is rumoured that the site was chosen by mistake by a government official who was told to requisition land at Kingsfold for the purpose (meaning at Warnham). He found Kingsfold, Billingshurst on his map and proceeded with the Marringdean site before it was too late to rectify the error. When the prisoners left in 1945 the buildings were first used to house homeless London families who had been 'bombed out' and later for stabling horses.

During WW II on 28th January 1944 a Hawker Hurricane fighter plane crashed at Steepwood Farm. Flt. Sgt. Wright survived. Another Spitfire came down in Daux Wood the following August. In 1943 a bomb-carrying Focke-Wulf 190 was shot down by a Mosquito night-fighter at Broadbridge Heath. The pilot, Fw. Jorga baled out and was captured at Cobb's Wood, Billingshurst. He was taken to his aircraft wreck the following day, much to the astonishment of schoolboys looking for souvenirs, which boys did in those days, often cycling for miles to 'incidents'. An Advanced Landing Ground was created at Coolham to support the D-Day Normandy Landings. Squadron Leader Horbaczewski, the Polish CO of 315 Squadron RAF landed his Mustang aircraft in France to pick up a fellow pilot and bring him home in his lap in the single-seater aircraft.

In 1943/4 20 Allied aircraft were lost in Horsham Urban and Rural District and two German craft crashed. Throughout the war 715 allied aircraft fell over the whole of Sussex, with the loss of 533 aircrew and 152 enemy aircraft crashed. 11,486 High Explosive bombs fell, about 90,000 incendiary bombs, 907 V 1s (Doodle bugs, flying bombs) and 4 V 2 rockets. Over 1000 people died and nearly 4000 were injured.

Farming and Business

Anglo-Saxon riddle: Who am I?

'My nose is pointed downwards; I crawl along and dig in the ground. I go as I am guided by the grey enemy of the forest, and by my Lord who walks stooping, my guardian at my task, pushes his way in the plain, lifts me and presses on, and sows in my track'.

After the war Kingsfold was back in the market. In June,1947 Messrs Lynn sold it to R. W. Cornell who owned it until July 25th 1952 when Cornell was succeeded by to Mrs. G.I. Scolding. Mrs. Scolding was obsessively keen on animals and tried to farm all her land with Shire horses. John Wilding, the horologist, who farmed at Duncans where the Beck sisters had lived, used to help her out with his tractor on the most intractable soils. She it was, who gave St. Mary's Church the original four wheels that are suspended with candles at Christmas-time, in memory of her equine friends.

Billingshurst clay is notoriously hard to cultivate, waterlogged in winter and baking hard and cracking in summer, so that many farmers had a second trade. Local historian, Hugh Kenyon, said that local clay was so hard to work that farms were seldom in the same family for more than two generations, whilst those on greensand lasted for ever. There is still one substantial working farm along Marringdean Road, Kingslea Farm, run by the Stocker family who are also Agricultural Contractors.

Farmers in Billingshurst usually had alternative strings to their bow, related to the opportunities and raw materials locally available. They could be millers, brewers and maltsters, timber dealers or run threshing tackle outfits for example, and deploy labour in winter when it was not needed on the land. A ready supply of skins would encourage various kinds of leather work –shoes, gloves and harness, which latter trade in tack and equipment for horse-drawn vehicles led to rope-making, blacksmithing and the craft of the cart and wheelwright. The demand for tiles and drainage pipes and building bricks encouraged the development of brick-making, using local clay. The exploitation of sandstone and winklestone offered another valuable alternative industry.

The answer to the riddle is: The plough!

The existence of Stane Street as a traditional route from London to the coast encouraged a continuing opportunity to offer ostling and staging facilities for horse-drawn transport and commercial hotel-keeping. There were numerous public houses for the benefit of both local people and the passing trade. This type of business was enhanced by the arrival of the motor-car and charabanc, especially when the practical range of vehicles was more limited than it is today, and road speeds slower and more hazardous. Cyclists and cycling clubs too contributed to hospitality businesses from late Victorian times.

More business was encouraged by the Wey and Arun rivers so that industrial development to feed distant markets could begin; and of course the coming of the railway triggered not only more shop-keeping but also a shift to light industry, the form of employment which still prevails.

One of the earliest of these factories was hoop and barrel making. The timber trade in all its forms, coppicing with 'standards', pollarding, collecting oak bark in spring for tanning, faggot making from the underwood for the baking oven, charcoal burning, fencing with oak, hurdle-making using hazel which was also used for thatching spars and wattle panels, basket-making with osiers, carpentry and general building had always flourished alongside arable and pastoral farming as normal local Wealden practices. Certain woods had special uses: ash for pegs, gates, bean rods, walking sticks, cart shafts, wheel felloes and tool handles; willow for cricket bats, elder for skewers, hornbeam for troughs, and way back, dogwood for arrows. From the time of the Napoleonic War it was customary to plant oaks widely spaced to secure short trunks and many curved branches providing *crooks* and *knees*, ideal for building ships' hulls. Oak bark was used for tanning and the timber made excellent charcoal. The Wealden topography had always dictated a complete integration of agriculture and woodcraft. Until wire became available, in the middle of the 19th century, cattle-proof hedgerows, usually with ditches and hand-made wooden hurdles, were vital to all farmers who kept stock. The woodcraft tradition is still honoured. Four Seasons at Coneyhurst, Potbury at Five Oaks, Burroughs at Fewhurst and many other suppliers, deal in charcoal, tree surgery, fencing and logging and there is an extensive wholesale fencing business, McVeigh Parker, established at Stane Street on the road to Adversane.

The older style of agriculture we would characterise as mixed farming, involving some arable fields for the growing of wheat, barley, oats and root crops. After 1874 when the price of wheat and barley fell because of cheap imported grain farmers ploughed less and turned to stock, especially dairying, 'From corn to horn' as the saying went. Most land remained as pasture, supporting horses, cattle for milk products and beef, sheep, pigs and goats, together with fowls for eggs and meat.

With the coming of WW II many pastures again went under the plough to grow wheat to save shipping in the hazardous conditions of war. Since then attention has shifted to more diverse crops such as oilseed rape, linseed, maize for silage, peas and beans. Most recently the number of dairy farms has shrunk to one as milk production and local distribution has proved uneconomic on smaller scale holdings and with the advent of refrigeration, supermarkets, and plastic containers.

Recent Ownership

On April 26th 1960 Mrs Scolding sold Kingsfold to Messrs. Tulloch and Maslin who held it for four years. The Maslin daughter, Jabeena, was a renowned horsewoman. She had all the old huts at the POW camp made into stables. She taught riding to all the schools in the area and was "Chef d'equipe' and trainer of the British Equestrian Pentathlon Team at the Seoul Olympics. Kingsfold was then sold to K.P.Hicks who was the owner for another six years until selling to Mr. And Mrs. Arthur Paton on 4th Jan 1971.

Mrs. Jane Paton was a magistrate on the Petworth Bench and an early Governor of the Weald School, acting with distinction as Chairman for many years until her retirement in 1991. Mr. Arthur Paton OBE, M.C. was born in 1916, the son of the Consul of Korea shortly after the Russian Revolution. The family later were in Moscow and Istanbul where father was Consul General. When Arthur came to school in the UK he had to forego the Cyrillic handwriting he had learnt from a White Russian Governess. He won a scholarship to Christ's Church, Oxford. He was summoned to Cardiff Arms Park to play rugby for Harlequins. He was commissioned into the 11th Hussars and won his Military Cross in desert battles in Libya and Egypt. On one occasion three armoured cars were shot up by a German aircraft. Luckily all the crews were having a brew-up some yards away. The sergeant, a former London bus driver cannibalised the three cars to make two, capable of returning them all to base. After the war he worked at the Foreign Office dealing with the problems of GI brides. Next he was into a fishing business in Kenya for four years and finally with the Bombay Trading Corporation from which hub he and his wife Jane travelled extensively in the Far East and the Mediterranean in the days before popular tourism.

In 2009 the Kingsfold property was sold for £1,100.000.

Other Older Buildings

There are other interesting properties along the road. One of the oldest which now gives the road its name is Marringdean Manor. Colin de la Mare, son of the poet Walter lived there for a time. Then the house was in poor repair. A visitor recalls seeing a bird's nest in one of the bedrooms. Other older timber-framed buildings, other than Kingsfold are Great Gilmans, South House and another small timber-framed dwelling.

South House is a hall house dating from the early 15th century. It was originally open to the roof before a chimney was inserted and the roof rebuilt. The chimney has a chamber halfway up probably used for smoking flitches of meat though some think of it as a 'Priest Hole'. Another curious possibility is that the house was first named 'Sow House' where pigs were used to clear woodland for cultivation.

South House, off Marringdean Rd. 2013

Great Gilmans is of 17th century date, or earlier, refaced with painted brick and weather-boarding.

Oakdean was one of the earliest erections after the 1903 sale. Mr. Jack Leaman lived there. He was a redoubtable village character, always smartly dressed like a pin-striped city stockbroker with a military air and authoritative voice. He had indeed been the Commanding Officer of comedian Spike Milligan during WW II and in his later years was the doyen of the Billingshurst British Legion and a stout supporter of the Dramatic Society.

Beke Place, a high status building, was where Mr Tom Flynn conducted a 'crammer' school to sharpen the prospects of candidates for the Common Entrance exam to public

Jack Leaman and Jack Easton, Bank manager, Chairman of the Parish Council and President of the Tennis Club

schools. The name is otherwise spelt – Beek and Beak.

Beke Hall, a Tudor house, originally built in 1495, was brought in pieces from Boxford in Suffolk by Captain Reginald Cosway in 1926 but burnt down in 1967 while being worked on by builders who were doing it up ready for Ms. Diana Dors.

Fure House in 1637 was known as Pocokes. High Fure is an Edwardian building on land which was part of the Manor of Ferring and Fure where the Bishop of Chichester was the Lord of the Manor. The many Manors with lands in Billingshurst were quite distinct from the ecclesiastical Parish. They originated as grants of land, under the feudal system, allotted to Lords who owed fealty, military services and paid taxes to the higher tier, the Tenant-in-chief of the Rape of Arundel. The Lords either farmed these economic units themselves, calling on labour from their tenants, or rented out the lands under 'copyhold' to yeoman farmers. They administered landholding rights and enforced the law through their own courts.

The actual Manor headquarters for Fure was way south at Ferring, but a strap of land, two fields wide from Fewhurst in the north east, through Jeffries Farm, South House and beyond High Fure to Greater and Lesser Woodhouse was an outlying unit of Ferring as a kind of colony. Students of hedge history, dating them by the number of species to be found, have postulated an early date to the distinctive strong hedgerow boundaries of Fure. Gervase de la Fure is first recorded as a tenant holding one yardland, paying rent of 7s 7d plus 4 hens and 25 eggs and required to perform services. Philip Hogheles (Howles) succeeded him in 1379 [Chaucer's time] at double the rent. The Pannel Roll of 1530 indicates that a Mr. Palmer had South lands and Gervase Goldings had South House though Jos. Grynfeild had the buildings and the land that was 'of old used by Maurice Grenefeild'. [There are farms named Palmers and Goldings in the north and east of Billingshurst. Sir Thomas Palmer had land at Five Oaks until 1609. He held Kingsfold until the last years of Queen Elizabeth I which he sold to William Penfold but the Greenfields had both that and Southlands by the end of the Civil War].

Edward Greenfield was in possession of High Fure from at least 1504 and his successive heirs held the High Fure land together with South House until 1811. Between 1563 and 1630 Robert and Morice Grenefeild are mentioned some 10 times in the Churchwardens' Accounts. In 1560 'Robert Greenfield bought for 3 shillings 2 black sheep, one ram, one ewe, which had been unclaimed for a year'. From 1609 to 1636 Maurice and Thomas were granted 20 trees for repairs and in 1617 the tenants of Fure were ordered to repair the parish pound there before the Feast of St. Michael the Archangel 'on pain of 20s'. [Michaelmas -29th Sept, a

Quarter Day, traditionally the end of the farming year and harvest is over when roasted goose was eaten, lands changed hands and farm workers were engaged at Hiring Fairs].

Between 1636 and 1740 Greenfields and their relatives, the Slaughters (Slaters), acted as Churchwardens, Overseers of the Poor, Waywardens, Collector and Surveyor of Highways on 14 recorded occasions. Whenever a new heir took over a payment called '*heriot*' was payable, at early times the best ox and a fine to the manor court. The custom lasted until at least 1843 when Mary Allen had to pay £6 heriot and £100 13s fine on taking over from her late husband, William Allen.

Inventories

Four inventories of South House were taken just before and during the Civil War (1633 – 1645). These records of the goods and chattels, stock and crops, offer us a valuable insight into the way of life of yeoman farmers in the 17th century. Some 16 rooms are listed on the site. In the following description the four inventories are conflated to identify significant items and the clerk's spelling as in the 1645 version is largely preserved:-

Imprimis: his wearing apparel and money in his purse - £10

In his lodging chamber [best ground floor room, also called 'The Parlour] – 1 bedsteddle, 1 feather bed, 1 straw bed, 3 blanketts, 1 rugge mat & cords & 2 bolsters -£5. I presse, 2 chests, 1 box, 1 side board, table, 3 small chayres and 1 other little box- 15s.

In the hall – 2 long tables with frames, 8 ioyned stooles, 1 ioyned forme, 3 chaires, 1 glasse case, 1 glasse cuppboord, cushions and 1 old table - £2

In the buttery [an above-ground 'cellar'] – 6 barrells,1 long table, 2 stands, one old table, 3 flagons, baskets -£1

In the kitchin- 1 long table, 1 forme, 1 cradle, 4 chaires -£1: 1 dussen of pewter, 5 candlesticks, 1 lanthern & divers small peeces of pewter - £1.10s: 1 furnice, 2 brasse kettells, 2 skillets and 1 warming panne and an yron pot -£3 pott hangers, pott hooks, fire shovel & tounges and yrons and a dripping pan & s gridgeon ? spits -30s: a fowling peece and a sword, 1 stone mortar, 1 cleaver - £I: 5 payre of tyre sheets & 7 of towe sheets [?towel] - £4.: 2 fine table cloths, 4 of a courser sort, 2 dusson & a halfe of napkins, 4 pillowbers [cases] & other lynnen - £3: books, bottles, baskets & divers other small things forgotten - £1

In the Lower kitchen were a caldron, 4 posnets [3 legged pots], a trough and a coop [basket poultry pen].

In the chamber over the buttery [also called the loft} – 2 bedsteddles, one trundle bedsteddle,2 chaffe bedd, 1 straw bed, a rug, a bolster, matte & cords - £3.

In the last two inventories it held 4 quarters of wheat, then flax and 3 bushells of buckwheat.

In the cheese loft, over the parlor: at first beds, tables chests and 10 cheeses. Later just beds etc. and a corslet and sword - £3

In his lodging chamber[the Little Chamber]- 1 bedsteddle,1 feather bed, 1 straw bed, 3 blanketts, 1 rugge, matt & cords & 2 bolsters - £5: 1 presse, 2 chests, 1 box, 1 side boord, table, 3 small chayres and 1 other little box -15s.

In the out or servant's chamber – 1 bedsteddle, 1 chaffe bed,1 blankett, 1 coverlidd and 2 old chests - £1

In the malting chamber over the Kitchen – flock, chaff or straw bed, rugge & cords etc. - £3

Wool was stored in the garret loft.

In the bake house – 1 powdring trough,1 tubb, 1 kneding trough, 1 stand, searchers and other lumber -£1.10s.

In the smoke loft -12 flitches bacon, 4 flitches beefe, 3 quarters malt -£5. This room was later named oast house with an oast hair, a wimsheete, fatt, linen wheel, sacks etc. – 5s

In the milk House – powdering tub, 6 tragges [trugs], 4 butter crocks, 8 kivers [covers] etc. – 10s

In the wash house -1 renning tub [? for curdling milk with rennet], brasse kettells, a little kiver, a coop, 2 barells - £1 16s

In the brew house – 1 furnice, 1 mesh fatte, 1 keeler [shallow tub], 4 tubbs, 2 cheese presses etc. - £4

In the entry – great saw & other tools, poke [bag] of wool.

The farm dead stock comprised in 1645: shelve and other boards at Beeke wth other lumber – 13s 4d: weanes [wains or carts], plowes, 1 oxe harrow, 3 horse harrowes, 2 dungcarts, cheynes, yokes & other things - £6: boords, bees, planks & other things - £2: caseway stones, a grinstone, & 2 ladders £1 10s: 6 pronges, 1 sledg, 2 sickels, wedges, 1 yron ringer, mattocks, axes, bills, shovells, spitters [spades], augers, & other husbandry tools - £1

The live stock comprised: 7 hennes & a cocke 6s: 2 fowre yearling steeres £7 10s: 2 three yearling steeres £6 10s: 3 2 yearling steeres - £7: 9 twelvemonththings £11. [which suggests that the Greenfield wealth derived from beef and other meat!]: 6 kyne [dairy cows] £19: 31 sheepe & 12 lambes -£11: hogs & pigs £4 10.

Draught animals comprised 5 oxen - £20 and 1 horse, 1 mare & 1 colt with bridles & saddles -£6.

In store were: 20 bushells of oates - £1 10, wheate in the barne -£10, 3 loade of hay £3, wheate in the house -10s, wood, faggots, post and rayles £4.

In the fields were: 11 acers of wheate - £20, 26 acers of oates - £26, 5 acers of pease - £5

Early inventories show how all fabrics were relatively expensive before the industrial revolution. Wool was the main constituent and flax was grown to make linen. The value arose from the domestic labour involved in turning the raw materials into cloth, often the work of 'spinsters'. Bed linen was particularly valuable as were napkins and cloths. Clothing was often particularly identified and costed in wills. All households were working houses where the necessities of life were created from what nature and cultivation could provide. Money might be used for such goods as could be bought from pedlars, but much was won by barter and by do-it-yourself traditional craftsmanship.

The 'summa total' of Elizabeth Greenfield's estate she inherited from Maurice was £229 15s 4d.

This inventory of John Barkhall, late of Billingshurst, of 1692, illustrates the point about the high value of cloth and clothing to our ancestors:-

Imprimis – his wearing apparel and money in his purse £5 -0 -0

Item   - in his bedchamber one bed and all there unto belonging

£3 -0 -0   Two joyned chests, one box and the linnen in that chamber
£3 -1 -0   In the inner chamber one bed and all thereto belonging
£4 -0 -0   Two kine and a mare
£4-10-0   Six sheep
£1 -10-0   2 swine and six piggs
£2 -15-0   Item – on money
£45-0 -0

All the pewter, a silver bowl and three silver spoons only amounted to £7 -2 -0. Mr.Barkhall seems to have kept his cash under the bed or some other safe place! The value of a pound at that time was relatively quite low, about £45 in today's money, so John had the equivalent of over £2000 to hand.

Later History

Sussex marble at South House Stable (Coarse winklestone)

The records show that Sussex marble, the coarser of the two types of winklestone, was quarried. In 1634 Thomas Greenfield was granted a licence to dig and sell the stone for 7 years. Sarah Greenfield was allowed 'to dig marble stone at High Fure, burn it on her land [for liming the clay] and sell the same already burnt'. Maurice Greenfield was granted a similar licence for three years in 1641 'at Southouse' for 10 shillings. The superb barns and stable at South House have complete walls built of this Sussex marble. There was a 'horseway' linking Jeffries Farm via South House and Wellers to High Fure. The Manorial Court ordered Maurice, albeit he was a Collector and Waywarden, to repair it under threat of a twenty shilling fine in 1679. A later Maurice upset the Manor Court in 1727 when he ' required 6 timber trees for repairs to his customary holding in Fure, but licence was not granted to him as he had formerly greatly damaged and cut down trees growing on his holding without licence'. Copyhold had its limitations!

The Greenfields seem to have lost much of their wealth during the Napoleonic War. In 1806 High Fure and South House were surrendered by William Greenfield to Charles Farhall, yeoman, for £800, as a mortgage, then again in 1809 to George Henty of Ferring, and in 1811 to Peter Martin (Surgeon of Pulborough), comprising one messuage, 2 barns, 1 stable and 80 acres. These mortgages were duly paid off. In 1808 William had '5 sittings' reserved in St. Mary's Church pews. Finally in 1813 William 'surrendered [the property] for £3800 to William Allen, junior, of West Chiltington, in full and absolute purchase'. The Allen family held the property, raising and repaying three mortgages, until 1857 when Mary Allen, now a widow of Pulborough, was granted a licence to let the property for 21 years. The mortgage she raised from Edward Pettar of Petworth, Gentleman, was repaid in 1871. The acreage rose from 80 to 140. The Allen family probably included the wealthy maltsters who in 1857 cheated the revenue, as related here in the section about Adversane and graphically described in Deborah Evershed's book about the hamlet.

Other occupants, judging by the parish burial records, included May Johnson (1819), Esther and William Turner (1858) and Esther Luxford (1899). By 1879 Robert Evershed was hiring South House and Gardens and six fields. George Ireland farmed High Fure in 1890. In 1898 there is record of a mortgage between G.C. Carew-Gibson of Kingsfold and Lionel A. Vaillant when South House was included with other premises in Surrey and Sussex.

The property, together with Jefferies Farm was farmed by the Ireland family in the early 20th century. Listed as 'buried from South House' after the turn of the century were Solomon Wadey (1908) and James Hard (1919). Two months before the outbreak of WW II William Nash Wadey of Newbridge Farm, who already owned Steepwood and Jefferies Farm, bought South House farm for £1050. The estate was held in trust in 1960 and sold for £26,000 in 1965 to William and Pamela Harries. They held it or a year and then sold it on to a Dr. Louis Bohm of London, NW 11. Dr. Bohm broke up the estate, the moated farm 'Jeffries' going to Frederick Sopp, now a flourishing motor car business. The other land passed to Stanley Stocker, an eminent farmer. The house and 10 acres was conveyed to Nicholas and Maureen Rowe in 1965.

South House took on a more swinging look appropriate to the times. It was converted into a Country Club by the Rowes, equipped with a splendid bar, roulette wheel and all the paraphernalia of a well-concealed pleasure palace for a well-heeled clientele. They left for Pythingdean, Pulborough. Dignity and respectability were restored when Mr. C.E. and Mrs. Sheila Van den Bergh took it over in 1967. They re-established this fine house and stable building as two modern dwellings with total respect for what has remained from just short of a millennium of occupation and development. The main Barn was wrecked by the great storm of 1987 but it too has been restored by Robert Van den Bergh to its former splendour.

South House, barn, stables and pond

Barn timbers, restored after the great storm

Exterior of South House Barn

Mr. Taylor's account of his life as a garden boy, aged 14, at Kingsfold in 1932.

Written in 1977, slightly abridged.

We worked every day from 7 in the morning until 5 at night, 7 shillings a week. I don't remember any holidays in those days. There was Cherryman – he was the

45

head gardener. He lived in the Lodge and Mrs Cherryman made butter in a churn at the back, proper little dairy there was there. One of my jobs was to bicycle two or three times a week to Oakdene and Clevelands with pounds of butter. Palmer, he was the under gardener and cowman, lived behind the wall. He was quite a character. He had an accordion, the kind with keys and one of the early radios set up with big loudspeakers – used to make a terrific noise. He'd lost his wife but he had several daughters. One of them worked as a kitchen-maid here. There was a big fat cook, wasn't very kind to her, used to make her scrub the kitchen floor and I'd find her in tears scrubbing this big floor. Palmer used to clean the windows and when he did the top ones I'd have to stand at the bottom of the ladder. The only trouble was he was a tobacco chewer and I'd be at the bottom dodging the bits he spat out.

There was a big Aga in the kitchen and the sink was the other side. I used to come in here to clean the knives, hundreds of them, valuable I think they were. The shoes too. I used to clean them in the garage, and there was an electric light engine next to it. I remember one man staying had the most enormous shoes – must have been a size 15.

Mrs Clark, she was a very old lady, all wizened and bent. She didn't go out very much. It was a big old car she had and Parminter was the chauffeur. He lived on the other side of the road. He didn't really do much work – used to spend his time polishing this car, but she'd only go out about once a month.

Outside there was the rose garden with roses in figure of eight beds. Mrs Clark would knock off the dead heads or spotty leaves and I'd have to pick up the bits. That's all they gave a boy to do in those days, just the dull jobs. Cherryman would cut the hedges and I'd pick up the cuttings. On wet days the two gardeners, they'd be in the shed sawing away and I'd be next door chopping wood, just the dull jobs. When they thought I was getting a bit fed up, they'd let me go over the field there and let me start the motor for the water pump in the mornings. That was an interesting job for a young boy.

We never used weed killer in the old days that I can remember, wouldn't spend the money on it. I'd be out with a knife pulling weeds out of the gravel. I lived over the road in Kingslea cottages. That was how I got the job in the first place because my father used to go to the Station Hotel for a pint on a Saturday with Mr. Cherryman. We boys used to hide in the bushes to see them staggering home, three forward and two sideways we always thought they took.

The plantation didn't have a nice path like this, but we used to spend a lot of time in the autumn sweeping up the leaves, pine needles and that. That was Mr. Gray's field over there. Gray was the farmer. They came from Somerset I think. He was a great character. He fell off a big hay cart and landed too heavy on his feet and he was stone deaf ever afterwards. It was his daughter married Mr. Stocker. In the field out there was an old donkey – if you touched him a cloud of dust came up. He was just a pet with a little shed for him.

We had good asparagus beds in the vegetable garden here. There were lots of polyanthus under the wall and over there where the swimming bath is was the compost. There was no grass on this side, just paths intersecting and there were raspberries, blackcurrants and fruit trees. I remember when a blackbird got to the raspberries under the net and Mrs. Clark came out. I caught the bird and she shouted at me, "Wring its neck" and again "Wring its neck" – I thought that was a bit hard. We used to weed round the pond by hand, but it wasn't as pretty as it is now.

Right up to where the wall is here there was great piles of coal, the big stuff, great huge lumps. That was another of my jobs, breaking it down with a hammer and I got grumbled at if I made too much dust. Down between these hedges there was a grass walk with herbaceous borders on either side'. The grass wasn't too wide and the borders went right up to the hedges. There were dogs' graves along the grass here (outside the cellar windows). Mrs. Clark had little hairy dogs, Cairns I think they were. You could hardly see their eyes for hair.

Mrs. Clark used the billiard room as a sitting room and there was a little conservatory with a door outside the kitchen window. That's where I gave my notice. Up the road I got 15 shillings [75 pence!] – that was double. Mrs. Clark couldn't believe it. "I can't afford to pay you that" she said.

We bicycled a lot in those days. I remember going all the way to London to see the Lying in State of George V. When we got there we had to wait about four hours in the queue. I wanted to have something to eat before we started home, but this other boy he said, "Wait until we get to Epson Downs". When we got there everything was shut. It must have been 4 a.m. when we got home. It quite put me off, doing it without any food!

"Our England is a garden, and such gardens are not made'

By singing:-

'Oh, how beautiful!'
and sitting in the shade,
While better men than we go out
and start their working lives.
At grubbing weeds from garden
paths with broken dinner knives."
[Rudyard Kipling]

Wedding at Kingsfold

From Mr. Chitty's deeds - Mediaeval Farms

In 1306 we learn from the deeds that one John le Pratt de Billingshurst granted land called Brokefield to Rogo Buchi de Shepele (Shipley), paying one red rose for it. He had the land from Elvicus the Bold. The Pratts owned several farms, and it is likely that Laura le Pratt married a Merlot, the family that owned Muntham House in Itchingfield from 1300 to 1877.

John Pratt's son, also John, granted land at Billingshurst in 1317 to Roge Buchi's son, also Roger. In 1318 Roger passed the lands to his brother, Lawrence Buchi. Witnesses to the transaction included Richard ate Putte (? Puttock) and Richard Gylemin (as in Great Gilmans?).

Lawrence's son Robert had land – meadows and a water mill – in Billingshurst and Shipley, which Robert Traylemere and his wife Maria 'held for their lives'.

Another Pratts Farm is marked on Budgen's map, opposite Summers, together with Pinkhurst, Muntham House, Itchingfield, and Hadfold. The Pratts Farm mentioned in the deeds is today a two-bay late 16th C end chimney-stacked house with extensions, refaced in brick in the 18th century.

In 1338 William de Hadfolde of Billingshurst granted 1 and ½ acres of land in Wassington to Robert Bouchi of Shipley. His name relates to Hadsfoldshern, Old English – Hadesfoldeshyrne – Hedefoldeshurne 1279 –Hadfoldsherne 1711 – Hadfordshern c 1800, corner of land relating to Hadfold (fold is an enclosure) – or Adversane.

Among the 40 or so names listed as paying a wealth tax in Billingshurst on the Subsidy Roll of 1332 are the following which have clear modern derivatives both as place names and surnames:

Johne de Pemefold – who paid most – Penfold

Robt le Tote – Toat

Petro Prat – Pratts Farm

Willmo Kockebrok – Coxbrook, East Street

Malill de Hadfold – Hadfold and Adversane. Hadfold was originally controlled by the Priory of Tortington.

John le Carpentir - Carpenters

Ancient Buildings in Billingshurst

There are 80 old houses in the Billingshurst area originally of timber-frame construction though they have all been altered and adapted through the years according to the fashion of the day. Twenty of these are in the heart of the village. All were first built for the more affluent yeoman farmers and traders. Subsequently they were often occupied by farm workers and humbler folk, but of recent years have enjoyed the status of antiquity and are eagerly sought after by well-to-do people of independent means. All 'listed' buildings are now strictly controlled by Horsham District Council to preserve their original features which are of special architectural or historic interest, as required by the Town and Country Planning Act of 1990. All buildings erected before 1700 should be listed and many up to 1840. Only St. Mary's Church is Grade I. There were 108 addresses in Billingshurst as entries listed at Grade II in 2013.

Fewhurst (late 14th century farmhouse) in Coneyhurst Road has a crown post and an end-aisle construction. The chimney extension uses local winklestone, which is also used at Jeffries Farm (part 17thC), nearby. An ancient L-shaped barn at Little Jefferies Farm was burnt down in 1969.

Pennybrooks, in Birch Drive set amidst modern housing, is a 4 bay house with two areas still open to the roof. Its original name was Broomfields, a name pre-empted by a Victorian building in Station Road while the old house lapsed into labourers' cottages until restored and renamed.

Okehurst

At Okehurst, beside the slab-roofed farm house, is the Clock Gallery in two bays and two storeys of about 1530. The ground floor was originally used for dairy purposes and the upper floor as accommodation for workers. In most of the older

49

timber-framed houses the buttery, where barrels and bottles were kept, and the milk house were incorporated on the ground floor adjoining the hall. Here such rooms are provided in an out-house. Dallaway in his *History of the Three Western Rapes of Sussex'* (1811) says of this house:

"Okehurst is held in the honour of Arundel as parcel of the Manor of Bury and was a constituent part of it when Domesday [Book] was compiled. ....A family named 'de Okehurst' were the mesne tenants for many generations. In the reign of Edward IV Thomas Bartelott of Stopham, having married the heiress of de Okehurst, became possessed, and in their descendants it remained vested till 1579, when it passed to John Wiseman, one of whose daughters conveyed it in marriage to Edward Goring Esq., second son of Sir H. Goring of Bodecton, the immediate ancestor of Sir Henry Goring, Bart., the present proprietor." Edward Goring paid £340 for it in 1572. His monument is in St. Mary's s Church. Likewise Thomas Bartlet, MP for Midhurst, is represented in a monumental brass with Elizabeth his wife (1499). She was grand-daughter of William de Okehurst who fought at Agincourt. Okehurst was not a Manor House, in the strict sense, as the headquarters of a manorial court and demesne but part of the Manor of Bassett's Fee.

The Gorings sold it in the 1870s and the next owner we hear of is Shepley-Shepley followed by Peter Locke-King. The shield and baton of Sir Charles Goring, Sheriff of Sussex in 1827 adorns the Hall ceiling. Radiating from the shield are twelve pikes, each inscribed with name of a Botting. Smuggling was at that time going on along the Fosseways, and the story runs that the Sheriff's guard consisted of the two Botting brothers and the five sons each of them, twelve in all. Pikes are said to have been better than firearms. William Botting was the miller at Rowner and Francis Botting farmed Okehurst in 1867. The Fielding family followed Hugh Locke-King.

Other listed buildings in Okehurst Road are Rowner, Spurland, The Clock House, Gatefield Cottage and Bignor Farm House, all 17th century in whole or in part. Frogshole and Pound Cottage are 16th Century.

South House, off Marringdean Road, is L shaped. It had a buttery with chamber above it, similar to Hammonds in East Street. The barn is 18th Century.

Great Daux is an early example, unusual for the area, of close-studding where the studs and spaces between are of similar width. It is 15th Century with a slab roof and diamond-shaped windows.

Buckmans (17th C) at Five Oaks is very unusual in that it is tile-hung all over. It has fishscale tiles.

Buckman's, Five Oaks with tile-hanging overall

High Seat (18th C) at the north end of Billingshurst has a wall with 'mathematical tiles' designed to look like bricks and a slate roof.

Old Cottage at Andrew's Hill is a 17th century 3-bay house with a central smoke bay.

Great Grooms, once also known as Parbrook, until recently the Jenny Wren restaurant, is largely of 16th Century date. It was named from a John Gretgrome and its early history dates from the early 14th century. Some floors are laid with Sussex marble and it has a bread oven inglenook fireplace.

At Marringdean Manor the south wing is 15th Century with a 16th Century crosswing.

Knob's Crook, Adversane is a 16th Century open hall house.

Fossbrooks, in Parbrook, a two-storey timber-framed building with plaster infilling with casement windows, is 16th century.

Fossbrooks in Parbrook

Duncans Farmhouse in W. Chiltington Lane, (17th C or earlier), has a Horsham slab roof.

In East Street are Gore Farm House and Hammonds.

Coombland House, Marringdean is 17th Century incorporating sandstone and red brick.

Great Gilman's, Marringdean Rd., is 17th Century or earlier.

Marringdean Cottage is 17th Century.

Grainingfold at Five Oaks exemplifies a mediaeval farmhouse.

Copped Hall, Okehurst Road, is an L-shaped house. The North Wing is 17th C or earlier.

Wynstrode, also in Okehurst Road, is 17th C, L-shaped.

Many of these houses have wide hearths built to accommodate standard four-foot cordwood logs. It was economical of labour to use long wood for fires until the invention of power-driven circular saws made 10 inch billets feasible for use in stoves and small fireplaces.

Wide hearth in South House inglenook

The Unitarian Chapel

After the Toleration Act of 1689 dissenters from the Anglican Church like Matthew Caffyn (1624-1720) were no longer prosecuted and imprisoned for heretical teaching. By 1726 a Baptist Meeting House had been founded at Horsham, with two of the Trustees living in Billingshurst.

In 1742 William Evershed, known as 'The Preacher', came to Great Daux Farm where he raised four children. From there he attended 64 Baptist meetings at Horsham in 56 years! The Billingshurst members were keen to have their own chapel, so Evershed and William Turner bought land from a Mrs. Elizabeth Sendall and her son Edward for three guineas (£3.30). The Chapel they built was transferred to 10 Trustees for 1,000 years. Extra land was acquired in 1759 and 1799 when William died. He is buried in the yard. In the early 19th century the inter-denominational Sunday School was the only education available to village children. It was held in the Market Room behind the King's Arms. In 1825 the Vestry Room was built and yet more land obtained.

At first the Horsham and Billingshurst Meetings had joint Elders, but by 1818 a theological dispute about the 'Laying on of Hands' led to rupture and independence at Billingshurst.

Mr. Dendy Evershed published a comprehensive history of the Chapel in 1991, including a record of all burials since 1755. Baptism by immersion was practised until 1872, using water from a spring near the Women's Hall gate brought in buckets to the Baptistery behind the Chapel. When the water ran out sprinkling was substituted for general baptism. Marriages were solemnised after 1839.

In 1877 the Jeffery family paid for a new roof and repairs. In 1886 more structural work led to the making of a library with bookshelves, the only forerunner of the County Library in 1944. An organ was installed in 1911 shortly after it was renamed The Free Christian Church [Unitarian]. Services steadily improved with rewiring and a new heating system in 1985.

Some land was sold to CALA homes and subsequently an extension added in 1990. In 1999 the name was changed to Unitarian Chapel.

Pear Tree Farm and Frank Patterson

In 1898 Frank and Emily Patterson hired a derelict Elizabethan house at a rental of 9 old pence per annum (3 and a half pence). They had it repaired by a local builder and lived there for 54 years, renaming it Pear Tree Farm. Its old name was Hookers at Eastlands. It is a 16th century two storey, timber-framed building with a tile-hung south gable.

Frank was born in Portsmouth in 1871 of seafaring stock. His sailor father wrote for 'The Boys' Own Paper'. Frank attended Portsmouth Art School. There he set up a shooting gallery in the loft! He enlisted in the army in his teens but wisely bought himself out of it. To seek work he walked to London and began his career as an illustrator of books and magazines – mainly 'Cycling' magazine. He worked for the magazine for 63 years. He was an enthusiastic cyclist until 1909 when a leg injury restricted him to walking, sometimes up to fifty miles a day! His drawings were mainly not drawn from life however but based on pictures and postcards. He was a thoroughly reliable journalist, always on time, submitting up to ten drawings a week. It is estimated that he made 26,000 drawings, always displaying 'a joyful celebration of our beautiful countryside' [Gerry Moore]. He was an exemplar of the Golden Age of Cycling in the 1920s when touring to welcoming inns was a popular pastime. His riders would be dressed in plus fours, long socks, strap-over cycle shoes and an alpaca jacket, equipped with map, panniers and a saddle-bag. By contrast Frank himself dressed and behaved like a local Billingshurst yeoman farmer in tweeds, boots and gaiters who kept gun-dogs, though in fact he rented out his land, kept no stock and earned his living as an artist.

He did not drink tea, but had 4 and a half gallon barrel of IPA delivered from King and Barnes Brewery at Horsham every fortnight. He was a good shot, in demand at local shoots to boost the bag of pheasants, using his trusty hammer 12 bore shotgun with Damascus barrels, a perfectly weighted weapon in his grandson's opinion. Being a professional man he was often called on as a juryman. He saw this as a penalty and craftily arranged with the local policeman to be arrested and convicted for not buying a dog licence. In those days a criminal conviction was enough to debar you from jury service. In 1933 he found a piece of sandstone with footprints which were believed to be those of a stegosaurus dinosaur.

In 1934 he floated a correspondence course from Pear Tree Farm and produced a prospectus, 'The Patterson School of Sketching', but it did not flourish. One of his nephews was a pupil artist but they fell out when he tried to pass off some of Frank's work as his own. They never spoke again.

Pear Tree Farm by Frank Patterson

Billingshurst's Heritage No. 2

Frank and Emily had two daughters, Molly and Peggy. Emily had consumption and needed nursing for several years. Agnes came as a companion and when Emily died she and Frank married. They had two sons Jock Angus and Gordon Andrew, both of whom served in the RAF in WW 2. Jock's son Roger, now a retired master beekeeper of national standing, remembers only seeing Frank taken off to hospital by ambulance. In 1991 an exhibition of his work was staged at Sotheby's in Billingshurst. He died in 1952 and his ashes were scattered at the Farm.

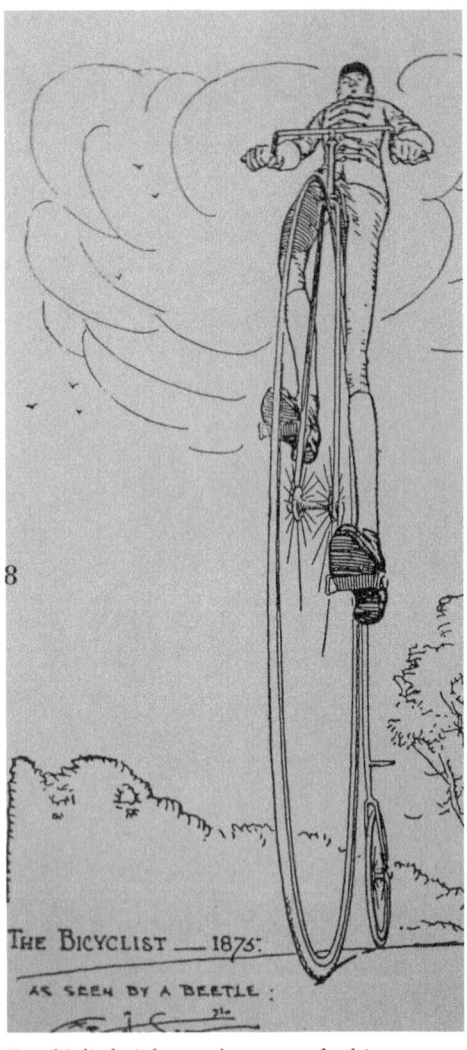

Frank's little joke on the penny-farthing

Frank greets a friend with his 12 bore

Notable local people with Billingshurst Connections

Maggie Gee – novelist, daughter of the first Headmaster of the Weald School, V.V. Gee. Her autobiographical work '*My Animal Life*' includes fond and anxious recollections of her childhood and schooling in the village as well as brave, frank and profound meditations on her family and personal life.

Edward Enfield – Writer, educational administrator, wit, cycling tourist, professional stickler and paterfamilias, unswervingly loyal to traditional values.

Harry Enfield – Comedian and satirist of contemporary manners. Creator of TV characters Stavros, Loadsamoney, Kevin the belligerent teenager, etc.

Lizzie Enfield – novelist, journalist and contributor to 'The Oldie' magazine

Diana Dors, England's answer to Marilyn Monroe, actress and 'sex symbol', lived for a time in the 60s at Palmers Farm, Coneyhurst.

Mary Law, Actress, personal friend of Agatha Christie, once filmed with Diana Dors and played in *The Mousetrap* and with Laurence Olivier's company at Stratford-on-Avon.

Nancy Roberts – TV 'hostess' with Hughie Green of '*Double Your Money*' from 1955.

Paul Darrow – TV actor and author. Robin Hood, Blake's 7, Dixon, Z cars etc.

Dave Gilmour D.Mus, CBE- Singer of popular music and guitarist with Pink Floyd. The group are believed to have sold 250 million records.

Stroller – show jumping pony. A gelding once owned by Miss. Sally Cripps that won Silver in the 1968 Olympics, exercised by Mr. Des Wakeling.

Max Faulkner OBE (of Gay Street) – Open Golf Champion 1951 at Royal Portrush. Owned 300 putters. Flamboyant dresser who once walked on his hands to the next tee 'to get some blood to his brain'. Co-founded and designed West Chiltington Golf Club with son-in-law, pro golfer Brian Barnes.

David Sainsbury – National and International Level Rugby Union Referee

Arthur Paton OBE, M.C. – rugby footballer, soldier, and businessman.

Aileen Walker MBE of Stonepits – for services to Billingshurst. She was the principle founder of the Billingshurst Society. She designed the village signs.

Mike Read – radio disc jockey of Steepwood Farm. Twice bankrupt, the first time for debts to Horsham District Council.

John Wilding MBE – expert horologist, prolific writer on antique clocks, known as 'Meccanoman' because of his childhood enthusiasm and subsequent love of precision engineering. He played the French horn in amateur orchestras and formed his own chamber music group. Patrick Moore, the astronomer, composed a march dedicated to John's group. Mr. Wilding was Clerk to the Billingshurst Parish Council. They presented him with a watch on his retirement with the dates 1966-70 inscribed on it.

Billingshurst's Heritage No. 2

John Wilding with clock and French horn

Dr. Richard Lane – expert entomologist, international authority on fruit flies.
Frank Patterson – artist and remarkable character.
Roger Patterson – Frank's Grandson, 50 years a beekeeper and pillar of Wisborough Green Beekeeping Association. Author of beekeeping books, contributor to Journals and recognised national expert.
Kenneth Alwyn (of Broadford Bridge) – Celebrated Conductor, writer and international recording artist. Royal Ballet, Covent Garden, LSO, BBC Concert Orchestra etc. He composed *'The Young Grenadier'* for Trooping the Colour on the Queen's birthday and *'Fighter Command 1940'*, ceremonial march of the RAF. Pilot.
Gillian Yarham, County Organiser of Women's Institutes in West Sussex, Chairman of the W. Sussex Federation of WIs and Director and Trustee of the Company.
Dr. Arthur Evershed (1836-1919), painter, etcher and lay preacher. Etchings include studies in Chichester. Work at the British Museum and the Victoria and Albert
Thomas Evershed, born 1817. Emigrated to America in 1835 where he became a leading engineer in the construction of railways and canals. In 1842 he returned

to England and made sketches of local scenes, including St. Mary's Church.

Henry Charles Fox – landscape painter (1855-1929) lived in Upper Station Road at 'Cricklewood' for many years.

Deborah Evershed, author of *'From Hadfoldshern...to Adversane'* published in 2006. This is a record and celebration of her own family, Miles, Puttocks, Greenfields and Hards in late Victorian times who, time out of mind, had peopled the hamlet of Adversane embellished with anecdotes and stories of their doings and enterprises.

Hugh Fortescue Locke-King. Founder of Brooklands racing circuit. Landowner at Five Oaks and probably Billingshurst's richest man.

Dame Ethel Locke-King, wife of Hugh was the organiser of a number of military hospitals during WW I.

Sir Charles Fielding KBE, business-man, Chairman of Rio Tinto, proponent of the College of Science and Technology, Director General of Food Production in WW I, agricultural writer on the international food trade. He had Ingfield Manor built.

David Arnold of Brampton House. Navigator of first submarine, 'Nautilus', to go under the Arctic Ice Cap in 1958. Deputy Vice-Commander of Royal Yacht Club and navigator for Ted Heath on 'Morning Cloud'. Author and County Councillor.

The Beck sisters, Ellen and Edith of Duncans Farm, off West Chiltington Lane, from 1905 to 1930 were supporters of Women's Emancipation and Mrs. Pankhurst. Donors of the Women's Hall, the Children's Garden and other village amenities such as the 25 uniforms of the Billingshurst Band formed in 1919.

Rev. Stanley, donor of the Old Village Hall.

Sheila Van den Bergh – 24 years a District Councillor and sole person twice Chairman of Horsham District Council.

Maj. Gen. Renton, Horticulturist of Rowfold Grange, President of The Horticultural Society, Chair of Weald Governors, and donor of Working Men's Club building and other village amenities.

Mr. Robert Morris, of Five Oaks. The family dairy farm supplied eggs and milk, cream and butter from Guernsey cows from 1930 to the 1980s. Robert was first Chairman of the Parish Council, 1894. Donor of Five Oaks Iron Mission Room in 1891. Two of his four sons were killed in WWI, Francis in Mesopotamia and John at Gallipoli. They are remembered by oak memorial doors at St. Mary's.

William Verling Sherlock was Born in Georgetown, Demerara and batted for West Indies cricket team on the 1910/11 tour. He died at Wynstrode, Okehurst Road in 1937.

William Penn (Blue Idol) Strictly speaking the Quaker Meeting House is in

Thakeham parish. William Penn School is in Coolham and Penn Charter School in Philadelphia. Charles II bestowed Pennsylvania upon William which territory the family 'owned' until the American Revolution.

William Cobbett (1763-1835), Billingshurst visitor

Cobbett was a self-taught, anti-authoritarian agitator, and radical reformer chiefly remembered for his book 'Rural Rides'. He was a great champion of impoverished farm workers during the depression after the Napoleonic Wars, a whistle-blower against corruption on both sides of the Atlantic and an opponent of the Corn Laws. Yet he was a traditionalist who saw the Industrial Revolution as the ruination of rural society. Brighton Pavilion he likened to a turnip stuck on top of a box. However he holds Billingshurst and district in high esteem. "I saw, and with great delight, a pig at almost every labourer's house". "The people are very clean, the Sussex women very nice in their dress and in their houses". "This village [Billingshurst] is seven miles from Horsham, and I got here to breakfast about seven o'clock. A very pretty village and a very nice breakfast, in a very neat little parlour of a very decent public house [The King's Arms]. The landlady sent her son to get me some cream, and he was just such a chap as I was at his age, and dressed in just the same sort of way, his main garment being a blue smock-frock, faded from wear, and mended with pieces of new stuff, and, of course, not faded. The sight of this smock-frock brought to my recollection many things very dear to me. This boy will, I daresay, perform his part at Billingshurst, or at some place not far from it. If accident had not taken me from a similar scene, how many villains and fools, who have been well-teased and tormented, would have slept in peace at night, and have fearlessly swaggered about by day!

When I look at this little chap – at his smock-frock, his nailed shoes, and his clean, plain, coarse shirt, I ask myself, will anything, I wonder, ever send this little chap across the ocean to tackle the base, corrupt, perjured Republican Judges of Pennsylvania? Will this little lively, but at the same time, simple boy, ever become the terror of villains and hypocrites across the Atlantic."

Cobbett was angry about the enclosure of the 800 acre heath north east of Horsham by an enclosure act of 1813 secured by the Lord of the Manor, the Duke of Norfolk, the cost paid for by the sale of a small parcel of land. "A large common...cut up, disfigured, spoiled, and the labourers all driven from its skirts. I have seldom travelled over eight miles so well calculated to fill the mind with painful recollections". A verse of the time catches the spirit of Cobbett's criticism:

'The law locks up the man or woman,
Who steals the goose from off the common;
But lets the greater villain loose,
Who steals the common off the goose!'

He would have been yet more incensed had he lived to know how shrewd had been the Duke's investment in development land. 'By 1911 land thus acquired was fetching £850 an acre. No doubt as a small compensation to the burgesses of Horsham, he rebuilt the Town Hall, in a singularly ugly pseudo-Norman style' [J.R. Armstrong]. It has recently become a restaurant. Fortunately no enclosure acts affected the people of Billingshurst. There were no open fields or commons to be exploited because the farm landscape of small fields had originally been won by 'assarting' or grubbing up the trees from the time of the Saxons.

Horsham Town Hall

'Soon after quitting Billingshurst', Cobbett wrote, 'I crossed the River Arun which has a canal running alongside of it. At this there are large timber and coal yards, and kilns for lime. This appears to be a grand receiving and distributing place'.

Billingshurst's Heritage No. 2

The Wey & Arun Canal

The most remarkable archaeological feature in Billingshurst is the relic of an astonishing feat of engineering undertaken by our ancestors in the early 19th century. In truth it is an attribute shared both with Wisborough Green, since much of the enterprise was on the west bank of the Arun River, and also with Pulborough, since that village claimed the river frontage until boundary changes gifted it to Billingshurst in 1933. The Arun named after Arundel was originally called Tarrente or Trisanton meaning 'trespasser', and is recalled in the name of Tarrant Street in Arundel.

As early as 1641 a Bill was introduced to Parliament to link the upper reaches of the River Wey to those of the Arun by a canal between Cranleigh and Dunsfold. The Arun waterway, from the coast at Littlehampton, had been made navigable as far as Stopham Bridge at Pulborough in Queen Elizabeth's time. Cargo boats are even said to have been able to reach as far as Pallingham Quay by 1637. However the Bill was not proceeded with. A century and a half later, in 1785, The Arun Navigation Act was passed and the section between Pallingham and Newbridge opened two years later. The Wey & Arun Junction Canal Company was formed in 1811 and the Act of Parliament authorising the work between Shalford and Newbridge was passed in 1813 when construction began. An authoritative account is to be found in P.A.L. Vine's book *'London's Lost Route to the Sea'*.

In 1816 the Wey & Arun Junction Canal opened for business. At the opening ceremony in a spirit of euphoria at 'The Compasses' inn at Alfold an ox was roasted whole and the navigators who had done the spade work drank 200 gallons of ale. It had required the construction of over 18 miles of canal and 23 locks. It could accommodate 50 ton laden barges and cost £101,370. This is the equivalent of well over £100M today. It was a spectacular feat of civil engineering, of enterprise and of strenuous physical labour. Freight could now travel by water back and forth from the Thames at Weybridge via the Wey, the Junction Canal and the Arun to Arundel docks and the coastal harbour at Littlehampton. More importantly for strategic military purposes the government had secured a safe inland passage to Portsmouth when yet another canal linked Chichester and Portsmouth to Arundel. Ironically the security aspect of the project was never realised as the threat of French invasion was over after the Battle of Waterloo, only one year earlier.

Southwards from Loxwood Bridge beside the Onslow Arms are the following features:

Brewhurst Lock
Baldwins Knob Lock

Drungewick Aqueduct over the Lox River
Drungewick Lane Bridge
Drungewick Lock
Malham Lock
Rowner Lock
A272 Bridge (Newbridge)
[From here on we are on the Arun Navigation]
Orfold Aqueduct
Orfold Lock, now called Lordings
Lee Farm Lock
Pallingham Quay
Pallingham Lock – a double 'staircase' lock.

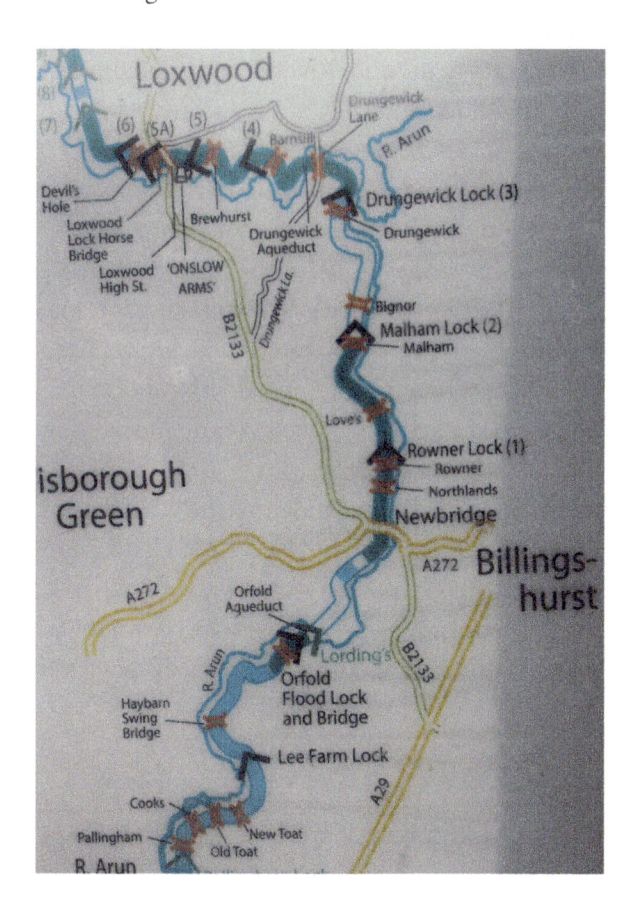

George Wyndham

The third Earl of Egremont, George Wyndham of Petworth was the main sponsor of canals in West Sussex. He is remembered as a patron of the arts who sponsored the emigration to Canada of thousands of poor Petworth folk. He saved the Arun Navigation Company from bankruptcy by buying shares. He also invested in the Portsmouth-Arundel link and his own canal on the River Rother. He bought 250 shares at £100 each, some 28% of the value of The Wey & Arun Junction Company. Dividends ceased altogether in 1865 and never exceeded 1%! By 1850 shares had fallen in value to £10. By a cruel twist of fate, the toll income had improved a little in the late 50s when the company undertook haulage of building materials for the new Horsham to Petworth rail line, the true instrument of the canal's own demise. The last dividend paid in 1865 was 6 shillings, about ¼ %. Closure was inevitable and the shareholders put the company into liquidation. The other two Navigation Companies, the Arun and River Wey (Godalming) Navigations, raised legal objection to abandonment, but after no buyer for the canal business could be found at auction in 1870, the necessary Act was passed and closure came in 1871 after which the land was sold off. The Earl's heirs were affluent enough to support the losses, though when George Wyndham died in 1837 he might well have still been nourishing hopes of better financial returns.

Wyndham was a power in the land, part of the influential Whig aristocracy. He, like Lord Byron, had an affair with Lady Caroline Lamb and is reliably reputed to have been the natural father of the young Queen Victoria's mentor and Prime Minister, William Lamb, Lord Melbourne, the statesman well commemorated in Australia.

Besides the goods mentioned by Cobbett, timber, coal and lime, the wharfingers dealt in imported groceries and shop goods, grain for the watermill, chalk, sand and gravel and seaweed for fertilizer on farms. Exported were timber, oak bark, hoops and other woodcraft products. The toll on a ton of coal from Arundel to Newbridge was 1s 8d plus 6d for using a tunnel at Hardham which by-passed a loop in the Arun.

The Working Years and Demise

Commercially the Wey & Arun Company enjoyed moderate success in the 1830s, paying that small 1% dividend but prospects steadily deteriorated. In the best year 23,000 tons of freight were moved. Most trade was from London, mainly coal and groceries, porter beer and pottery. Such things as bullion guarded by red-coated troops, furniture and soldiers' equipment went north. A wharfinger's house had opened at Newbridge in 1839 beside the entrance to the wharf. It continued in use until 1888 when the last barge to and from the south put an end to river traffic. At one time it housed a beer house called The Limeburners. It is now a private residence and The Limeburners Arms is on the opposite side of the river by Lordings Road, converted from a row of 17th century cottages. Rowner water mill on the Arun River was demolished in 1966.

Rowner Lock under reconstruction

Restoration

The Wey & Arun Canal Society was formed in 1970 and became the Wey & Arun Canal Trust in 1973. Enthusiasts have combined to rehabilitate the 'lost route to the sea' with the idealistic and laudable vision of restoring the entire derelict canal to the state of its heyday as a delightful leisure amenity. There are many obstacles. Many riparian landowners are reluctant to cooperate, some stretches have been built over, locks, bridges and aqueducts have collapsed. Nature has reasserted its dominion of the channel bottom requiring judicious reclamation from the wild before any dredging or restoration work can begin. The costs are formidable even with modern machinery and volunteer assistance.

Passenger barges at the Onslow Arms

The Wey & Arun Canal Trust has dredged half the old 18 mile canal bed, built a new lock and road bridge at Loxwood at a cost of £1.9M and restored 10 other locks, 24 bridges two aqueducts and many culverts. Rowner Lock, last used in 1871, was completely restored in 1982 having started in 1971. Pleasure cruises on three boats, the 'Wiggonholt', the 'Zachariah Keppel' and the 'Josias Jessop' (named after the consulting engineer) now operate from the Onslow Arms to Drungewick and northwards from the Inn as far as Devil's Hole Lock, (2012) and probably as far as Southland Lock in 2013/14. Once the stretch to Pallingham is repaired the waterway will be open for small boats to go all the way to Littlehampton.

Canal Tourist 1869 – a neo-Pickwickian idyll

J.B.Dashwood, with his wife and dog, stayed in the village on their sail-boat journey from 'The Thames to the Solent' at a time when the canal company was foundering and already up for auction. He wrote:

'Loxwood... boasts of a neat clean little inn close by the Canal side...although we did not pull up here but pushed forward to Billingshurst. There are five locks between Loxwood and Billingshurst. The country here is decidedly ugly with flat water meadows on either side. Just before reaching Newbridge...[the weeds] became so thick that it seemed almost impossible to cut our way through them.'

'We found Billingshurst a charming little place with a neat little Inn by the name of The Kings Arms...We had the gratification of sitting down to as good a dinner as I believe it is possible to get in a quiet country village! Fresh eggs, butter, bread, fruit, cream, all excellent with mutton chops done to a turn with excellent beer and a very fair sherry.'

'After dinner we took a stroll up the village...all seemed peaceful and happy; little family groups sitting at the entrance doors of their houses, others strolling up and down the hilly street, while the young ones besported themselves on all sides. Judging by the appearance of the old men we saw crawling about in every direction the place must be most healthy...for it stands on high ground and appears beautifully clean and thriving.'

'Next morning the Inn was a bustle by 5. Hot and cold water for shaving and baths to any amount and boots polished like mirrors. The breakfast is a capital one. Our little table was filled with cold meat, eggs, toast and coffee at our going hour of 5.45.'

'At a little before 7 o'clock we reached Newbridge where our boat lay quietly at her moorings, wet with the morning bath of dew...[at the first lock] we watched the lock-keeper's wife and two pretty daughters making butter in the early morning. Though flat the meadows on either side presented such a lovely English picture with cattle dotted about, ...the larks sang aloft sending forth their melodious morning song and the banks of the Canal clothed with wild flowers of every hue and colour that we enjoyed this part of our journey almost as much as any.'

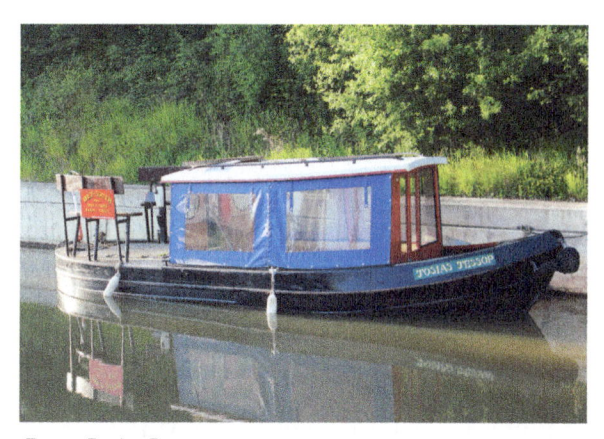

Barge Josias Jessop

Rowner Watermill

Probably the oldest recorded relic of the past in Billingshurst, though originally in Pulborough parish, is the watermill on the River Arun which may predate St. Mary's church. It is likely to have been included in Domesday Book of 1086 as one of the two mills listed in Pulborough. It was actually two mills of differing dates both raised on a small island to prevent flooding. A William Rowner, whose surname was taken from the place, had it in the late 15th century. He passed it to Thomas Stydolf in 1503, then it went to Richard West, a Billingshurst yeoman. In 1593, late Elizabethan times, 142 oaks were sold off to John Ede, woodbroker, of Wisborough Green. From 1678 Guildenhurst and Rowner were occupied by the Garton family of Billingshurst where John Garton is buried. From 1685 the Greenfields were in possession, having been granted an eight year lease, less one week, granted by Kathren Garton, widow, to ' Thomas Greenfeild of Kensfold'. This was for Rowner farm house with buildings and 120 acres. The mill is shown on Budgen's map of 1724.

In 1732 Richard and William Garton and 19 others petitioned Lady Elizabeth Goring, who had the rights to the Great Tythe, to continue to honour a verbal agreement on the rate to be paid over at Rowner House [2/6d in the £ of the rental value] and to keep up the enjoyable tradition "of being there treated with best ale and roast beef according to the said agreement with the late Sir, as hath usually been". The good widow gave them a dusty answer. In 1773 she turned them down in a letter from her Secretary.

The Carter family worked the mill from 1809 to 1842, succeeded by William Botting to 1870 and the Hammond family are believed to have been the last regular occupants. It is said that the mill was used briefly during WWII to grind animal feed. The West Sussex River Board inherited the mills in 1958 and, in the interest of the flow of the river, had them demolished in 1966. Only the wheelpit of the older mill remains.

Sketch of Rowner House

    The only rival in antiquity to the Mill, other than the parish church, may be Newbridge itself, though not the present structure which crosses both the canal and the river. Records suggest that it was 'new' in 1279, implying that there had been a yet older bridge. Nearby was the site of the lost chapel of St. Elyn raised in the 14th century.

The Tedfold Estate and Streele Farm

The name Tedfold suggests that the place was an original Saxon settlement. John Hurd's researches reveal that in 1164, 100 years before St. Mary's began, it was held by a John Tregoz who was in dispute with the Abbot of Fecamp about a wood called Durehurst. The monks got the quarter next to Tuddesrode. Henry Tregoz was also in dispute in 1203 with a William Mordant, who provided him with a day's entertainment and a horse for his son and heir!

In 1321 the pasture of Toddesrode belonged to the Manor of Dedisham. In 1478 Thos Portbury, a tenant, stripped leaves from an oak belonging to the Lord of the land without licence. He suffered a 4 pence fine. John, the Elder, another Portbury is on record as paying 'to Our Lady of the Assumption 12d, the High Alter of the same church 12d, to the Chapel of Saint Elyn at Newbrigge 2d.' That Chapel is now quite lost.

By 1602, at the end of Queen Elizabeth's reign, the estate had passed to the Manor of Parham which leased it to John Wales for £4. A rent of 'reape sylver and horse sylver' was paid at 'midsomer' in 1605. By 1628 it was in the private hands of Anthony Wales and became a Manor in its own right. During the century and a half between 1628 and 1795 the ownership passed to Rich Haler, Wm Skinner and a farmer, Giles Brown. His son, also Giles, was a notable dissenting Anabaptist but when he married his first wife, Anne Naldrett, she put a stop to Baptists meeting at Tedfold. He was a Trustee of the Billingshurst Meeting House and an Overseer of the Poor. When he died in 1762 he was buried as he wished beside Anne 'who came to Church' in the Anglican churchyard.

It was written of the Baptists that 'They were more serious-minded than their neighbours but in Sussex they did not adopt extreme puritanical attitudes and behaviour. They enjoyed their smoking and drinking, went to fairs and to the races, watched cricket. Day by day they carried out their trades and occupations within the wider community and were often elected to serve as Overseers of the Poor and Waywardens'. After the deaths of Brown's sons, Tedfold passed to his three daughters. One of these daughters married John Evershed. He was Waywarden in Billingshurst in 1770 and another four years, and four times Overseer of the Poor up to 1805. In 1812 their eldest son, William, bought the estate from his mother and aunts. He and Thomas Evershed were often Overseers too. Three generations of Eversheds remained there until after the death of William in 1865.

The Greenfields were Billingshurst's most dominant agricultural family for several centuries but relatively little is on record of their doings and relationships. The Eversheds by contrast, who were also considerable farmers, were culturally and religiously important in the life of the village, albeit of a chapel-going rather than Anglican bent. The family has kept up and recorded its manifold membership world-wide. The family is thought to predate William the Conqueror. Thomas de Eversherd is on record in 1215. William Furlanger, a yeoman of Billingshurst had a daughter who married Thomas Evershed (1636 – 1695).

The Head of the family, Mr. John Dendy Evershed, whose father was born at Tedfold, has an article written by Sarah Evershed (1818-1907) in 1883 about her memories of Streele Farm where her grandfather lived amid the fields full of cider apple trees. She lived in Canada and her memoire offers an insight into domestic life in a Victorian yeoman farmhouse.

'On all the cottages flourished vines; some years the grapes ripened beautifully and they were always sufficiently good to make barrels of grape wine. The quince yielded ...enough fruit to make a barrel of wine....Grandpapa's gardens were well stocked with walnut, filbert, quince, medlar and rare apple trees....at the bottom of the garden the nightingale sang in the dewy evenings.' She describes the house with its inglenook fireplace in the hall where grandpa sat and smoked his long white pipe and read his Chronicle with the aid of his tortoiseshell spectacles, tied on with black ribbon. His clay pipes were put twice a week into an iron frame and burnt beautifully white and clean in the red embers of the big brick oven.

His counting house led off the Hall 'in which he transacted his business with his labourers'. On Saturday nights the cottagers came to pay their rents and the labourers trooped in wearing their heavy hob-nailed boots with their wooden tallies, notched for each day's work or a half notch if for only half a day and were paid accordingly. There were two staircases, one going to the principal bedrooms, one to the servants' quarters. The stone floored kitchen had a pump with a deep stone sink. 'Built in the chimney was a chamber large enough to hold many flitches of bacon and ham in process of smoking. On each side...in the chimney place were rough oaken settles for the use of the men and women servants. Beyond were seen two large coppers – one for boiling the clothes and the other for the lard, hogs puddings and sausages'. Faggots were used for heating the brick baking oven. The men drew their mid-day beer in the small beer room 'ad libitum' and in the milk house were the immense pewter dishes and plates used only at Harvest Home. To light the kitchen they used bundles of rushes drawn through the refuse lard. 'The youngest serving boy sat by the upright iron rush holder constantly moving up the rush as it burnt out while the women sat at their needlework, and the men wrote to their sweethearts, or sang the old English ballads'. October ale and 'small beer were brewed and cider in the brew houses'. Twice a week the big oven was heated, bread was made and when it was baked 'rice puddings and

Brobdignagian apple pies took their place'. 'The servants had plenty of bacon, cabbage and plain flour dumplings to eat or pork with cabbage steeped in vinegar. Grandpa had roast beef or veal or a slice of streaky bacon with his apple dumpling or tart. At bedtime the servants heated the beds with a large brass warming pan or a cradle made of hoops with an iron frame in the middle containing red-hot embers from the kitchen fire and by half-past nine everyone was in bed'.

Over 120 Eversheds are buried in the graveyard of the Baptist Chapel. 100 living Eversheds visited the Chapel in July 1999 at the fifth Family Reunion when Dendy was 87 years old.

The Tedfold estate was put up for auction but withdrawn because the reserve was too high and it was not sold until 1871. It comprised 420 acres, including the farms known as Tedfold, Leyhold, North Eaton, Jefferies, Coppid Hall (Coppid spelt with an 'i') and Old Hayes, or the Hole all in a picturesque and beautiful part of Sussex. There is no record of who bought it.

Auctioneer's map of Tedfold Estate

In August, 1920 Mr.C.E.G. Gordon offered for sale this large landholding in the northwest quadrant of Billingshurst parish. The sale particulars describe the estate as follows:

"A large family residence within a well timbered park, three farm homesteads with excellent pasture and arable lands, woods and plantations. The whole extending to 344 acres with vacant possession, for sale by private treaty." The description follows of 'An excellent family residence, in red brick ...within a park of 90 acres, through which runs a long carriage drive with a picturesque Lodge Entrance.' There were 7 rooms on the ground floor with Adams mantels and French casements and 14 bedrooms all with 'modern grates' with access to balconies 'from which beautiful views are obtained'. There were 'ample offices' –Kitchen with large range, scullery, larder, servants' hall and butler's pantry, well-fitted cellarage and cool dairy in the basement, 2 coal sheds and W.C. and septic tank. Well water pumped by electricity and an electric power station 12 h.p. Pelapone and 54 accumulators installed 'this year'." [These Pelapone engines built in Derby are now collectors' items].

The gardens boasted ornamental trees in variety and a large spreading oak, kitchen and flower borders and shrubberies together with an orchard. There was stabling for four horses. The farm buildings included a large barn, a 14 horse cart-horse stable, cattle shed for 22, cow shed for 8 and loose boxes, a 3 bay cart shed with granary over, implement shed and stair over, chaff house and mixing house. The engine house was fitted with a Fairbank Morse engine mill, cake crusher, chaff cutter, root cutter and saw bench. There was a pump house in the yard and a range of piggeries – 'exceptionally good accommodation specially built for pedigree stock'. There were good quality grass-lands, 90 acres of arable and 21 acres of well-timbered woodland 'which affords good sporting'. 'Hunting may be had with Lord Leconfield's and the Crawley and Horsham Foxhounds'.

Ancillary holdings were Hampshires and Leyhold Farm, a small homestead with barn and sheds, and a pair of brick-built cottages – Leyland Cottages – formerly the farmhouse. In one field 'red sandstone is obtainable.' At Hole Farm, then in Pulborough village, was a 'picturesque old half-timbered cottage in black and white', a barn with threshing floor, a 6 horse stable and a 4 bay cattle shed. Additionally there were South Eaton Cottage, two other brick and timber dwellings (Weaver's and Burnt Row) and two five-roomed Ringwood Cottages.

These attractive sale particulars offer a picture of a well-to-do gentleman's estate just after the Great War, electrified but as yet largely unmechanised, but well equipped in traditional fashion for the enjoyment of mixed farming, high quality livestock and generously appointed as a prestigious rural seat for leisure and pleasure. The original building date of the house is unknown. It was modernised in 1831 when it was given a new brick front.

Subsequently it was up for sale again by auction in 1944 and 1966. Unsuccessful applications were made for various building developments at Tedfold Stud including one to build a by-pass and 300 houses in 1988.

The Railway Network

The great British Railway Age was initiated in 1829 with Stephenson's Rocket and reached its frenetic climax nationwide about 1846 by then known as 'Railway Mania'. But in our geographical region the Railway Age flourished somewhat later, lasting for 100 years from the 1850s to the 1960s when Dr. Beeching's drastic recommendations were implemented and the network of branch lines that had grown up was mercilessly eradicated. The main factor which had made the railway uneconomic was the switch of freight from rail tracks to metalled roads. Lorries and buses ousted locomotives just as trains had replaced canal barges, even though passengers still made good use of the facility. At Billingshurst the railway service has continued, since the London-Portsmouth line has remained a strategic and economic necessity.

At first the only line from London to the south coast went from London to Brighton which was finished in 1841. In 1846 the London, Brighton and South Coast Railway Co. was formed as an amalgamation of five pre-existing enterprises. It had built a coastal branch line west from Brighton, first to Shoreham and then, circuitously, to Portsmouth. Shortly afterwards another rival company, the London and South Western Railway ran trains from London to Portsmouth through Surrey and Hampshire via Guildford and Godalming.

It was not until 1859 that serious progress was made on the third access, this time more directly to Portsmouth via Sussex, first to Horsham in 1848, next to Billingshurst and Hardham Junction in 1859. Four years later the line would push south, via Amberley and Arundel, to Ford Junction. (1863). This extension would link in to the coastal line already established westwards from Brighton via Chichester. Thus the first line south of Horsham through Billingshurst actually terminated on a spur to Petworth on what, subsequently, became a branch line to Midhurst.

Deborah Evershed catches the excitement of the very first steam engine to arrive at Adversane, which unloaded the household chattels for the new crossing-keepers' cottage (Thomas and Mary Smith) on October 10th 1859. A large crowd had assembled to wonder at this amazing occasion!

"Don't you go near it, George," Grandmother Deborah exclaimed ..."It might blow up".

These three main lines survived Beeching's axe, but the branch lines which developed from the London-Horsham-Billingshurst-Ford line all succumbed.

The first of these ran from Hardham Junction by Fittleworth to Petworth in 1859 and on to Midhurst in 1866. North of Billingshurst another junction at Christ's Hospital allowed a new line linking West Grinstead, Henfield, Steyning and Shoreham (1861). The station itself was built between 1899 and 1902 when the school moved there from London. The Christ's Hospital junction caused yet another branch line to be built running north-west to Cranleigh via Slinfold, Rudgwick and Baynards. This line opened in 1856 and closed a100 years later, being adopted as part of the Link Way between The North and South Downs. Cyclists may still use part of the old railway from Christs Hospital through West Grinstead.

These local railway linkages were invaluable connections and in the days before sophisticated road transport and reliable roads they were welcomed by traders and farmers. They afforded ready routes to fresh markets, and also gave access to London and the seaside at acceptable prices and less expense of time to otherwise isolated people. A cheap day excursion from Billingshurst to the Crystal Palace, including admission, cost 4 shillings [20p], though cheap is a relative term. Most farm workers then would work for a whole day to earn that money. Before the trains came, coach fares were prohibitively expensive to ordinary folk. Mr. Thomas Ireland paid 10 shillings for a trip from Billingshurst to London in 1820, equivalent to some £40 today. When Mr. Pickwick was gadding about the country at that time Dickens' readers must have recognised in him a very wealthy gentleman.

The branch railways had become ridiculously uneconomic when Beeching made his report, and though today we might welcome having the routes back, it is questionable if we would try to reinstate the old service. Had the branch lines survived the 1960s the pattern of subsequent housing development in the region might have been quite different. It is the continued existence of the railway station that marks out Billingshurst as a 'sustainable location', so deemed by officialdom as vulnerable to further development.

In 1922 the two rival rail companies were amalgamated to form The Southern Railway, a company which was nationalised to become Southern Region of British Rail in 1948, only to be returned to private ownership by the Major government of 1993.

Billingshurst Station

The photographs from the footbridge, looking north, illustrate how the area has developed since 1922. Milk churns stand ready on the down line to go to the coast. Daux Road is a track to Great Daux Farm and beyond the platform are open fields.

View from railway bridge looking north

Recent view from same spot

The listed Signal Box is to be moved in 2013, doubtless to be preserved elsewhere, probably on the Bluebell Line. The crossing is to be widened so the bridge steps on the west side are to be rerouted requiring the demolition of part of the Station building.

At the level-crossing at Adversane another gateman, George Piper, was employed more recently until automatic barriers were installed in 1966.

Billingshurst's Heritage No. 2

Gatwick Airport

In 1957, the year the Weald School was opening, work was in progress turning an old RAF Station and former aerodrome and racecourse into Gatwick, London's second Airport. The world of the rabbit in Billingshurst was that year being rapidly depleted by myxamatosis but the human population was about to undergo rapid expansion, in no small measure as a result of the traffic of aircraft to and from world-wide destinations. Billingshurst is well-placed within the catchment area for staffing airport services so that much recent development of housing and light industry must be attributed directly or indirectly to the stimulus of air traffic. Pilots and cabin crew typically took up residence in restored labourers' cottages and new housing estates.

In many respects the airport has revolutionised and urbanised the lives of the people much as the steam train did in the 19th century, steam, smoke and cinders being only marginally more obtrusive than the roar of giant jets belching carbon dioxide and tracing vapour trails overhead. The coming of the railway transformed the distribution of consumer goods so that ordinary Victorian Billingshurst people could shop for such as Sheffield cutlery, burn coal, roof buildings with Welsh slate and enjoy products sourced round the Empire instead of depending almost entirely on things grown or made locally. They could afford a break and enjoy a plate of cockles at Bognor Regis too. Similarly the airport enabled a new and yet greater cosmopolitanism, bringing unfamiliar exotic foods, pasta, paella, pizza, tikka massala, won ton soup and 'genius' chicken wings. The chefs to prepare them came too in a more fluid society stimulated by international tourism and economic immigration. Billingshurst families ate paella and played golf on the Costa del Sol and drank wine and ate Camembert in Provence. Gardeners started to plant garlic and olive trees. Wine sales rocketed. In 1959 Gatwick handled some 368,000 passengers. Nowadays the annual figure averages about 33 million with up to 55 aircraft movements every hour from the single runway, nearly one a minute! Should a second runway be built there would be yet more development of housing in the village and the expansion of tourism, services and manufacturing.

Station Road Maltings and Whirlwind Limited

The old Malthouse in Station Road was owned by Mr. James King, (1824-84) maltster and corn dealer, who also had the maltings in the High Street. He lived in later life at Broomfield Lodge and had the wall built on his land which for many years formed the west boundary of the cricket field and is now embraced by the new recreational gardens. The Malthouse burnt down in 1883 but was soon rebuilt. The premises were taken over by Mr. N. Ray Stiles in the early 1920s and his company was eventually manufacturing over 400 Whirlwind Suction Sweepers a week. Further premises at the side were acquired for additional shops and offices. During WW II the factory made aluminium ammunition boxes. In 1947 Mr. Stiles sold the patent rights to what was only a moderately successful appliance, and the factory became Barralets (Pressform) Ltd. makers of water heaters then Lorlins Electrical. Finally the whole lot was demolished and became Saville Gardens and residential accommodation.

Printing in Billingshurst

From 1929 to 1941 Mr. Charles Tiler ran a printing business at Alick's Hill. He published a village news sheet up to the outbreak of war in 1939.

Oct. 3, 1936. THE BILLINGSHURST NEWS. 3

Streeter, K.O.M, (one of the founders of the Maple Leaf Lodge).

Bro. Streeter said it was a great surprise to him to be asked to conduct the ceremony. He wished to thank their Worthy Chaplain for all the work he had done for the Lodge and the example he had shown to all brothers. Buffaloism had high ideals, and they would have to be supermen to carry them all out. One of the highest of their ideals was to elevate their brethren. The basis of the Order was charity. The Order numbered over seven million brethren in all parts of the world, and wherever a Buffalo went he would always find members to welcome him.

Bro. Gardiner thanked the brethren for their good wishes. He had enjoyed his visits to the Lodge and had met there men whom he might not have known otherwise. He well remembered on the occasion of the visit of another Lodge, one member coming up and asking him to shake hands as he had not shook hands before with a parson! The Maple Leaf Lodge had always been against anything that was lowering to the Order.

The Rev. Brother was given musical honours and cheers as he left the Lodge.

CHURCH SOCIAL.

All Parishioners (children under 16 excepted) are invited to meet the Rev. E. and Mrs. Streete at the Women's Hall on Monday evening next. Tea will be provided from 5 to 6 30 p.m.

FOOTBALL.

Billingshurst Wednesdays visited Arundel on September 23rd, and came home winners by four goals to nil. Phillips was the first to score with a long shot two-thirds to half way line up the field. Some minutes later a good pass from Hayes was taken by G. Voice, who scored a neat goal. "Mutt" also scored another goal soon after. Play was more even in the second half and D. Payne headed in the fourth goal from a good centre by R. Knight.

The K.O. Cup tie on the 30th was against Petworth (at Newbridge Road), who have been champions of the League for four years and are the Cup-holders. Billingshurst were up against a fine and fast combination, but held their own fairly well until after the interval. Petworth then scored a quick goal almost from the kick-off. Billingshurst attacked, and Pierce headed into the net from close up. The goal was disallowed for off-side, wrongly in our opinion. This rather made the homesters dispirited, and two more goals from Petworth put paid to the

---

Trinity Congregational Church,
BILLINGSHURST,

MONDAY, OCTOBER 5th, at 7.30.
RE-OPENING OF
TABLE TENNIS CLUB.
October—April.   Subscription 2/-.

THURSDAY, OCTOBER 8th, at 7.15.
OPENING OF
TRINITY GUILD.
October—March.   Subscription 1/-.

SATURDAY, OCTOBER 10th, at 3.
ANNUAL RUMMAGE SALE.
ADMISSION 1d.
All Gifts gratefully received.

TRACTOR
FOR HIRE.
(WITH PRIZE PLOUGHMAN.)
ALL FARM WORK UNDERTAKEN,
including Sawbench Work.
Terms on application to
CULLEN, Grainingfold, Billingshurst.
Phone: BILLINGSHURST 50.

We can undertake Printing of any kind.
CHARLES W. W. TILLER,
The Printing Works, Billingshurst.

Billingshurst News – Ancient Order of Buffaloes

Village Memories

Things that have changed in Billingshurst since I can remember

Written by Mrs. G. Maria Ireland, who was born at Billingshurst Vicarage, May 5th 1837, the year of Queen Victoria's accession to the throne.

The Curfew Bell was rung at 5 am and 8 pm for a quarter of an hour from November 2nd to February 2nd. There was no policeman. An old man (watchman) walked about during the night.

A four-horse coach from Worthing to London came through the village and changed horses at the King's Arms every day. Vans went to and fro to London for grocery etc. Coal, Flints and all heavy goods came by barge on the canal to Newbridge, where lime-burning was carried on.

A small stream ran in the village between the pavement and the road from the Rising Sun [now long gone] to the Blacksmiths Shop. Mops were dipped in it.

There were two nursery gardens, one from Townland to the Rising Sun, used by Philip Puttock who left the money for bread to the poor. The other from the Baptist Chapel yard to the Wheelers Corner, was used by John Alman whose son John died in 1844. His favourite tree, a cedar, was planted to his memory in the Churchyard near the East Gate. [In 1978, a large tree at the east end of the church was felled by a gale].

There were two windmills, one on the hill by the lane near the Six Bells, burned down November 5th 1852, the other Hammonds Mill, the top blown off.

There was a pond and waste ground on Alex Hill where osiers were cut and stripped by the village women.

The Church was altered in 1866. Before that there were high pews all along the west entrance, with a three-decker pulpit by the middle pillar. There was no organ or harmonium but a Bass Viol, Flutes and other instruments, the metrical psalms being sung and a few hymns. The second service was held in the afternoon and no lamps were needed.

The Sunday School was held in a building attached to what is now the Lady Chapel, since pulled down when the Church was altered, used only as a Vestry and a Day School, when there was one. The Churchyard was enlarged about this time.

The Railway was begun in 1833 [sic. 1855 intended?]. At that time there was no house along the fields walk from the Vicarage to Kingsfold, except the farmhouses at Broomfields and Dawks and no road through from Alex Hill to Nats Lane.

The new Vicarage was built in 1858/9. The old one was on the same spot, facing north. The Hilly, Blacksmiths' Fields, the meadow and fields on the north side of the road by the shop was Vicarage ground.

Paraffin or Petroleum was not known. Candles were used, moulds and dips, some rushlights (pith of rushes dipped in fat). I once saw flint and steel used for striking a light. Tinder was used to catch the sparks and then small thin chips dipped each end in brimstone put to the sparks to make a flame.

Photography was unknown, and some people had their profiles cut in black paper. There were no bicycles or telegrams. There were three turnpike gates on the road to Horsham, one after Five Oaks, one at Lyons Corner and one this side of Broadbridge Heath which was then Common Ground. Dogs were used to draw carts. Fish was brought from Worthing drawn by four or five dogs.

Billingshurst Jottings by Ruth Kelleher

Ruth was born at the turn of the 19th Century

I don't think that many people know that our first library was in a hall at the back of the Baptist Chapel. When I went to borrow books I got to know the Librarian, a Miss Weeks, who lived in cottage at the entrance who showed me the little chapel. In the next cottage we met for meetings of the YWCA.

Across the road in Price's meadow we always had the bonfire and fireworks until the Misses Beck bought it and had the Women's Hall built

We had penny readings, so called, for a weekly variety show, all the local talent. One man always brought the house down when he came on stage in a Sussex 'cowgown' and sang Sussex songs. The Village Hall was always packed. One show I remember was Hiawatha. My eldest sister took the part of an Indian girl, never knowing that she would marry and go and live in Canada.

Courtney Laker had an orchestra; my brother played the violin in it, and there were always dances. We went to what was once a market hall in Myrtle Lane at the back of the Station Hotel. The music was provided by Len Voice on a cornet and by his future wife on the piano, which we all enjoyed.

Coronation Parade, High St. 1911

We went to all the fairs and shows. The first one was in the Jubilee Meadow at Little Daux, to celebrate King Edward's Coronation. We had sports and a nice tea and we all wore a medal.

Mr. Towner farmed at Rosier. I remember we picked cowslips in one of his meadows. Daux Wood was our delight when we gathered bluebells and other flowers and went blackberrying. Where the bungalows are now in Daux Avenue was our way to the woods. We danced in a fairy ring and gathered heaps of mushrooms there.

When we came to Billingshurst there was just one little post office in the High Street, one grocer, one draper, one baker and two butchers. We must have been good customers since at Christmas the grocer gave my mother a bottle of port; the baker gave a cake and the butcher 2lbs of his nice pork sausages. The butchers used to kill their own animals and all the boys used to go to watch.

Mr. Voice had a grocer's shop at the station and we went there to buy his nice lardy rolls. Across the road was a shop where we bought eggs at a shilling a dozen from free range hens in the field where Keatings is now.

Memories of Mrs. M.E. Marten, 1 Daux Avenue, born 1864 (abridged)

The village street had paving stones of all shapes and sizes. [In the High street lived] the Vetinary surgeon who was always called the farrier. Further up the road was the harness-maker; he had a long garden where there was a rope walk, and a man with a bundle of hemp in front of him could be seen walking up and down from post to post making a rope. Opposite lived a Currier in a shed close to the footpath putting the finishing touches to big pieces of leather. After the present Congregational Chapel was built the old one in the Jengers Meadow, an octagonal building which reminded one of a huge summer house, was used for Sunday School and entertainments called 'penny readings'. The Post Office was at a little shop at the beginning of the Church Causeway. At the top of Osier Hill was a pond, quite close to the road. This, at certain times of the year, was filled with osiers which were used for making baskets.

The old Congregational Chapel and Meadow House, Jengers Meadow

I also remember the brickfields in the Wildens. They were called 'The Potteries' and I well remember seeing flower pots made there as well as bricks in my very early days. Where the Post Office and the other new buildings now stand there was a meadow with a low brick wall upon which men used to sit and chat together about the affairs of the village.

Memories of Billingshurst- Tom Topper

Extracted from a talk with Mr. Mike Coxon, slightly abridged. Tom Topper was born in 1912. He had six brothers and two sisters. He came to Billingshurst in 1918, the end of the Great War and the year of the great flu epidemic

We lived near the Station, opposite the cricket field. The houses at the bottom of Station Road where the grocer and garden shops are now, used to be one big house. [Hereford House]. Then came the original houses and next a block of houses where the Malt House had been sited. Then there were two cottages and Brookers Road, beyond which were three or four more houses and Saville House (now Saville Gardens). An old man who lived at the Station used to come out on Armistice Day and blow the 'Last Post'. We kept two minutes silence. It was not organised – he just liked to do it.

Where there are now flats and a bungalow, which lies back a little, there used to be a big house, Saville House, occupied by Admiral Holmes. They had a big apple tree – I know because I scrumped the apples many times.

Beyond there was only hedge and field until you reached the Lodge (to Cleveland House), which is still there. They had conker trees all the way up the drive to the big house, which no longer exists. Then there was an empty field, and on that as you came down Alick's Hill, on the right, there was a wagon shed. (Carpenters is named after it [sic. This is a mistaken belief]). I remember the shed had a lovely beam across the middle, so you could hang from your feet.

On the hot summer days the steam trains used to catch the fields alight. We kids would say, 'The field's alight!' and rush out and stamp it out.

There was a shop at the Station, the post office and village shop. They had a taxi service with a Model T Ford. The driver would stand in the station saying 'taxi, taxi' and then he would run across to his brother in the sheds at the back and say, 'Jack her up, Percy, and get the handle going', because you always jacked up a Model T to start it. During the war the Canadian soldiers came and had the taxi, just for the sheer fun. They couldn't believe their eyes. This old thing must have been 20 years old before the war started!

People would take a taxi to Wisborough Green or Kirdford, for example, but if it was local they would only have the horses and trap. When it came by we kids would slip up behind without them seeing us and sit on the back axle. People coming along and seeing us sitting there would shout, 'Whip behind, Guvnor!'

We used to call the coaches 'charabancs' that came through the village. As they came over the hill we would call, 'Throw out your rusty coppers'. They were going to Goodwood races. Goodwood was a big week with lots of traffic and we could collect several pennies. The police stopped it. Kids were running all over the road amongst the traffic though it was only doing about 25 mph.

When there were police speed traps the AA man would stand in the road further down, so that members not receiving the usual salute from him, would know and slow down. This sort of warning was quite legal. Often a trap would be set just outside the village. The best local bobby we had was Sgt. Dutton who was here just after the war. [The AA men also worked at Five Oaks corner in Goodwood Weeks].

Not far from where we lived were the gas Works at the bottom of Groomsland

Drive. My brother, Bert, used to work there after the war in the mid-fifties, but when North Sea Gas came they were closed down, although the site is still there and they still use the pipes and controls.

As you go through Parbrook from Station Road, you pass the school playing fields and then, just before you reach the first of the new houses, there used to be a very old one with oak beams. My aunt lived in it, but when I was about 14 they knocked it down. Great Grooms was where the Jenny Wren Restaurant is now [currently a private house]. There is a footpath across the fields by the school, coming out by those new houses and when we were children we'd walk across to get skimmed milk from the farm. We always knew the direction from the whining noise of the separator, which sounded right across the field. [Cream separators were well established before WW 1 but milking machines, though invented in 1904, were adopted only very slowly].

Hillview garage was just one side of the road, the east, and was owned by Mr. Merrikin. Ted, his son, runs it now [recently redeveloped as private housing].

The original Hillview Garage

Where the Junior School is there used to be one big field running right down to the railway – as far as where the bowling green is – and then one awkward shaped field to square it off before the line. It was a lovely sight to see it being ploughed; two teams of horses, one going down, one up and the men walking behind them. At harvest time it would be stacked up with stooks and sheaves for the horses and wagons to come and pick up.

Then as you come further down Alick's Hill there was another orchard – I knew where all the orchards were! At the bottom two or three houses which are still there, and then, next to Badgers, on the other side of the bus drive was a baker's shop. It stood a little back from the road, and I used to work there as a boy.

The bake house itself was just at the back where Billingshurst Coaches are now [presently retirement homes]. Behind was an open field with a footpath to the Church and a pond.

As you go up the High Street there was a corn merchant's...not far from the Unitarian Church. Barclays Bank was an ironmonger's, but the slaughterhouse is still behind the butchers [now redeveloped]. As a lad I used to watch them kill the bullocks. After the war it was used for only pigs and sheep. Then come the King's Arms and Six Bells, and next to that, where a Building Society is now, was Miss. Laker's house. One of the rooms was used as a dental surgery. The dentist came out from Horsham on Tuesdays and Thursdays. West's has been a confectioners for years, but the Post Office used to be a barn. A farthings worth of sweets bought as much as 15p now [? 50p].

They used to play football on the Jengers then. There was no shopping precinct, but fields stretching away from the old white house and the red brick one, on whose site the old Congregational Church once stood. There was no Coombe Hill, and a footpath ran across the fields to Tedfold and finally to Rowner. It does still, but starts later because of the housing estates.

Turning up East Street from the High Street everything on the left is new until you come to the red-tiled farmhouse, Gore Farm, where the steam engines are [Lugg's Yard]. Up School Lane there are some old cottages; the one on the right hand side has been knocked down and the other rebuilt. Those on the left are still the same. At Hammonds, where Dr. Kilsby lived, there used to be a Mr. Trower and his two sisters. This old house was a farm once. I remember passing it in the evenings and seeing it lit by oil lamps. Just past it are the remains of the old mill. You could see the basic shape.

East Street rises fairly sharply from the High Street. The coal wagon used to go up pulled by a horse. There was always an iron shoe dragging behind one wheel so that if the cart slid backwards it would run into the shoe and be braked. The hill used to curve right round to the Church. At the top, where the Vicarage car park is now, there was a cafe. The old cottages, Rose and Chime are still there. Mr. Rhodes started his shoe business in the front room of one of them. Then, of course, came Gratwick Manor, with only fields between it and the Catholic Church.

To get to School Lane from Station Road we used to walk up the Church Path. At the bottom of the hill below the school was common land – The Bowling Alley. This was a great place when it was snowing. We used to slide down on tin trays.

Beyond the Catholic Church, by a big house called 'Trees', on the right was Red Lane where they used to play football. [Jubilee Meadow] The lane goes down to the Railway, past Little Daux Farm. I spent a lot of time in Daux Wood. In those days there were lots of brown squirrels, who nested in the oak trees. We used to climb up, take one of the babies and bring it home for a pet. We'd put him in a wheel like a gerbil and he would play in it.

One day when I was going through the woods a bird flew in front of me, looking as if it had a broken wing – so I ran after it, but once it had taken me far enough away it few off normally. I wondered why it had led me astray, flying a limping flight, just few yards ahead of me, so I retraced my steps, and sure enough, there was its nest with young in it.

In those days people had to make their own fun. Cricket was one amusement, and men came from far away to spend weekends playing here. There was no organised team for young people, but you could always go down on practice nights, and if you'd helped clear the ground of plantain weed, you'd be allowed to play while the team was practising.

Bonfire night was the big event, and as villages go, ours was a huge one, bringing in thousands to see it, one of the biggest in Sussex apart from Lewes. They used to build it where the Junior School is now. We were living at Hillview Cottage then and had a fine view. One year (1937) someone set it alight about three evenings before the night; but Colonel Drew came and said we would have one all the same, by hook or by crook. The farmers rallied round with tractors loaded with stuff. They had another bonfire built in two days flat, put an all-night guard on it, and ran electricity to it over the fence from our house. There was a Bonfire Society when I was a kid and the torch-light procession was quite intense and frightening. We used to watch it from the top of Alick's Hill where there was a high bank. The procession would wind down through Parbrook and past the Station, calling at all the pubs. They had fireworks and torches which they had made weeks before, at the back of the King's Head, their Headquarters.

When I was married I was earning only £2 a week and paying 1s-6d rent, and money seemed as short then as now. A new house probably cost £300! A trip to Littlehampton was terrific and one went to London once in a lifetime. No cars for us. We used to cycle everywhere. Street lighting was gas, and homes had it as well or, if not, oil lamps. But it was a great life all the same.

[Note: The Bowling Alley was not, properly speaking, Common Land, but an important footpath link from a Duckmore in the High Street to another Duckmore house near the present house of that name at Wooddale.]

Madeleine Woods also tells more of Tom Topper. His friend Cecil Rhodes' father the cobbler in East Street, also served as village lamplighter. He was so skilled at judging the distance from chain and stick that he lit the whole High Street without getting off his bicycle. Tom came from a family of 7 boys and 2 girls, headed by a fiery naval stoker. The Toppers supplemented their diet with nettle tops for greens, dandelion leaves and wild mushrooms. They had their hair cut for 3d a trim at Parbook and collected acorns to get 3d a bushel at Blunden's corn store in the High Street. The Miss Puttocks at Cleveland House provided their school caps and Major Renton gave them new boots at Christmas. At 13 Tom's friend Cecil was working for his father collecting boots from the grand houses where the cooks often treated him to a 'below stairs' meal. Tom's first job was fetching water and faggots for Lusted's bakery where he learnt the baker's skills. When he married he lived at Hillview Cottage paying 12/6d a week out of a £2 wage packet. There he caught rats by luring them into a dustbin and dropping the lid from a string suspended above. In those days you went to the Doctor's, with your shilling up front, sitting in the corridor of the Rose Hill surgery. Tom ran 'threepenny socials' at the Women's' Hall and used the collection to bake for and lay on a slap-up reception at the King's Arms Function Room for an unfortunate lady who 'had to get married'. This was so popular that he turned it into a regular weekend business launching Billingshurst couples into married life. Tom served on ten village committees including the Parish Council, Horticultural Society and School managers. Cecil Rhodes was 30 years with the Fire Brigade, 25 years as chief, rescuing cats from trees and pumping out water from High Street premises which flooded regularly until remedial work was undertaken.

Peter Stockwood remembers

Peter was a Weald School boy and has been 40 years at the School as Caretaker and now Premises Manager.

"I remember being caned by Mr. Gee for scrumping apples – "two strokes on hand, keep your thumb back" and how the bad boys would be marched back to his classroom as a further warning to other evil-doers. There was a terrific hailstorm in 1963 that dented all the green copper sheeting on the school roof. 6 oz hailstones, well over 2 inches across, fell from a tornado. Houses damaged and trees uprooted. Up at High Seat Nurseries Mr. And Mrs Hobson lost every pane of glass!

I used to see Diana Dors when I was a little boy at the Six Bells, then slim and glamorous with her red American sports car. I used to see Jimmy Edwards, the comedian, in the village too.

My school friend David Roberts slipped and fell into the flooded river at Newbridge and tragically drowned in 1959. The day before he had been selling goose feathers at the East Street School for a penny each.

I knew every tree in the orchard with a footpath running through where the Library car park stands. Mrs. Laker had apples, pears, plums and quinces and hazelnuts and lived in the High Street where the tobacconist's shop is now. The oak tree is still there.

Mr Cripps' the butcher's daughter owned a famous show-jumper pony called Stroller. They used to have gymkhanas just outside the village and kept the horses where Lakers Meadow is now. Marion Mould got Silver at the 1968 Olympics on Stroller. I read they won 61 international events.

When I was a boy I had a two hour paper round every morning all down West Street and out to Newbridge, then Lordings Road and Adversane, with lots of side turnings. Hard work in all weathers, snow, floods and storms.

I've long been an officer of the Angling Society and I've been all over the world diving and watching fish sub-aqua. Young Harry Enfield used to toddle down to watch us fishing at Rowner. I've seen him on TV shoulder a back-pack the way he saw us with our fishing bags"

Items of interest

In 1891 land south of East Street was purchased by Mr. E.T. Norris who had additions to Gratwicke House by his friend, Sir Edward Lutyens. Gratwicke Park was the venue for large fairs and, during the 1914-18 war used for the resting of cavalry detachments on their journey to Flanders battlefields. During WW II Gratwicke was commandered by the military authorities for a Home Guard Headquarters from Colonel and Mrs. Dudley-White, who had bought the property from Mr. Norris's soldier son in 1923.

In the early 1930s Mr. Hugh Maille bought part of Gratwicke parkland on which the present Catholic Church stands – a memorial to his daughter.

April 1982: ' There was great interest, indeed great excitement, when it was learned last month that the Southern Counties Garage had put in a planning application to demolish the garage, showrooms and workshops and the post office, and erect a large building incorporating a supermarket in their place'. [In the event the Post Office building stayed and a new office counter opened in Jengers Mead and Budgen's Supermarket was built].

Post Office and Budgens Supermarket

The old Village Hall was given to the village by the Rev, J Stanley and opened in 1906. Trustees included Rev. Stanley, Dr. Hubert and Mr. Joseph Luxford. Later an annexe was built to house a boys club. In 1939 the Education Authority booked the Hall for school purposes. Out of school hours it was used as a forces canteen and a Drill Hall for the Home Guard.

The Old Village Hall, High Street

> THIS HALL WAS ERECTED BY THE
> **REV. JOHN STANLEY, M.A.**
> VICAR OF THIS PARISH 1902-1914
> FOR THE BENEFIT OF THE INHABITANTS
> OF THIS PARISH.
>
> PAST TRUSTEES
> THE REV. JOHN STANLEY, M.A. DR. A. HUBERT, J. LUXFORD,
> J. HERRINGTON, W. TRIBE, E.A. GRAHAM, G. WARE,
> W. BERRYMAN, R.C. KNIGHT, R.S. HIGGINS, R. CRISP.
> F.O. CRAWFORD, E.W. CRIPPS, F. WILLIAMS.

Original Trustees of the Old Village Hall

The New Village Hall, now called the Community Centre, was officially opened on 30th January 1991. In that same year two other events of importance occurred. The new Doctors' Surgery opened in Roman Way and the Billingshurst Junior

School moved from East Street to Station Road. To mark the latter occasion the children made a symbolic march in Victorian costume.

The New Village Hall and Community Centre

Inside the Community Centre

Billingshurst surgery, Roman Way

Here is a report of a get-together at the Women's Hall in 1937. "The Social Evening on Thursday last, run by the Dinky Boys was a huge success...Games and competitions were organised by the Minister and Mr. Helsdon and were indulged by young and old. The great feature of the evening was a humorous item by the Dinky Boys which caused hearty laughter. Songs were given by Mr. Gravett and Mr. M. Harwood. Ronnie Radbourne gave a cornet solo and Mr. H. Morris told us some humorous yarns. Mr. Percy Wadey accompanied on the piano".

1999 - Billingshurst Millennium Map. "Chairman, John Hurd is working and reworking the actual map and Wendy Lines has compiled a draft list of Buildings to be included. She (Madeleine Woods) is to co-ordinate a growing team of artists (14 to date) to sketch out their ideas and paint in specific colours on the oak leaf corniches". (Madeleine Woods)

In 1940 the Sisters of the Immaculate Heart of St. Mary came to Billingshurst. Their Convent School at Newhaven had been damaged by bombing. They were first at the Corner House, Adversane, moved on to High Fure and in 1945 acquired Summers Place. There some 60 boarders and 200 day pupils formed a flourishing school which lasted until 1984.

William Evershed, who founded the Baptist Chapel with William Turner was born in 1717 near Lewes, and had no education except for reading. He was hired out as a farmer's boy but his ambitious nature overcame all his handicaps. He preferred Theology, Ecclesiastical, civil and Natural History subjects. It is recorded in his autobiography that, when following the oxen drawing the plough, he would have his task pinned to his shirtsleeve so that he could improve his mind at the same time that he was faithfully performing his duty to his master. In 1742 he took Great Daux Farm.

Elizabeth Carter, nee Evershed noted about another William Evershed, (1754 -1824):- [He] wore two fleecy nightcaps and then wrapped his head in a pillowcase. He wore a wig, so did his father and grandfather, but none of his brothers. Thomas Evershed (1680 – 1765) used to come to Billingshurst Meeting House wearing a cotton wig with one or two rows of little curls all round. John wore a bushy wig not a curly one. William wore curly one, large curls that he used to roll round his finger – his real hair was light brown.

The name Daux was current in 1369 in the name of Wiliam Daukes and it was also the name of Alice Dawkes who held one and a half virgates and a tenement called Crouchers in 1327. In 1400 there is a record of a William Dakons of Coucheslond. In Tudor times the name is variously spelt Daks when John Grynfyld bought it, and in Churchwardens accounts it appears as Daulkes (1563), Dawlks (1592) and Daukes again in 1630. In the will of John Sturt (1650) it is spelt Dawks but from then on it appears as Daux throughout the 18th century. Nevertheless the census of 1851 and that of ten years later has it as Dauks once more. Another authority writing about Great and Little Daux (pronounced Dorks) explains the word as 'Duhchae's hook of land', from the Old English Duhchaen hoc, written as Douwehok in 1296, Dawks in 1795 and Dorks in 1823.

St, Mary's Church Tower and Nave date from the early 13th Century. Subsequent additions are:-
Lady Chapel – c 1230
South Aisle - c 1280
North Aisle - c 1430
Spire 15th century
Porch rebuilt in 16th century
New clock   -   1800
Weather vane – c 1812.

The arms of the Garton family – three silver staves tied with a gold ribbon on a black shield – are on two of the church roof bosses. The Gartons, possibly originally from Yorkshire, had lands in Sussex in the 15th century and were probably enriched from the iron industry. Thomas Garton was vicar in 1478 and William, who died in 1560, was Churchwarden. In 1535 he was Steward of the Manor of Bassett's Fee which he subsequently purchased from Thomas Wroth who was gifted it by Queen Elizabeth. William's son Francis, 'Gentleman', became Mayor of Arundel twice. In 1588 he gave £30 to the Sussex Gentry Fund to help defend England against the Spanish Armada. The Manor then passed to Thomas Henshaw, a Royalist in Charles I's time, then his son Philip. After him was Thomas Tipping from Berkshire. His heir, Mary Anne, his niece, married Philip Wroughton. They sold to Collins who sold to Mr. Clear.

The Bongards of Wisborough Green were celebrated glassmakers until 1618. Isaac Bungar bought timber for his furnaces in Billingshurst and probably retired to a cottage in West Chiltington Lane called Horelands. Richard Greenfield, possibly the one who bought Clarks Land in 1645 and John Penfold of the family that once owned Kingsfold, were witnesses to the purchase deed in 1651.

Village worthies:-
Nathanial Short, weaver and Parish Clerk, paid £1 – 10s a year, 4 times married
William Frye, Vicar in the reign of Edward III
Old Ephrain Cooper, died aged 80, worth £58 in 1669, farmed Pounds, near Okehurst

Billingshurst's Heritage No. 2

Three village characters

John Gravett, 1530 paid 'to the light of Our Lady and St. Peter a cow for 10s, to be delivered to the Churchwardens'. Witnesses to a document dated 5th Jan 1365 were Thomas Gyleman [Gilmans], William at Hull [?], Richard Somer [Summers] and Adam Goore [? Gore Farm].

Two cottages in West Street on the north side were so low that that someone leaning out of the bedroom window could shake hands with a person on the ground below. They were occupied by the Truelove family and known as 'The Bank of England'. Ambrose Truelove was the village chimney sweep. They are sadly long gone.

We understood at the time of purchase that the building was Tudor, but have since learned that it, with the next door cottage, constitutes a Sussex Wealden House and dates from the late 14th or early 15th century! They are now listed Grade II and to think they were allowed to become derelict! [beside the Causeway] (Hilda Barton).

How many of you remember the floods in Billingshurst in the 1970s? My garden was inundated, and at 5 a.m. I was out in Stane Street rescuing my Grobags which were floating off to Pulborough!   (Michael Smith)

Floods, 2nd June, 1981. A little old lady, Miss Williams, lived in the cottage beside the Baptist Chapel path. 'Her living room carpet disintegrated and her piano fell apart. Her neighbours had a summerhouse. When it flooded the water floated it over the hedge onto her lawn where it rested like a Noah's Ark. her. "That's not mine. I don't know where that came from!" (Michael Smith)

Tues. 2.6.81 'Two heavy thunderstorms. The Six Bells had water up to the ceiling. School trips to the Downs were cancelled. The buses were needed to ferry passengers as the stations were closed. Mr. Edgar rowed up and down the new lake in his canoe. (Paul Smith)

Verena Bristow, aged 81 in 1982, was born in one of the three cottages known as 'Weavers', now demolished, down a lane opposite The Smithy, which is now SCATS, on the Newbridge road to Wisborough Green. She then lived in Bell cottage behind the Six Bells.

Geoffrey Rhodes is the fourth generation of 'snobs' or bootmenders in Billingshurst. There could be a day when Rhodes and Son are no more. Geoff laments, "It's a dying trade. We can't get the materials. Lasting tack, brass tacks – we have to ask the manufacturers to hunt around the dusty corners of their warehouses. Modern shoes are machine loaded. Tanned leather is very difficult to get hold of and very expensive and oak bark leather is discontinued. No-one is taught about bends and butts and how to buy and select any more". Fortunately that day is not yet. The shelves are packed with footwear of every shape and size.

Clare Luckin, the 'Billingshurst Egg Lady' styles herself "The Reluctant Farmwife". She writes of milking the cows on a three-legged stool, of the awful smell of the three goats that ruined her roses. "Whenever the wind was in the right direction I had to shut all the windows. In due course (the billy's) actions bore fruit and we had four baby goats scampering about the place on their thimble-size hooves". She wrote of the one that escaped and destroyed the Doctor's dahlias and the large and unpredictable horses, bought for the children, none of whom took to riding. "My husband heard a rumour that the Indian restaurants, which were just becoming established in the area, used rabbit, named as chicken in their menus and that the local market paid well for them. In due course the shed became wall-to-wall hutches...they needed cleaning out every few days...I put a stop to that project on the grounds that I had enough cleaning to do with my own family without having a similar task with the rabbits...We have had pigs too, and of course, chicken, bantams and ducks – one hundred and fifty of them at one time, but I endure them for their excellent product, and one does not have to have a relationship with them, only one's regular egg customers, which is the best product of animals that I can think of".

Hoops were used for barrels for the fishing trade. Whole trainloads would leave Billingshurst Station for the northern fishing ports. They were also used for barrels for sugar, glass, pottery etc. and the smaller size for tea chests. The industry declined during WWI and the years after and wood hoops had been superseded by metal ones. The hoop shed was demolished by a gale in 1949.

Billingshurst in the 1880s always had its Corn Market, held in the King's Arms in the Market Room, still in existence, and a great deal of local trade was done before the advent of railways. (Phyllis Adam)

Frederick Mursell, 1930s Fish Salesman, advertises his goods in Charles Tiler's Newspaper:-
There's Haddock, Herring, Bloater, aye, and Kipper,
Such as will suit a hearty English skipper,
And tempting sole, or eels to make a "pie"
With perhaps Rock Salmon in my basket lie,
And Cod and Whiting with some other fish,
Await inspection – please bring out your dish!
P.S. For your "Cats" I've always bits and scraps.

W.A Shepherd, Universal Supply Stores, Church Gate advertises his beers:-
Elephant Brand Ale, or Stout and Oatmeal Stout 2/6 per dozen, net
Pilsener Lager Beer 3/- a dozen net
Fremlin's Family Ales and Stouts
All our beers (lager excepted) are bittered entirely with English hops.

Died on 14th March, 1849. W. Wadey, a carpenter of Billingshurst, aged 90. For many years he attended a dissenting place of worship 9 miles from his residence and lately he often walked 14 miles to a place of worship. He married May Holden in 1788, now 83. She brought him 11 children, 9 of whom are still living. He had 69 grandchildren living and 14 died. Eight young men, husbands of his granddaughters, bore him to his grave.

At the entrance to Dell Lane there used to be a large pond known as the Holy Well where people came to pay and seek cures. It was filled in by the developers.

The Church Path has no owner. Apparently it is 'no man's land', or perhaps Common Land. It belongs to the people of the Parish. It was properly call Holy Well Lane. Brenda Twine recalled the 'small tree hung pond' at the end of the path, subsequently filled in, which was the Holy Well.

Church Path from Station Road

The Local History Society, guided by John Hurd, excavated a trench across the Roman Road at Parbrook in 1984 in conjunction with the Horsham Museum Society. The present road had been rerouted to the east, probably to avoid flooding and the site used for agriculture or waste. They dug a 6 foot X 66 trench. Beneath the overlying topsoil was the last road surface of flint, ironstone and clay, second was a possible mediaeval road surface of ironstone and clay, next the possible Roman foundations of large ironstone blocks laid on natural clay. This constituted the 'agger' which made use of a by-product of the local iron industry. It must have been in continuous use in this alignment at least until the end of the 16th century before the iron industry died out. The archaeologists had access to only one of the customary side ditches dug by the Romans. It was filled with clay and covered as part of the road thereafter. The road was estimated as being 10.2 metres wide, flanked by a wide and flat unmetalled surface.

"I worked at The Maltings in 1922/3 in the kitchen in the morning and a waitress in the afternoon. A plate of assorted cakes and a pot of tea was 10d a head. I worked from 8 a.m. to 6 p.m. for 7/6d a week. I remember a party of racegoers going home from Goodwood left a tip for 7/6d – a whole week's wages!" (Dora Allum).

"But we come to the countryside to see nature", they say. You won't see much nature in West Sussex. Almost wherever you look the landscape has been cut, dug, shaped and managed by Man. In fact if a farmer were to allow his farm to revert to nature, those same country-lovers would soon be complaining about 'that disgusting weed-covered eyesore' (John Richards)

Billingshurst's Heritage No. 2

Murders in Billingshurst

Miss Susan Lee, a student in the Lower Sixth Form at the Weald was killed with a knife by an employee of a local restaurant in 1978.

During the 1950s there was a double murder and suicide in the Argent family at Goldings Farm, Five Oaks which was subsequently renamed Oak House.

Billingshurst Institutions

The Angling Society

The Society was set up in 1919 when Pub angling teams used to compete for cash. It has grown to offer some of the finest coarse fishing in the Horsham District. In Billingshurst the main venues are on the Upper Arun and in the recently constructed fishing lake at Jubilee Fields. The Society also offers facilities at Shillinglee and Malthouse Lakes, Wisborough Green, and along the Lower Arun as far as Lee Place towards Pulborough. Chub, bream, roach, barbel, little bleak and pike up to 26lbs abound on the Upper Arun and carp weighing up to 30 lbs. Migratory 15lb sea trout coming upstream to spawn have been landed but they are always put back. Jubilee Fields Lake, where children may fish free, has been stocked with 4,800 fish recently and 750 barbel were introduced at Newbridge but they have migrated downstream to tidal waters. Roach, tench, rudd, gudgeon and crucian carp are now to be caught. Membership is currently 250, fishing matches are held and training is offered for children and novices. Some 25 trophies are awarded each year. Meetings are held at the Weald School and informally at the Limeburners Inn.

Billingshurst's Heritage No. 2

Peter Stockwood, Membership Secretary, with a carp

Billingshurst Dramatic Society (BDS)

The BDS company

During WWII men were allowed for the first time into the hitherto exclusively feminine 'Women's Hall' so enabling enthusiasts to form a Dramatic Society with facilities, however meagre, previously denied them. In 1941 the Workers Education Association ran drama classes and produced Sheridan's *'The Rivals'* the next year. Encouraged by Dr. Moreton, the village school headmaster, a Dramatic Society was formed. Their first two productions were *Tobias and the Angel* by James Bridie and *Arms and the Man* by George Bernard Shaw, Britain's second greatest playwright. Any proceeds from the later were to go to charity, so with some cheek the members wrote to the great man, still active at Ayot St Lawrence asking him if he would donate the royalties they paid to charity. They got an emphatic 'no', but with the reservation that so long as they did the plays for themselves they need pay no royalties, but if they were for other people he wanted his share! Remarkably he offered his help with setting up the Society and the constitution he helped with is still in use today.

Shaw died aged 94 in 1950 but the BDS prospered under the influence of Dr. Bill Bousfield, Jack Leaman, Ron Oulds, Francis Crisp and Molly Church. Stalwarts John Farmer and Nevin Davis made an entry in 1958 soon followed by John and Rene Humphries, a group whose influence shaped the present Society. Pamela Leaman, a former actress, brought professionalism to the troupe. Her first production was Rattigan's *Deep Blue Sea*. Jack Leaman thought up the idea of the Patrons, a subscribing supporters club, who would get special booking privileges, and soon an annual party with copious refreshments. The President, C.G. Davis, Nevin's father had to pay £2 to guarantee the party against a loss! Jack Easton, Bank Manager and Chairman of the Parish Council swelled the Patron's numbers to 120. Jack died in 1990.

Notable plays were produced in the 1960s. Francis Crisp did *The Amorous Prawn*, Ron *The French Mistress*, Nevin *The Reluctant Debutante* and John Farmer *Present Laughter*. Ron's *Alfie*, in 1968, with John Farmer as the libidinous scallywag met with puritanical criticism but was a theatrical triumph, winning the County Drama Competition, as did Ron's *Tom Jones* the next year at the festival. There followed a period of developmental liaison with George Rawlins, the WSCC Drama Advisor, when BDS actors dominated the casts of County productions. These experiences deepened the members' theatrical competence and many memorable shows ensued.

In the 70s Chairman, John Farmer procured the rights to stage the first amateur performance of *O Clarence* (based on P.G. Wodehouse) with John Humphries as Lord Emsworth. Pat Gierth joined the company producing remarkable posters and set designs in a hall and on a stage offering little encouragement. Don Campbell produced *The Lion in Winter* and in 1974 John Humphries directed his daughter, Sue Pollard, in *There's a Girl in my Soup*. In 1977 Ian Harvey, who became a professional actor, produced a wonderful *Sweeney Todd*, a show complemented by the talented pianist, Craig Pruess. For the Queen's Jubilee Ron Oulds produced a splendid tribute, *Send ER Victorious*.

The Company offer the local people intelligent popular theatre on their doorstep, and is bold in its choice of genres, tackling verse drama such as Edwin Pollard's *Murder in the Cathedral* by T.S. Eliot, performed at St. Mary's, social themes such as *A Day in the Life of Joe Egg* and *Abigail's Party*, farce such as *Noises Off*, musicals like *Guys and Dolls* and pantomime such as *Aladdin*.

For all its manifest shortcomings as a theatre the Women's Hall offers advantages to the Society. It is centrally sited in the village, readily available for rehearsals and set construction and enjoys its own peculiar old-world ambience. Of course the good companionship of the band of Billingshurst thespians has thrown up a host of anecdotes about drying on stage, missed cues and entrances, ad libs to fill awkward pauses and embarrassing gaffes by people in the audience. Jackie Charman, gifted actress and Secretary of the Society could offer an Evening of Entertainment of such yarns. John Humphries, as Wishy Washy in *Aladdin* once brought up on stage a little Chinese child from the audience and a lady when offered a programme replied "No thanks, I've got one from the last play".

When in 1979 Edwin produced *The Crucible* the West Sussex County Times wrote:

'The Women's Hall can hardly be regarded as an inspiration even to dedicated actors. The stage is cramped, backstage infinitely worse, almost depressing. Yet time and again the Billingshurst players produce works there that often emerge head and shoulders above anything seen elsewhere'.

The Company has staged 191 plays to date since its inception, a remarkable achievement and a demonstration of how great an asset the Society is to Billingshurst.

Rene Humphries and Nevin

Bowling Club

The Billingshurst Bowling Club is sited within the playing fields of the Weald School on three sides and on the fourth by Station Road Gardens. It is accessed from Myrtle Lane. A new pedestrian access, with disabled parking, has recently been built near the tennis court end of the Swimming Pool.

Mrs Puttock of Clevelands House originally leased the bowlers the land, carefully fenced off from her cattle, in 1932 at a peppercorn rent of 5 shillings a year. The freehold was purchased in 1968. Local tradesmen were the founders – Higgins the Ironmonger, Lusted the grocer, Crisp the barber and tobacconist, Cripps the butcher, C.E Wadey the builder and Watt the seedsman. At first the green had only three rinks, cut by hand mower at a charge of 6d an hour. The pavilion was 'basic' with a bucket and rota. The Club has been in continuous use by a band of enthusiasts except for the wartime years when it was utilised by the Red Cross and the Air Training Corps. In the early days matches were arranged against Graffham, Midhurst and Handcross.

Since the 1950s the Green was extended to six rinks, greatly assisted by the arrival of mains water and electricity. The original clubhouse was extended to include changing rooms, a kitchenette, lounge area and toilets. More recently a second pavilion has been installed for tea and refreshments after matches. Members reclad a Portacabin, previously used as a Parish Room at Clymping, and provided a pitched roof to complement the old clubhouse together with more toilets, available to the disabled. It has been named 'The Stocker Room' in honour of Jack who masterminded the project. An automated watering system has been an enormous advance on the loan of a standpipe and a long hose from the cricket club!

The Club now plays friendly mixed matches against 25 other clubs in West Sussex and Surrey, weekdays and weekends, afternoons and evenings with a full range of club competitions and friendly sessions. Newcomers are made welcome, all abilities are catered for and novices lent equipment and given free trial sessions. Garden seating is available for spectators.

The Bowling Club in 1960

Cricket Club

An early sporting newspaper called 'Bell's Life' of 1831 carried a report of a return cricket match between Billingshurst and Horsham, Nuthurst and Shipley. The Ordnance Survey map of 1869 shows a circle off Station Road marked 'cricket' which suggests that the game was played in the parish throughout the reign of Queen Victoria, possibly on the same site, though there was no Station Road until the railway came in 1859. Play continued there into the 21st century until fine new facilities became available at Jubilee Fields when the old pitch beyond the handsome wall was abandoned and redeveloped as recreational gardens.

Among the early players were the Hubert family, William Henry being a surgeon and his son William Arthur the village doctor at a house at Rosehill. They were renowned for hitting sixes over the houses in Station Road. Rex Haygate of a rival team, Wisborough Green, managed to hit a ball into a passing railway truck. No doubt a six was recorded for a lost ball, though it was recovered at Pulborough, the next stop on the line. The West Sussex Constabulary played their games on the village field and dinner was taken in 1878, as usual at the Station Inn where mine host was Sprinks, the miller's son. 'Later in the evening some capital songs were given'. W. Dalbiac was the Billingshurst demon bowler. The Eversheds, major Billingshurst landowners, like the Norfolk Edriches, once in 1892 fielded a complete family eleven, beating the village side in a low scoring, two innings match by two runs. Playing for Billingshurst, Rev Newcomb, A. Puttock and A. Hubert all scored 'golden ducks' and Maurice Ireland accumulated 4 runs. In 1885 W. Evershed went in first and 'carried his bat' scoring 90 not out against Horsham. In that year there was a match with Mr. Goff's team at Summers Place which is thought to have been another cricket venue in early Victorian times.

Ralph Wadey, dispatch rider during WWI

WWI disrupted cricket development, but interest revived in the 1920s with such stalwarts as Ralph Wadey of Five Oaks, R.E. Norris, Harold Wadey the builder, Arthur Spinks, Alf Burchell and three Bottings. Arthur 'Bumper' Voice provided transport from his Station Road business for the whole team in a Motor-van known as 'The Brake'. By the 30s the club could boast a Second XI. 'Old Winkle' (Bill Philips) was the groundsman. Again from 1939 war interrupted play though when peace came at last some Sunday cricket was permitted. In 1949 there was a danger of housing development on the site. Mr. Eric Puttock organised a fund-raising celebrity match with Sussex County and England players involved. Rev. David Sheppard, once of Slinfold, who opened the first Weald Sixth Form Centre and later became Bishop of Liverpool captained the side which also contained James Langridge, Jack and Charlie Oakes, Jim Parks and other famous players. Doug Wright and Godfrey Evans, England's wicket-keeper, played for Puttock's XI which won the match. Sufficient money was raised with a public subscription to see off the threat.

The club prospered. In 1958 the players made their first tour into Essex arranged by Secretary Tony Smith. They were well beaten in their first match against Tillingham, but rallied in their next game to beat the odds-on favourites, Rayleigh Cricket Club. More tours were arranged to the New Forest, Bath and

Norfolk in the closing decades of the 20th century. David Sainsbury, sports master and notable rugby referee of the Weald arranged the Hunstanton, Norfolk tour and the bowler, Barry Taylor, the others. David scored a remarkable 150 against Blackheath. Other notables of the time were John and Mark Upton, Roger Patterson, Justin Millais, Jim Burroughs, Tony Petras, Cheeseman, Steve McMurrugh and Roger Lusted. Some weekends three of four matches were played on both Saturdays and Sundays. Originally there was only a small changing-room at the Weald School end of the field. The Parish Council provided a most-welcome wooden pavilion in 1962 but that is now demolished after falling into disrepair. In its heyday the club provided sport for ladies, both cricket and stoolball.

The advent of generous space and comfortable pavilion facilities at Jubilee Fields in 2006 has enabled the club to flourish in the 21st century. Friendly and convenient as the old ground had been, it was often in trouble from neighbouring residents who had balls landing in their gardens. Two teams now compete in the Sussex County League. The club takes part in the League Cup and holds many friendly games and practices throughout the summer months. Juniors are encouraged and catered for by age groups, under 10, 12 and 14s. They play in the Colts' League.

Billingshurst's Heritage No. 2

The Club with Cups and Trophies 1984

Steve Nicholls, Beryl Lusted, Barry Taylor, Roger Lusted, Roger Patterson, Dave Patten, David Sainsbury, David Rood, Chris Michael

The Club with pots of ale – Bath Tour 1981

112

The Billingshurst XI 1957

In 2002 Mr. Joe Sillett of Billingshurst scored a century with an old bat which had been so holed by woodworm that he had had to shave off curves from the top edges. Inspired by his triumph he designed a new prototype on the same pattern and subsequently launched a bat manufactory, trading as 'The Woodworm Cricket Company' which sold 200 bats in its first year and rocketed to 15,000 by 2005. The company mistakenly branched out into golf clothing. Sadly the rocket ran out of fuel, despite big-name sponsors such as Freddie Flintoff and Kevin Pietersen, and went into administration. It was bought up by 'The Sports HQ' in 2008.

Billingshurst's Heritage No. 2

Association Football Club

The Club celebrates winning the League and two cups 1962/3

Three club programmes

The club old brigade, 1920 division 2 Trophy

Gordon New with a few cups

Billingshurst's Heritage No. 2

Association Football in Billingshurst has a lengthy history, a game deservedly popular with generations of men and boys. The West Sussex Gazette recorded its formation in November, 1890 on the first Saturday, after Mr. Skinner's side beat Mr. Newcomb's 8 -5 in a promising trial

Rugby Football has predominated over Soccer at the Weald School since the early 70s. Prior to that soccer was played and earlier was much enjoyed at the old East Street School on a field where the Catholic Church now stands. It was also played in the first 15 years of the Weald. Keen rugby players leaving the school must now continue playing the game at other clubs such as Pulborough or Horsham. Young soccer players, however, are now well catered for by Billingshurst Football Club, which offers continuity and sporting fellowship for life, if they remain in the village.

The old soccer club played in many different places. The first field was Hill Top north of Manor House. In the 20s they moved to different pitches at Little Gilmans, the old cricket field, Tedfold Park, Jengers Meadow and Jubilee Meadow near Little Daux. The team took the name 'Jubilee Rovers' for that period. After WWII they played at a site off the present Forge Way, land under what is now Carpenters and the present Recreation Ground. A regular pitch was at last assured when the Parish Council bought an orchard due west of the old cricket ground in Station Road. Changing facilities were shared with the cricketers in the old pavilion. That has gone too and the site is now car parks, the Leisure Centre and a Nursery School. This was the home ground of the club until 2006 when another Jubilee Fields became available as one of the side-benefits of a large new housing estate. The additional bonus was the use of excellent changing and recreational facilities.

The game was successful and popular long before the Great War. In 1909 the team played Horsham in the final of the local league, but lost 3-1. In 1932 Mr. Joe Pavey played in the team that won the Intermediate Cup in 1932. "We never used to speak on the football field: now they are like a lot of parrots," he said. Before WWII there were about 15 players, taking part in the West Sussex Wednesday League. Wednesdays were commonly Early Closing Days. Mr. Dick Jestico recalled, "We used to cycle to and from matches and pay 2s a week to have our shirts washed". Nowadays the club attracts some valuable supportive sponsorship. Mr. Glaysher travelled to games in a furniture lorry. Play was suspended during WWII but several friendly matches were played against the Italian prisoners of war from Kingsfold Camp. After the war the club revived still wearing heavy duty shirts and boots.

By the 60s the teams were winning numerous trophies and turning the club into the present efficient outfit with regular training and a warm social fellowship.

A note in the Oct 1965 programme reads, "Old Sonny Harrison, used to be a Billingshurst postman and now is an old age pensioner. He has given us 10/- (Ten shillings) for this week's tea, sugar, milk and oranges. What an example for our supporters! Our Centre Half, Derrick Elliott was taken off to Worthing Hospital with a broken thigh. We are starting a small fund to help his wife during his twelve weeks in hospital".

In the Centenary year, 1990, the Club had 60 registered players with three teams playing in the Sussex League, the first team in the Premier Division. Today the club's facilities and its excellent website would startle the pioneers and they would surely envy the facilities, the keenness, the social benefits, not to mention modern boots, kit, handsome match programmes and playing surfaces on three senior pitches and a number of junior ones.

In a recent Programme, cost £2, the club history is briefly recorded. It played in the Horsham League until joining the WS Football League on its inception. It had won the Premier League title the year before 'under the management of Mark Betts and Malcolm Saunders'. They then ran three senior sides, the first team competing in the Sussex County League for the first time. The Reserve and third teams continued membership of the WSFL competing in Division 2 and Division 4. As a 'Charter Standard Club it also ran ten junior sides, upwards from under 7 years up to 16, playing in the Horsham District Youth League.

Billingshurst's Heritage No. 2

The Tennis Club

Tournament players 2008

Five club members

Installing the Floodlighting

Lawn tennis has been played in Billingshurst at least as far back to the years before the Great War. The 'Flapper' generation of the 1920s, among the well-to-do, embraced the sport as a socially welcome diversion for both men and women, unlike football, cricket and stoolball. The convivial game was an ideal meeting and mating point. John Betjeman's poem about Miss Joan Hunter Dunn catches the spirit exactly. Mr. Joe Luxford, grand panjandrum of Billingshurst, had a tennis court at the turn of the century and promoted the game and there is record of other courts at Lordings Road and Newbridge. It is likely that the great houses of old Billingshurst would all have kept racquets, nets and balls and made a screened grass lawn for the family and friends.

We first hear of an organisation to control the use of a public facility which kept minutes of its meetings on 13th October, 1949. The Village Sports Association met at the King's Head and nominated a Tennis Courts Committee and decreed court fees of a shilling (5p) an hour. The Parish Council has provided two courts, expecting to collect fees from the public hiring it on a casual basis. In practice arranging use, selling tickets and supervising etiquette and upkeep of the balls, net and other equipment was a demanding task and the Council welcomed the volunteers who came together to form the "Billingshurst Tennis Courts Committee". On 2nd Sept 1949 it was formed with Mr. F. Crawford as the leader, under the aegis of the Sports Association, which then had oversight of games in the village. The Council were pleased to delegate control of bookings to the volunteers, requiring 10% of the takings. Mr. J.B. Sherlock was able to report the gift of £250 from the Ministry of Education to promote the game and the loan of £50 from the Sports Association to be repaid within 10 years.

American Tournaments were arranged, matches against other village clubs keenly contested for the 'Wynstrode Cup' and social events provided for members. [Wynstrode is a 17th century house in Okehurst Road where the Sherlock family lived] Dances raised small sums of profit, music by the 'Blue Quartet'. Jumble sales and Social Evenings were held. They even investigated some coaching for young players. Mr. Allan Dugdale, teacher at the village school ran the Village Youth Club and was allocated an evening for play. The Committee provided a simple pavilion measuring 20x15 feet. Calor Gas lighting was arranged. Sight screens were provided by using hessian sacks joined together and suitably treated. Hardboard was used to line the hut. They constantly harried the Parish Council as Trustees for repairs to netting and the surfaces of the courts. Mr. T. Topper was the go-between with the Parish Council. There was also conflict with Mr. Lawrenson about his building a wall to prevent 'the effluence from his works running on the courts'. A drainpipe was needed and they had to borrow the cricket club hose to clear the courts. They used the Railway Hotel's toilets and hired water from the Bowling Club at 5 shillings a year. They sought out a dozen tubular chairs from the closing down of the Maltings Hotel. Dances were held at Gratwicke House, hired from Mrs Page. In 1953 the Committee presented a Coronation Tableaux and won third prize. Regular suggestions of forming a Club were constantly rejected. The Parish Council was determined to ensure that the courts were available to the general public and not monopolised by a club.

Many of the group's doings are fondly reminiscent of the 1950s. The modern reader is taken aback by the effusive thanks to Col. B.C. Kerr for the gift of asbestos panels to line the pavilion. Raffle prizes were normally bottles of whisky and sherry, a box of chocolates and a pack of 50 cigarettes at whist drives and the like. The dance at Gratwicke in 1954 economised on the band by borrowing a radiogram. Tickets were 7/6d in 1956, the band cost £5.5s.0 and the profit two shillings and tenpence. The dance was deemed a success. When Mrs. Forster came to Gratwicke and charged £8 for hire and refreshments they went elsewhere. Meetings were held at The Market Room of the Railway Hotel or at the High Street pubs.

In 1962 the Parish Council sold the old courts and built two new ones encroaching slightly onto the football field. All play ceased until the work was completed.

In May 1963, the year John Kennedy was shot, forty people met at the Village Hall, Mr. Jack Easton, manager of Barclay's Bank in the Chair. It was decided to form a Tennis Club Committee to succeed the former Courts Committee. After meetings with Miss Joyce, Parish Clerk, the new Club secured exclusive use of the courts for 2½ days, (Tues. Thurs. and after 2pm Sun.) later 3½, at a rent £1 a week, plus use of the Youth Hut for changing, shared with the youth Stoolball team. The crying need was for a new pavilion and for the Club to take charge of maintenance and control instead of doing everything through the Council who had taken the courts out of use for resurfacing without notice. There were only 13 senior players left. More members were imperative. A plan to buy a Portacabin was rejected. Instead an elderly caravan was bought in 1966 renovated and furnished. A new agreement was made with the Council giving security of tenure and land for a pavilion. The club funds were invested in the new Premium Bonds! The idea of floodlighting was shelved. The club joined the Sussex County L.T.A.

Social events took in typical 60s style with barbecues, coffee mornings, wine and cheese parties, produce stalls, tombolas, a 'Cavalcade of Tennis' on Flower Show Day, sweepstakes, a bottle party at Gleniffer House, Slinfold and a Dinner-Dance at the Gatwick Manor Hotel. As the caravan steadily deteriorated the struggle for a pavilion began about 1967. The Council agreed to lease the site but funding, planning permission and bureaucracy were enormous hindrances. An offer from the then extant Stoolball Club to help with the fund-raising in return for a share of the building was politely declined. Mr. Easton, who was the second 'President', reckoned £2,400 would be needed. By 1968 they had assembled enough credit to place an order and secured planning permission from Horsham Rural. £540 Ministry of Education grant, £250 Parish Council, LTA loan £500, £109 donations, £90 interest-free loans, and £500 worth of guarantees! The new pavilion opened with a sherry party on 25th May, 1969. They sold the caravan for £20.

The Weald School courts became available in the 1970s as membership climbed to 94 seniors. There was now a continuing search for development. In 1975 floodlighting was installed costing £960 aided by a £500 loan from the LTA. Barry Barnes gave advice and service supplies. Prices rose sharply through to the 80s frustrating the demand for a pavilion extension, another court and more floodlights. Fundraising continued with the usual events which now included a barn dance. Annual membership rose to £20. By 1984 there were 110 senior members, but the fourth court would cost £6000.

Through the 80s the club prospered and in the 90s the 'old guard' gave place to new. Mr. Easton, doyen of the Club died in 1990. By the Millennium the roll of senior members had fallen to 53 and annual subs had risen to £65. The big question then was whether or not to move the Club to the imminent Jubilee Fields where a 4-court site was envisaged. A business development plan was drawn up in pursuit of grant aid, but in the event, like the rugby group, the Club voted to remain in its old quarters, with a renewed resolution to improve the facility. Its annual rent to the Parish Council had now risen to £1750 and the Parish, as Landlords, paid for basic maintenance and still required opportunities for casual public use.

Refurbished courts were opened in 2006 and new lights provided in 2008. Further refurbishment of courts 1, 2 and 3 and the provision of the long sought 4th court came in April, 2012 at a cost of £40,000. At this time new arrangements were made with the Parish Council. The Club were to pay a peppercorn rent rather than the current £2500 per annum, but from then on were entirely responsible for the upkeep of the facility, surfaces, nets, fences etc. The President, Di Burroughs, received the prestigious Tennis Sussex Robert Cushing silver salver award in recognition of her unstinting 30 years of service to the Billingshurst Club. Men's Captain and development officer, Rob Falkner, and Coach, Dave Almond, were also nominated for awards. David initiated a programme in 2013 for children from Worthing with disabilities. Senior membership is now £100 per annum. 250 people are enrolled, roughly half of them seniors and half juniors. Casual users pay £6 an hour. The Committee, under the Chairmanship of Jackie Bench has drawn up plans for a new clubhouse which should be completed in early 2014, wheelchair friendly with solar panels, at an estimated cost of £130,000.

Billingshurst's Heritage No. 2

Di Burroughs with the Wynstrode Cup

1984   David Watt, Ted Farmer, Jeremy David and Maggie Keyte

Di Burroughs remembers

I came to play at the Club in 1984 after a ten year break from tennis to discover that my short dress, frilly knickers and wooden racquet were no longer the done thing. They were as out of date as the Elsan toilet arrangements which required a rota to undertake the digging of holes in the days of the old caravan.

An intriguing mystery hangs over the Wynstrode Tennis Cup. The silver plaques go back to 1925 on the base of a splendid silver trophy intended by its donor, Mrs. Verling Sherlock, to promote competition and encourage fellowship among local village tennis clubs. Midhurst were the first winners, followed by Southwater. Billingshurst won it five times between 1932 and 1938. The competition continued throughout the 1950s, with a gap during WWII. A good deal of Committee time was spent debating how best to insure and protect the collectively owned imposing and valuable item. Sad to relate, Billingshurst were the last winners in 1960. Then nothing more is heard of the cup or of competitions in its name. No note of the loss is to be found in the minutes, so it seems likely that an end to inter-village rivalry was accepted without regret.

Then, out of the blue, forty two years later, the Cup was found in an attic in London and returned to the Mothersdales here in Billingshurst! There proved to be no enthusiasm locally to resume the old competitions between villages, most of which no longer had teams, so Billingshurst Club made use of it for the trophy for tournaments for five years. It has not been used since. Time for a rethink?

As for the future, we must keep up the impetus for improvement which will be the more likely with a new clubhouse and investment in young people. We can safely say that lawn tennis in Billingshurst has shed any snobbery, class consciousness and exclusivity and is now soundly based as a healthy mixed-gender sport with opportunities for friendly recreation as well as the development of skills at all levels. Novices are made welcome!

Billingshurst Choral Society

The Society (BCS) is an active and friendly choral group which sings in Billingshurst and the surrounding area. It currently has over a hundred singing members.

A chance remark, made at the right time, sealed the formation of the Society. Choral singing in the village had largely been confined to the church choirs, begun in 1985 when a group of singers joined together to sing madrigals. They called themselves 'Sundrie Voyces'. Following a successful concert at St. Mary's Church, a bass and experienced conductor, George Jones, commented that Billingshurst needed a choral society; a contralto, Jackie Bench, offered to do the administration. Much groundwork followed; visits to village church choirs, posting posters on notice boards, press notices in the local paper. As a reward 50 singers attended the first rehearsal at St. Mary's.

The Choral Society

By January 1986 a Committee had been formed, in the capable hands of John Cartmell, celebrated locally as a steam engine owner and enthusiast. Good connections enabled the employment of some of the very best soloists in the Society's concerts. Several up-and-coming stars travelled to Billingshurst who later rose high in their profession. Sarah Connolly CBE, opera singer, is just one example. From 1986 to 2000 performances had started locally, St. Mary's Church and the Weald School halls. Occasionally they travelled to Chichester Cathedral which has remained a popular venue.

George Jones has been the Conductor and Musical Director from the start. The Society has been performing a mixture of old and new challenging works ever since its inception. In 2000 AD BCS gave the first performance of the *Billingshurst Mass*, specially written by Stanley Vann, in Chichester Cathedral. The following year they performed the *African Sanctus* by David Fanshawe, a haunting mixture of African music and more traditional European melodies. The repertoire has extended recently with performances, in 2009 and 2011, of Will Todd's *Mass in Blue*, a popular and challenging jazz setting of the Mass. The following year BCS did Alexander L'Estrange's *Zimbe!* a celebration of the vibrancy of African music. 2013 saw BCS perform the UK premiere of Stale Klieberg's *Requiem for the Victims of Nazi Persecution*, as part of the Brighton Fringe.

In 2003 BCS and Angmering Chorale gave the first performance in the South of England of Karl Jenkins' acclaimed *The Armed Man*. The two societies travelled to New York in 2007 to join a performance of that work in Carnegie Hall. In January 2009 they returned for a performance of *Stabet Mater* in the Lincoln Centre. BCS formed part of the choir at the Royal Festival Hall to celebrate the reopening, following restoration, in 2007. They returned on stage there in October as part of a select choral group for the Royal Gala Concert to commemorate the same event. The choir perform regularly, by invitation, at the annual Brandenburg Festival in London.

BCS performs three major concerts annually, with the autumn concerts often in Chichester Cathedral and occasionally in Arundel Cathedral. Many concerts have been given jointly with the Angmering Chorale, also directed by George. The spring and summer concerts are performed at Billingshurst Leisure Centre at the Weald School.

The Society's Christmas Concert is usually performed at St. Mary's Church, which is also the rehearsal venue. Rehearsals take place there every Tuesday evening from 8 to 9.45 pm. BCS has a thriving social calendar and organises concert tours every two years. So far the Society has visited Belgium, the Loire Valley, Caen, Paris, Prague and Tuscany.

Bellringing

St.Mary's Church has a dedicated team of ringers and a peal of 8 bells, one of the best in Sussex.

Wendy Lines tells the story in an article in a Billingshurst Society Newsletter (No. 37 1982).

In the early part of the 16th century the sound of the bells in the tower was an integral part of the village life and from the Churchwardens' accounts we know that the bells were in constant need of repair and attention. In 1526 18 old pence were paid for "trussing of owre ilij th bell lytyll bel and second bell". On 1530 much work was carried out on the 'great bell' – 10d was spent on meat and drink when the bell was taken down and perhaps a jolly time was had after the hard work. The bellfounder however was not happy, because we find the item, "Paid to the bellfounder which was not content at the fyrst payment for the bell xxvjs viij (26/8d)" At the feast of All Hallows he was given a further fee and also paid 16d separately for food and lodging – for him and his horse.

At this time only four bells are mentioned by name, but there might have been five.

In 1532, in the reign of Henry VIII, the parishioners of Billingshurst undertook a mammoth task on behalf of one of their bells. They journeyed to a Reading foundry to have a bell recast. Expenses for "owre first goying to Redyng" were 5/7d. The carriage of the bell cost 8/- and the bell casting cost £6.0. 2d. Afterwards the suffragan bishop hallowed the bell and was provided with his dinner.

When Queen Elizabeth was on the throne in 1563 the bells were once again big news in the parish. Some 56 named parishioners and an unspecified number of 'bachelors' contributed to the recasting of the fourth bell. In 1580 a bellfounder must have been resident in the parish, because he rented two shops in the churchyard. Minor repairs were carried out constantly; for example "Item for taking downe the third bell and setting her fast in the stocks". Further recastings took place in 1593, 1616 and 1625. 1 shilling was spent on beer when it was loaded and 6d when "the bell was brought home". Think of the devotion, organisation, work and drinking involved on these occasions!

From the end of the 17th century the Churchwardens' accounts are not always so detailed, but in 1785 five bell ropes are regularly purchased. In 1818 the ring was increased to six bells. T. Mears of London this time recast or made the bells. The oldest of our present bells dates from then, as some bear this date and Mears' marks. [No 3 bell is dated 1812] At this time the bells were also hung in a new frame. The responsible officials in these years were Charles Farhall, Wm. King, Guardian, Richard Puttock, Overseer, Thos. Clear, Thos. Lathy, both Churchwardens and the Rev. G. Wells.

The ring was increased to a full peal of eight in 1897 [to celebrate Queen Victoria's Silver Jubilee]. After the death of George III there is an interesting entry, "to js. Champion for ringing the bell on the interment of the late King".

Originally the bell ropes would have hung to the floor of the tower. Today there is a charming ringing chamber that probably dates from the eighteenth (?) century.

Perhaps next time you hear the church bells, you can ponder a little on their long history and of the people of Billingshurst who have rung them through the centuries.

Mrs Lines acknowledged her indebtedness to Mr. J. Newman for his transcripts of the accounts and to G.P. Elphick for his book, *"Sussex Bells and Belfries"*

Loading up the bells

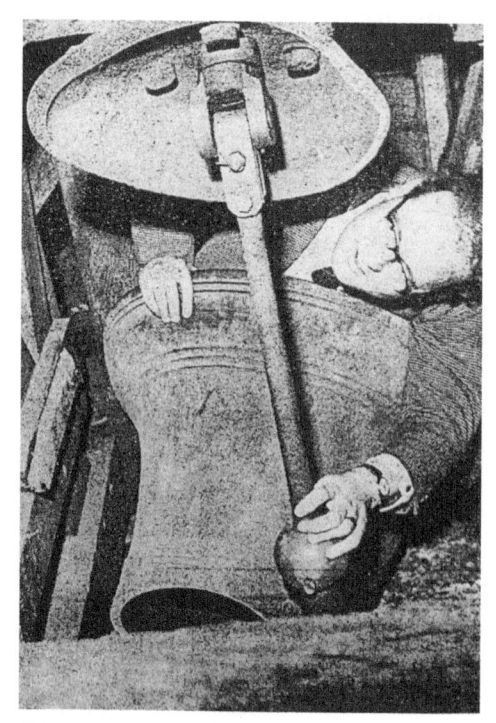

'Ring out, wild bells'

So far as we know then, three bells were installed prior to 1527, there were five in 1785 and a sixth treble bell was added in 1818. Two new bells were combined with the six in the belfry in 1897. In the 16th century accounts there is a record of constant expenditure on leather tongues for the clappers. The bells were no doubt silent during the Commonwealth period.

The Churchwardens Accounts in the Parish Records for 1823 reveal that they paid 7 shillings for beer for the ringers in 1821 and 5 shillings the following year, to James Fuller, landlord at the King's Arms, described as a public house. By 1823, however, James Trower of the King's Head was providing the beer. His hostelry was called an Inn and Wine House. By 1825 there was evidently no monopoly of the provision of beer for the bellringers at church expense as custom had shifted to George Puttock at the Blacksmith's Arms.

In 1965 the bells were again silent for a year having crashed to the church floor, mercifully harming no-one. Two were split so it was decided to recast them at Whitechapel at a cost of £1,500. Bell metal is commonly an alloy of copper and tin.

Lions charity bookshop

The Billingshurst and District Lions International Club maintain a comprehensive charity bookshop in Jengers Mead. Many people use this facility as an 'alternative library' paying a small price, subsequently returning books for re-sale. The club donates some £30,000 net on average per year from the bookshop and other sources of income to assist many worthy causes, both local and international.

The Lions charity bookshop, Jengers Mead

The Women's Institute

The WI movement started in Canada in February 1897. When Adelaide Hunter-Hoodless lost a child to gastro-enteritis she realised that women needed instruction in food hygiene and education as Homemakers and Citizen Builders. She worked hard to include Domestic Science in the school curriculum. The Farmer's Institute in Canada then formed a sister organisation – The Women's Institute. The movement thrived in the rural areas. In 1913 a member, Mrs. Madge Watts came to England to spread the word and establish the WI movement in the "Old Country".

Just after the end of WWI in January, 1919 a meeting was called in Billingshurst to encourage local women to form a WI. During wartime women had tackled many jobs formerly done by men, so they had greater expectations for themselves and a desire to share experiences, learn skills and better their education. A Billingshurst WI was formed. They still have a letter, dated 23rd Jan 1919, from the Board of Agriculture and Fisheries, Food Production Dept., welcoming the start. The rules were signed on 4th Feb. 1919 by the first Officers. A copy of the first six month's programme makes interesting reading. The lectures included Small Economies, Dressmaking, Pig Rearing, Keeping Fowls, Gardening and Keeping Rabbits. Also included were competitions, social time and, of course, tea.

A new nationally body was formed to govern the movement in England, with a Sussex woman as Chairman, Lady Gertrude Denman. She served for many years, building up the movement with the support of other strong-minded women. The organisation has three tiers. At the top is the National Federation followed by the County Federations and the local Institutes form the third tier. The Institute is a Registered Charity, and as such is non-party-political and non-sectarian but takes a wide-ranging interest in all matters, particularly those affecting women and their families. It does still preserve the crafts, cookery and needlework, most associated with the home, but takes pride in achieving recognition not only as 'jam makers' but also as women with much to offer in all walks of life.

Though not the first in Sussex, Billingshurst is among the first fourteen Institutes. Singleton takes the honours, founded in 1915. Nowadays the WI is thriving, meeting every month except August with an average of thirty members. Interesting speakers tell of events run by the County Federation, friendships are fostered and support offered to those who may be unwell or in need of help. The Institute meets with neighbouring WIs to share news and exchange programme ideas. The meetings are active and lively, eagerly anticipated by all the participants.

Leisure Centre

Billingshurst Leisure Centre

This community facility, built on the old association football ground at the approach to the Weald School off Station Road, was completed and opened for use in September, 2008 at a cost of £5.7 million. Karen Pickering MBE, an Olympic star and Britain's first world champion swimmer, performed the ceremony in the 25 metre, 4 lane indoor pool, equipped with a moveable floor. Alongside the pool is a 50 station Fitness Suite and reception and refreshment areas. Also available for hire on the Weald School campus are an all weather pitch, a gymnasium and a large four-court sports hall.

Aerial view of Leisure Centre, Wakoos Nursery, Recreational Gardens and the Bowling Green

Billingshurst's Heritage No. 2

BBC Situation Comedy – Ever- Decreasing Circles

This BBC TV programme was screened between 1984 and 1989. 27 episodes in four series were set in what was ostensibly a suburban close in Surrey. The filming was in fact mainly done in Dell Lane, Billingshurst and other Sussex locations. The series, considered by many critics to be one of the wittiest and intelligent productions of the Corporation, starred the late Richard Briers and Peter Egan. Richard played Martin, an obsessively orderly middle-aged committee man and Peter, his adventurous philandering neighbour, Paul, who had his 'salon' filmed in Lower Station Road.

Retail Businesses in Billingshurst

The earlier well-to-do businessmen in Billingshurst were the master butchers. The Penfolds (1530) and Greenfields (1649) are so described. Later men of affairs were the maltsters and brewers. They, together with the bakers, nurserymen, grocers, blacksmiths, leather workers, timber merchants and haberdashers supplied most of the needs of the people until well into the 19th century.

From Victorian times more shops opened and closed accordingly as fashion and perceived needs grew increasingly sophisticated. For example toys, bicycles, confectionary, fashionable clothing and hardware were in demand and services such as hairdressing, plumbing and photography afforded increasingly diverse opportunities for trading. Independent small shop-keeping provided a secure livelihood for many Billingshurst people until the challenge of the supermarkets and an increasingly mobile society began to rob them of their resident clientele. International Stores was the first national chain retailer. There is now one supermarket, one national convenience store and a large country store, not to mention massive competition from outlets in Pulborough, Storrington and Horsham, with other rivals readily accessible at Crawley, Guildford and on the coast. Enterprising entrepreneurs continue to accept the challenge offering local access to niche supplies and services such as computing, opticians, gifts, wine, travel and gambling with varying degrees of success. Regrettably however, as elsewhere, charity shops and empty premises continue to signal the steady decline of independent shopping. Many desirable outlets for books, art supplies, music, videos, antiques and other cultural desirables have faded away. Estate agents still prosper.

The Gastronomic Revolution

Kelly's Directory for 1962 listed only Jane's Tea Garden and the Shirley Cafe near the Station as places where one might buy a meal, together with the seven pubs which then dealt mainly in sandwiches and snacks. People did not eat out except on rare festive occasions. At Billingshurst since then there has been a truly remarkable gastronomic revolution. The businesses of the village can now be said to be predominately in the service of the inner man. Today there are no fewer than 28 outlets where hot food or ready meals may be purchased, eaten or taken away. In 13 of these it is possible to sit down and be waited on; 12 are 'ethnic' in character. They include 6 public houses, two fish and chip shops, a country store [SCATS], supermarket, convenience store and two bakers.

Billingshurst's Heritage No. 2

Takeaway Restaurants, Lower Station Rd.

Parbrook

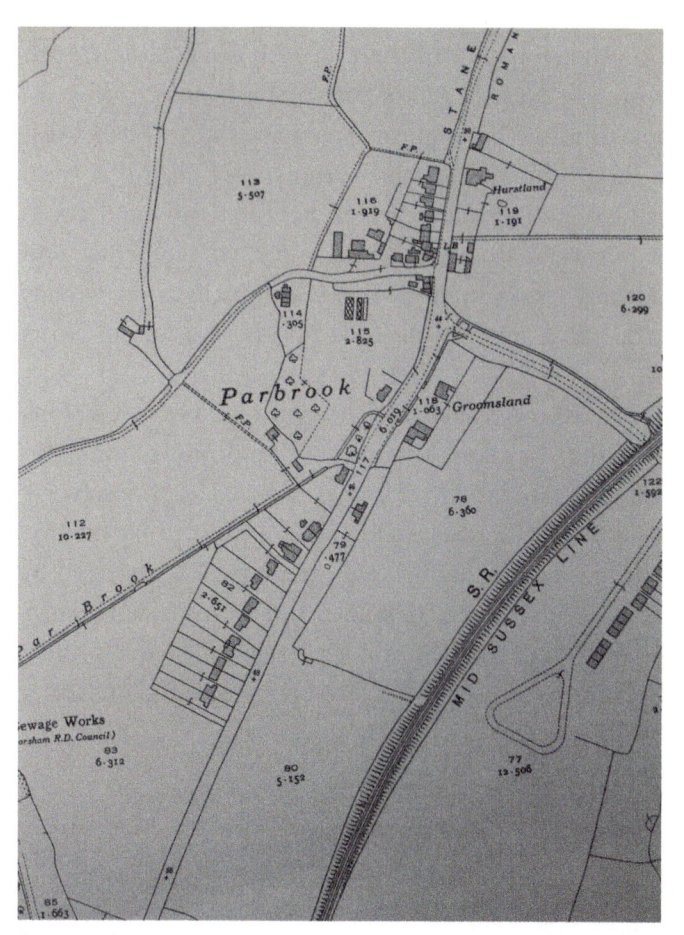

Staggered Junction at Parbrook

Street scene at Parbrook at the corner of Natt's Lane

South of Billingshurst along Stane Street lies the distinctive and separate set of dwellings beside the stream which is named Parbrook. The little hamlet stretches from Hurstlands, now a small estate in the corner of the Weald School playing fields, as far as Andrew Hill on the slope out of the valley on the road to North Heath, Adversane and Pulborough. Natts Lane is part of Parbrook leading off Stane Street beside the brook to join Marringdean Road and on towards West Chiltington. Before Station Road was built in mid 19th century all traffic from places south east of Billingshurst joined Stane Street at Hurstlands and could turn north to join the main Petworth Road or Billingshurst village centre and Horsham making it an important road junction. It was originally a crossroads with a more direct farm track going directly towards Newbridge at the Natts Lane junction.

The two oldest properties are Groomsland and Fossbrooks. Great Grooms about 1400 was recorded in the Fitzalan Survey as the property of John Gretegrome possessed of 'half a virgate [about 15 acres] 1s 8d & for ripeselver 1 cock, 2 hens 15 eggs and 9d'. The building has a chequered 20th century history. It became the Jenny Wren Restaurant for many years but has now reverted to private occupation, with another house recently built in the grounds. The barns and farm buildings were given planning permission for change of use to an office block and were transformed into an extensive antiques emporium for many years. It has recently become private apartments.

Sketch of Great Grooms

Fossbrooks was the home of Ephraim Wadey, the builder. He owned the brickyard at Gilmans, south of Natts Lane. This fine old timber-framed 16th century house with casement windows is now divided into two dwellings. The extensive builder's yard at the rear is being developed as a small estate named

Imperium Gate. Groomsland Drive was built after WWII on the site of the old Brickyard together with the modern industrial estate called Gilmans.

Further north, opposite the Weald School, set back from the road is Cedars. Its original name in 1480 was Bondwick after its owner. Then when Laurence Clark married Mr. Bondwick's sister and took possession it was retitled Clarksland subsequently developing into a considerable farm estate. So it remained until 1912 when it was renamed Cedars.

Cottage life – by Mrs. Doris Garton, slightly abridged

"I was born in 1916 in a small primitive cottage in Parbrook, Billingshurst. My first memory is of my father coming home from the war in 1918 when I was two. I remember him opening his kit bag and producing a beautiful baby doll for me and a clarinet for my brother brought from France. Our cottage consisted of five rooms, sitting room, larder with shelves for keeping food and produce and a large scullery. All the downstairs rooms had flagstone floors and were very damp. The only floor covering was coco-matting, laid in strips and peg rugs made by my mother from old clothes. These could be replaced when the damp penetrated and caused them to rot.

The rickety wooden stairs led to two bedrooms, one door opening between the two. Under the stairs was our coal store. The coalman used to shoot coal straight from the sack into it. Imagine the dust! At the far end of the scullery was a large copper and built into the outside wall, a bread oven. The water was heated by faggot wood. My father had bought a piece of the wooded area nearby to provide faggot wood, pea boughs and bean sticks each year. He hired a horse and cart to bring them home

We had an outside loo which we flushed by taking pails of water with us on each visit. There was a well in the garden in which we used to keep butter, milk and meat. The provisions were placed in a bucket and lowered into the well by a chain. All vegetable fruit waste went into the hole for composting – true organic gardening.

My mother was a wonderful laundry woman and washed ironed and polished evening shirts and collars, worn in those days by the gentlemen for evening wear. She also goffered frilled caps and aprons worn by the maids for big houses.

I used to watch her heat the irons and polishing irons standing on bricks against the open fire. It was specialised work, goffering with tongs made hot in the red coals. My mother was a great wine maker so the larder with its stone floor was ideal for standing the crocks containing the fruit while it matured, feeding it from time to time with sugar candy. My mother bought spotted fruit from the greengrocer and put in a crock to soak to make wine. I used to go into the fields to pick dandelions, cowslips, winter pinks, parsnips, potatoes. The wines and ciders were made from all kinds of wild flowers, vegetables grown by my father.

My father worked in a small hoop yard, he was a hoop bender, these being used round barrels and casks. This was a small business at the end of Station Yard.

Making a bundle of hoops

Delivery of milk was by horse and trap, ladled from churns. Coal, bread, fish straight from the coast, all was delivered this way. We had steam trains. When I was about 9 a spark from a locomotive ignited a field of hay. Some livestock was lost with damage to sheds and some houses. People were evacuated from nearby cottages which I and my family were part. The fire brigade fought the fire with water from our garden wells and the brooks. Our well became permanently dry.

At the station was a taxi service run by horse and cab, some closed in carriages and landaus, used by ladies taking pleasure trips. The same family owned the station shop run by a small plump man [Mr. Voice] who always wore a bowler hat, selling everything from candles, sugar, tea, fruit and paraffin. No such thing as hygiene in those days.

I walked to school at the top of East Street. The Infant school had three classes and the big school was where we stayed until leaving at 14. I was taken to school by two older girls past the Vet's, where the Westminster Bank is now. It was a large house [Brick House] entered by a yard which housed an aviary and ravens. We walked up Rose Hill along a path on the top of a sloping bank where now stands the Rose Hill estate.

One big feature of the village was the Maltings Oast House. [It had, in its heyday, provided malt to the Swallow Brewery and run an in-house public house known as The Ship.] It was used as a 15th Century restaurant owned by a Scots family. All the waitresses wore long black flowing dresses, Dutch hats and aprons, 15th century style. I worked there, when aged 10, looking after a little boy of 2.

We used to walk across the Jengers meadow for picnics where now stand all the houses in Coombe Hill and Rowan Drive.

Opposite the current WI Hall there was an old corn merchant's, Blundells, sacks of corn and dog biscuits outside, and we kids used to help ourselves to the dog biscuits. Then there was the Unitarian Church and the butcher's where Cripps now is. Next was the King's Arms and Six Bells then the sweet shop owned by Lakers, World Stores, Post Office, Garage, International Stores, Drapers, Ironmongers, (Pilchers) Tribe the butcher, little cottages- old Mr. Jones had a clock business – a great character going round to all the big houses carrying his Gladstone bag and winding up the clocks once a week for the local gentry.

The only music we had at home was an HMV wind-up gramophone. We had a cabinet wireless powered by accumulators. Our lights were oil lamps and candles. Later we had a pump action Aladdin Lamp and then gas, a great step forward. The first street lighting was gas. A man used to cycle round the streets with a long-handled taper to light each lamp. [Mr. Rhodes].

I left school to start work after a disagreement with my father, who wanted to apprentice me in dressmaking with Hunt Brothers in Horsham. Being headstrong I wanted to serve in a shop but was not allowed, so I had to go into domestic service. There began a very hard but interesting 10 years, viewing and serving in many different households."

Farm work

"In the 1920s my father did contract to local farms at Parbrook. He would set off [from Hunston] at 6.30 am with his tools and hay knife strapped on his bicycle. According to the seasons he did hay cutting and tying, harvesting and threshing, thatching and land work, draining, ditching, ploughing with a horse, hedge-cutting and layering of hedges. He was also sometimes hired as a water diviner, using a hazel twig. Sometimes he would be away only returning home at weekends and at other times he was able to work locally. He also sharpened blades and shears using a home-made vice he erected in the garden".

Parish Yarns

Village Humour and other stories

In Sussex humour often involved jests at the expense of village rivals. This scrap of satirical verse is an example:

"*Rudgwick for riches, Green for poors,*
Billingshurst for pretty girls, Horsham for whores!"

Ridjik was the pronunciation for Rudgwick, (Wisborough) Green had the Union Workhouse, and Horsam was used for Horsham, hence the puns.

Bob Dames writes to the Billingshurst Society: We read last month that BILLA's people, having created BILLINGSHURST and moved up to BILLINGSGATE, finally settled in BILLINGHAM –what a long trek for a Saxon family all the way from London to near Middlesborough! Did they dilly-dally at BILLINGFORD in Norfolk, BILLINGBOROUGH near Grantham and BILLINGHAY towards Lincoln and later at BILLINGLEY near Doncaster? Who was it then, who settled in BILLINGTON near Bedford? Maybe they quarrelled with some of the family who traversed by BILLINGSLEY in Shropshire, thence to BILLINGE near St. Helens, Lancs. and finally to BILLINGTON north of Blackburn. Or, was the name BILLA a bit frequent like SMITH nowadays – and were they all different families? Think about it!

Billy Hoad goes courting in the rain at Billingshurst 1894

Billy Hoad grew up as a Horsham schoolboy. His fascinating 'Diaries and Reflections' are available online.

'Caught the 10.00 train to Billingshurst to pay first visit to Rose [who lived at Kirdford]. On arriving there found out the G. Baptist Chapel and went to service. While there the rain came on very hard so after chapel stayed in the schoolroom and had a snack I had brought with me with (the) Minister who seemed a very nice 'old Johnnie'. Stayed there till 3 then went to meet Rose. Found her then spent the afternoon under the railway bridge raining all the time. Went to chapel again in the evening. Only nine present including parson, choir, organist and ourselves but they still managed an anthem somehow. After service made for the station, caught the 7.37 train and got home soaking wet. Not a very good day for the first time!

The Railway Bridge, Natt's Lane

Scandalous behaviour and a lesson in tolerance

Reminiscent of Thomas Hardy's novel '*The Mayor of Casterbridge*' is the case mentioned by Harry Burstow in his book '*Reminiscences of Horsham*'.

"I have been told of a woman named Smart who, about 1820 was sold at Horsham for 3 shillings and sixpence. She was bought by a man named Steere, and lived with him at Billingshurst. She had two children by each of these husbands. Steere afterwards discovered that Smart had parted with her because she had qualities which he could endure no longer, and Steere, discovering the same qualities himself, sold her to a man named Greenfield, who endured, or never discovered, or differently valued the said qualities till he died."

The Haunting of the Kings Arms

Judy Middleton in 'The Haunted Places of Sussex' writes:

'As a coaching inn it is only fitting that a coachman should haunt it. On a cold February night, circa 1800, the coachman had imbibed rather too much beer and was unsteady on his feet. As he went to make his final check on the horses before turning in, he stumbled across the yard, missed his footing and fell down the well. It is said that it is exceptionally deep and his body was never recovered.'

Empire Day

"This was a special event, celebrated each year on 24th May. Parents attended our school at Billingshurst and Britannia and her attendants were always represented on stage whilst the rest of the schoolchildren represented the countries of the British Empire. All children wore white marguerites to school on this day. It was always celebrated in the morning and then we had half a day off."

Guy Fawkes Night

"The fancy dress competition was judged in the old village hall in the late afternoon. In the early evening everyone assembled outside the King's Arms to start a torchlight procession led by Billingshurst Band and bands from other villages.

The guy was carried on a cart of torches. Fireworks were let off – squibs, bangers and jumpers – as the procession wound its way around the village calling at one or two big houses and the Station Hotel and returning to the field at Alick's Hill which is now Hillview Garage and a housing estate. Here there was a very large bonfire. Someone would climb to the top of the bonfire to recite the bonfire prayer and position the guy, after which the fire was lit by torches. This was a major village occasion between the wars".

"One particular custom was for a man dressed as a devil to run to the top of the bonfire as the villagers recited their Bonfire Hymn – and then run down again as fast as possible before he got caught in the flames. The tradition came to an end one year when the 'devil' got badly burnt.

At Mr. Wadey's field beyond the Manor House there was the bonfire… Here poor 'Guy' was taken from the tumbrel and hoisted to the top of the bonfire. He must have made up his mind to make a quick job of it for he fell off the stake as soon as the bonfire was well alight and disappeared amidst the flames and the smoke. Mr. Radbourne read the 'prayer' from the top of the pile, and he too made a lightning disappearance as the flying torches went whirling through the air."

Bonfire Night
Remember, remember the fifth of November,
The Gunpowder, treason and plot.
I know no reason why gunpowder treason,
 Should ever be forgot.

Guy Fawkes, Guy Fawkes, 'twas his intent
To blow up King and Parliament.
Three score barrels of powder below,
Poor old England to overthrow

By God's providence he was catched,
With a dark lantern and a burning match.
Holler boys, holler boys, ring boys, ring.
Holler boys, holler boys, God save the King.

Additional lines were available for those of a particularly anti-papist disposition who recalled the burning of seventeen Protestant martyrs at Lewes in Mary Tudor's time:

A farthing loaf to feed old Pope,
A pennorth o' cheese to choke him,
A pint of beer to wash it down,
And a faggot o' wood to burn him!
Burn him in a tub o' tar,
Burn him like a blazing star,
Burn his body from his head,
And then we'll say old Pope is dead!
Hip, hip, hooray!

The bonfire was built on several different sites; one of the earliest was Price's Meadow where the Women's Hall now stands.

The Weald School, a history

In the Beginning

Weald School, Station Road entrance

The Butler Education Act of 1944 had decreed the creation of three sorts of Secondary School to be built to cope with the expected 'bulge' of babies to be born shortly after the armed forces had returned home from WW II.

The former 'all age' schools, such as Billingshurst School off East Street, Pulborough and Wisborough Green School, would be able to cope with children aged from 5 to 11 when the older pupils (12-15) were moved elsewhere. It was envisaged that the old dream of 'Secondary Education for All', previously enjoyed by only a small minority of children, might be realised. A Secondary School at that time was, normally, a selective Grammar School. All youngsters were now to be educated to the age of 15 in new premises designed to match the abilities and aptitudes of their pupils. The Grammar Schools, locally Collyers for boys and Horsham High School for girls, would continue to recruit the cleverest children from Billingshurst and district, selected by the '11 plus' or scholarship examination. They would be taught foreign languages, the classics and three sciences as well as the basic subjects. All the other children would attend new 'Secondary Modern schools' equipped and staffed to meet their assumed needs. These were broadly and mistakenly estimated to be largely non-academic and practical in nature, the 3 Rs, religious knowledge, woodwork, metalwork, technical drawing, domestic science, needlework, shorthand and typing, history, geography, physical education and in Billingshurst, rural studies. A third cohort was also envisaged comprising competent youngsters with a technical or commercial bent, who would be educated in Technical Schools. These latter were never actually built though one such existed for a while in Horsham.

So it transpired that on 12th September 1956, 80 pupils started secondary school off Station Road in the partially built Weald Secondary Modern School picking their way over planks laid in the mud. These children came by six coaches from local villages, but not at first from Billingshurst or Pulborough but as far afield as Cowfold and Petworth. 'First Year' boys wore short flannel trousers and school caps. In summer girls wore uniform frocks. Mr. Victor Gee, a headmaster from Bromsgrove, had been appointed at Easter to order equipment, recruit staff and prepare for the opening. Parents' Meetings were held at the Women's Hall. Only five classrooms were in use until after Christmas when 300 more children were enrolled. General Renton, horticulturist of Rowfold Grange, was made Chairman of Governors, and Mrs. Foster, nee Wilberforce, vice-chair. The children were tested on entry and allocated to 'streams', the cleverer A streamers having lessons broadly similar to grammar scholars, B streamers getting a good deal of practical tuition and those in the C stream offered simpler work and remedial lessons.

Early ideals of the Secondary Modern School

The parents of the children attending the school had high hopes for their youngsters but were understandably disappointed that their offspring had been 'overlooked' by the 11+ examination. A 'Sec. Mod. School' was deemed 'second best' and an unproven asset. Adverse criticism of the green copper roof as being too costly for the education of people who were not high achievers did little to boost the morale of those who were enthusiastic for the new school system. An ideal education was envisaged as a ticket of entry to the 'officer class' as promulgated by the public schools and the Grammar Schools which were modelled on a similar ethos, curriculum and teaching practice. Most of the teachers there were graduates who wore academic gowns. The pupils of these exclusive schools would be inculcated with a desirable body of knowledge and given the self-assurance and confidence that would authorise them to issue orders and expect to be obeyed; a ladder of success for those, with the high intelligence, tenacity, perseverance, and the necessary parental income, who wished to climb it.

Since 1951 Grammar Schools had prepared their more able 16 year olds for an Exam called Ordinary Level of the General Certificate of Education, which unlike its predecessor, the School Certificate, could be taken in just a single subject. [The older exam had to be passed in at least five approved subjects.] At the Weald the Governors supported the Staff in a determined effort to secure success in a public examination that would serve their aspirational pupils well and prove that all was not lost if a child failed at 11+ which, of course 9 out of 10 of them had . An early start was made using the UEI exam [Union of Educational Institutions] so that pupils who volunteered to stay on at school till 16 could achieve a valuable certificate to improve their career chances. This policy was highly successful. In 1960 the school had two girls who achieved Advanced level at GCE and in 1968 two boys gained places at University. By 1972 three-quarters of the students were taking extended courses taking a new exam, the CSE (1964) or the much desired O levels in a variety of subjects. Success in this demonstrable way brought enormous prestige to the Weald, soon recognised as one of the more desirable Secondary Modern Schools. Parental support was generous. By 1961 they had raised enough money to build a swimming pool. Anxiety about youthful rebelliousness as exemplified by the fashionable 'Mods and Rockers' led the County Council to provide the school with a Youth Tutor, and in due course, a purpose-built on-site Youth Wing for day and evening use.

Up until 1989 Heads, Staff and Governors of schools were responsible for both what was taught in the curriculum and how lessons were conducted. They were unconstrained by a National Curriculum, but strongly conditioned by their training and accepted good educational practice as recommended by the advisory service of the County Council. The Secondary Modern ethos of the time expected schools to broaden children's horizons by hosting visiting speakers, promoting sports, music, drama and the arts and by opening the pupils' eyes to the world of work and life in Britain and abroad. The Weald management responded well and it is fair to say that the initiatives of those years by the Secondary Modern Schools have left our present schools a legacy of breadth in education which we would be ill-advised to overlook in pursuit of narrow academic examination scores.

Mr. Gee was especially concerned to promote foreign travel. Under his influence many hundreds of Weald students visited Copenhagen, Amersfort in Holland, Germany and St. Augulin in France. He was a long-term trustee of the Central Bureau of Educational Visits. In 1968 he led 60 British Children to Lucerne where a plaque commemorating the centenary of a visit by Queen Victoria was unveiled by the Mayor. More local destinations were also exploited regularly like Cobnor for sailing, London for the National Association of Youth Clubs, Lodge Hill, the Lake District and local shows and theatres.

Mr. V.V. Gee. Headmaster, 1956 to 1974

Going Comprehensive

In 1965 Anthony Crosland, Wilson's Education Minister, issued Circular 10/65, a document which was to change the face of secondary education for the next half century. Local Authorities were asked to reorganise their schools 'along comprehensive lines'. The Conservative members of WSCC were against making changes, but the Independents, who normally backed the Conservatives, took a different view and supported the various proposed schemes. These involved creating three Sixth Form Colleges in West Sussex, served by 11 to 16 schools, several Middle Schools and, as in the case of The Weald, some few 11 to 18 all-through Comprehensives with their own Sixth Form. When 300 Weald parents attended a meeting to hear about the proposals for going comprehensive by 1969, all but one voted in favour. Billingshurst district parents were well aware that the 11+ exam was a game of snakes and ladders, played at too early an age, and there were 9 snakes sending you back towards 'go' for every single ladder leading to the glittering prizes. The new system would bring with it up-to-date buildings and equipment and a better-qualified staff.

From 1968 children of all abilities and aptitudes living in the catchment area and not in private schooling would come to The Weald, the 11+ exam having been abolished. The school would be fully comprehensive by 1973. By that date also the raising of the school leaving age to 16, called 'ROSLA', obliged all children to be prepared for a public examination, either the Certificate of Secondary Education or O Level. Some 25% of each school year group would have to stay on rather than leave to find jobs. Pessimists predicted disciplinary disaster but in practice the staff and students coped well. Though behaviour did deteriorate somewhat during the 80s 'punk' years, nevertheless good order prevailed and the dreaded 'ROSLA', was soon forgotten. The young are now expected to be in either training or education until they are 18!

A Change of Headteacher

This was Mr. Gee's chosen moment to retire to finish his days in 1992 in Norfolk.

Mr. Geoffrey Lawes, a Headteacher in Brockley, South London, was appointed in his place to begin in the summer term of 1974, bringing his experience of by now well established London Comprehensive schooling. Among early appointments was that of Miss Angie Clark, confirmed as Senior Mistress, a position she had held in the last year of Mr. Gee. She had come to the Weald as Head of Girls' physical education. No-one made a longer or more conscientious career at the school than Mrs. Burroughs, as she later became. She retired only in 2013.

Subsequently numerous changes of policy ensued. For example corporal punishment was discontinued. Mr. Lawes championed abolition in two national TV debates. The House System and division into Upper and Lower Schools disappeared. Forms were no longer streamed for registration and 'setting' was introduced for teaching purposes, so that children were taught in groups according to their ability in particular subjects rather than by a general assessment. At that time it was a fashionable judgment that good 'pastoral care' of pupils was just as important as any other aim in education and that large schools needed sub-division so that no child became an overlooked anonymous unit. Consequently each year group was allotted its own permanent staff under the management of 'Heads of Year' acting, for welfare and disciplinary purposes, like schools within a school. The excellent tradition continued of extra-curricular activities, music, drama, sport, visits and foreign exchanges. Association football gave place to rugby union. The familiar uniform school blazer and badge and logo gave way to a V-necked jersey, and the Sixth Form were allowed smart casual dress. The influence of ever-increasing numbers and the admixture of higher ability pupils together with a major building programme of laboratories, a new Sixth Form Centre, opened by Rev. David Shepherd, Bishop of Liverpool, and a teaching block boosted morale. By 1979 some 22 students were beginning degree courses, two of them at Oxbridge. A successful Modern school had morphed into an equally successful comprehensive. The teaching staff of 1981 had had at some time 40 of their own children on the school registers, a silent testimonial of their confidence.

Progress has continued unabated so that today over 90% of Weald pupils achieve 5 or more passes at the current equivalent of the old O level, the GCSE, grades A to C. [The CSE and O Level were merged in 1988.]

Community Schooling

A popular concept from 1976 onwards was that of the 'Community School' successfully pioneered by Cambridgeshire Village colleges. In a nutshell it envisaged the use, by the whole community, of expensive school halls, classrooms, gyms, swimming pools, libraries, playing fields, educational equipment and teaching expertise. They ought not, it was argued, to be used exclusively by secondary aged children. Anybody in the neighbourhood should be enabled to use or hire the facilities from the cradle to the grave. By uniting adult education, youth provision, and providing crèches and hosting clubs, societies, public meetings and celebrations, a Community School could make available both continuing education and public amenities and leisure facilities, comparable to a small local university. Older 'late developers' could enjoy refresher courses and learn new skills. The premises would be particularly welcoming in school holidays and at weekends. The beauty of it was that the taxpayer had already paid for it. Mature adult students could study for A level with the Sixth Form on payment of a small fee. Evening classes were arranged to meet in local primary schools. A crèche was opened in a school hut, the origin of the present Wakoos.

The concept was enthusiastically adopted at the Weald in 1978. A Community Tutor was appointed in liaison with Horsham District Council to run the thriving Evening Institute and Youth Wing and to organise lettings of the premises. The Parish Council held its meetings in the Library, there were regular discussion group and Society Meetings, the Annual Flower Show used the Hall, Sports Clubs hired the pitches, dances, music concerts, keep-fit rallies and carnivals were held. Together with a handful of other West Sussex Schools the Weald was officially designated a Community School by a supportive County Council. During 1988 25,000 customers paid to use the Weald Recreation Centre. The previous year 80 Adult Education Courses were run with 2,386 enrolments, plus 246 for children of junior school age. Where did it all go wrong? The answer was, of course, 'Events, dear boy, events'.

Economic strictures and troubled times

Progress was made during the late 70s and 80s in the face of difficult political and economic circumstances. Financial constraints meant that the maintenance of buildings was most often left to working parties of staff and parents, and fund-raising was a necessary means of securing minor building developments. Numbers on roll continued to swell resulting in dangerous overcrowding in narrow corridors. Temporary buildings proliferated. 1536 pupils were on roll in 1982, a figure similar to today. In 1983 some temporary relief was obtained as a result of a complex fund-raising collaboration of the County and District Councils, the Sports Council and the local parishes to build the Sports Hall and changing rooms and a new library, so designed as to create a quadrangle west of the old Assembly Hall. The designation as a Community School helped to secure these funds.

Then in the mid-80s there came industrial turmoil. Chancellor Lawson announced £500 M of public spending cuts. The teachers' unions were seeking a pay award to remedy ten years of steady deterioration of their salary. At the Weald between 1984 and 1987 a fairly normal service was maintained through a difficult period of 'work to contract' by staff. [withdrawal of goodwill to do anything other than teach their classes]. Only by dint of introducing a 'concentrated school day' was it possible to deal with supervision of pupils at break and lunchtime. When, after months of national discord peace was restored to the teaching profession, a short interlude of peaceful reconstruction followed.

The so-called 'Continental Day' was continued, the afternoon sessions becoming periods for voluntary clubs and extra-curricular activities, with two separate home runs on the buses. This lasted until the next set of major political interventions in the life of the school.

In 1988 all schools had to adopt the American style grade numbers for school Years, so that what had been the 'First Year' of secondary school became the 'Seventh Year' and the Upper Sixth was 'Year 13'. Curiously the 'fossil' term Sixth Form has persisted.

This was the first of a flood of more profound changes. Teachers were now subject to a tighter contract. More importantly, the school curriculum, hitherto determined by Staff and Governors, was to be prescribed in some detail by the Government. The National directives would shortly swamp the school with paper in pursuit of 'one size fits all' reforms which were over-ambitious, over-prescriptive and, after much wasted effort, proved unworkable. The documents required a so-called 'entitlement' range of subjects which it was felt necessary for every child to follow, regardless of its age, ability or aptitude. Silk purses could be created from sows' ears. Every student could learn a foreign language, for example.

The political consensus was that English education was in a parlous state, desperately in need of drastic 'reform' from the wisdom of governmental 'experts', and it was reckoned no longer wise to leave the curriculum, and to a great extent how it was taught, to teachers and governors. Not surprisingly the Weald management which had conscientiously tailored its own curriculum to the needs of local pupils resented this imposition of a national orthodoxy but were obliged to comply. Teachers began to make some limited use of Information Technology. From 1985 another sea-change in practice swept away the traditional crafts of woodwork, metalwork and technical drawing, needlework and domestic science, together with the lathes, forges, benches and circular saws in dedicated rooms. They, and their teachers, gave place to computer science, design and technology, correctly assessed as the working media of the future. In retrospect we may have washed away the baby with the bathwater. Traditional craft skills still remain in constant demand.

In 1989 Mrs. Burroughs returned to the Weald after a ten year break to raise a family in the role of Head of Special Needs. By this time children who found school a challenge, abused as 'Dunces' in Victorian times and offered poorly resourced 'Remedial' treatment more recently, now attracted extra funding and individual support. Wherever possible they were taught in 'mainstream' rather than 'special schools'. It was to Mrs. Burroughs credit that with the Weald quickly established such a service to successive groups of disadvantaged pupils.

A new Head, new initiatives

In 1991 Mr. Lawes retired after 17 years as pilot of the Weald and Mrs. Virginia Holly, a Deputy Head from a school in Greenwich was appointed.

Efficiency and progress needed, in the Thatcher government's view, to be brought about by vigorous competition between schools, so that parents could select the good schools and failing schools would either wither away or could be disciplined and reorganised. The key instrument would be the exercise of parental choice of secondary school at 11+. To further that choice, annual league tables of measurable achievement such as examination successes and attendance would be published. The accompanying tool was a new machinery of 'accountability'. Governors were required to publish written policies on all aspects of school life such as bullying, health and safety, illegal substances and sex education. Regular assessments would be carried out on all schools by an inspection regime called Ofsted. Its judgments would be published for the benefit of parents and for remedial action by local authorities when deemed necessary.

The effects of this were mixed. Sharper competition did develop between local schools in pursuit of 'top billing' and energy was invested in advertising and public relations. School uniform was elaborated. However enhanced parental choice for Billingshurst catchment parents had little effect. They had always been free to select other schools providing they could afford their own transport. Parental choice is an urban concept where there is practicable access to alternative schools. In practice Weald annual enrolment stayed steady and of recent years the school has been fully subscribed by satisfied parents of the neighbourhood. A series of excellent Ofsted reports from their first introduction has endorsed their encouraging judgment.

Mrs. Holly soon made some changes. The Continental Day was discontinued as it breached certain new legal requirements for hours of tuition and the focus of practice was, of necessity, subtly shifting to improving pass-rates in examinations. Standard Achievement Tests at 14 were introduced to support the regime. A substantial budget surplus was invested in a more attractive redesigned entrance to the school. A public Gold Awards Annual Prizegiving Ceremony in the Sports Hall was instituted to promote the growing prestige of the school and the successes of the pupils. Mrs. Paton resigned as Chairman of Governors and was succeeded first by Mr. Tony Bolden who declared that the Governors should 'market the school'. When, in 1993, four pupils won Oxbridge places public esteem indeed stood high.

Mr. Bolden was shortly succeeded by Mr. G. Puttock. For a short time there was some anxiety lest falling rolls would cut back available school resources. Since 1990 schools had been obliged to manage their own finances, being granted an annual budget according to the number and age of pupils on roll. The management was then free to spend this on teachers' salaries, ancillary staff and equipment as they thought fit. This was just one example of how power over policy and practice was shifting away from the County Council both to the Head and Governors locally and also to central government in respect of the curriculum, inspection, institutional discipline and financial provision. Responsibility for funding the Sixth Form was removed from the LEA and entrusted to a new agency called the Further Education Council. Special subsidies were then offered to schools which could earn themselves special status for particular excellencies. The Weald explored 'Technology Status' and was eventually duly rewarded, though it underwent some turmoil in the process.

The national purse-strings were now loosening. The 1996 school budget was for £3.25 million. A splendid new library, the school's fourth siting, was opened in March by the Duke of Kent and permission given for a new music block. There would soon be an all-weather pitch and 'Solutions', a fitness suite, as an enhancement of the Community School. Some playing fields had been lost to the major development of 550 houses and the building of the western by-pass, and £1M was promised for a new swimming pool. The reduction of traffic on the A29 at last allowed the possibility of a major lay-by and coach park. From the school's inception in 1956 the need to use Station Road as a bus park for 17 coaches twice a day had proved a daily hazardous headache for the staff and local residents.

Sadly in 1997 the pioneer Governor, Mrs. Pamela Foster died, a lady whose counsel and wise judgment had contributed to the growth and achievements of the Weald.

A Hiccup in Progress

Enormous energy by two staff members was now dedicated to achieving 'Technology Status' which required sponsorship with local businesses and a commitment to develop and propagate good practice. British Aerospace was highly cooperative. However negotiations and details of the bid for government funding were limited to the Head and her small circle. £147,000 worth of support was promised from local businesses. The rest of the staff, hitherto always accustomed to consultation, began to take umbrage. The bid for recognition was successful, ready for a start in 1998, one of only 18 such approvals nationwide. The Governors were delighted but many staff felt side-lined and unconsulted.

Meantime other negative issues emerged. Rolls had fallen and would not revive for two years until new pupils arrived from the new housing development. Resources would probably shrink and certain unwise expenditures and promotions were being called into question in the staffroom. There was disapproval of the Head's presidential style of management which frequently deliberately excluded the advice of the three popular Deputy Heads. Matters were exacerbated when she announced that one of them would be made redundant with other teachers to help meet the expected financial shortfall. The Governors backed the Head and Chairman, entrusting them with any necessary decisions. They also foolishly turned down the scheme for a bus park lay-by. The Senior Management Team in response devised a set of alternative proposals to balance the budget without recourse to any redundancies.

The staff rebelled. In February 103 of them signed a crucial document giving a vote of no confidence in the Head's ability to manage the school. The damage was done. The story spilled into the local newspaper. The Governors supported the Head, but the County Council sent in a team of officers for a week to explore the situation. No bulletin was issued but Mrs. Holly, who had been on sick leave, resigned to take up a temporary post with the Central Bureau of Educational Visits.

Adverse publicity was minimised by this resignation and the rapid restoration of good relationships by Mr. Bunker, the Director of Education, drafting in Mr. Ted Hickford from Midhurst Grammar to restore morale as temporary Head. In this Mr. Hickford was eminently well-qualified by experience and personality. He paved the way for the next Headteacher, Mr. Peter May, to put the school once more into the public good books. He joined in January 1999 from a headship in Witney, Oxfordshire. Mr. Puttock had resigned in exasperation as Chairman of

Governors, and Dr. Graham Parr took on the responsibility.

21st Century Schooling

After those few steps backwards the staff, pupils and parents and governors were enthusiastic for a new leap forward into the 21st century which with evident vigour of the new Head was keen to promote. Technology status led to a marked investment in Information and Communications Technology. The computer now began its significant invasion of the classroom as a standard medium of research and instruction. Within a year 230 stations on the internet network came into operation, all with e-mail and internet access. Through all the difficulties exam results remained excellent. A 66% pass rate at GCSE (A-C) was recorded. An 'exceptionally good' Ofsted report in 2000 boosted morale. By 2002 the Weald had won two Achievement Awards and the Head attended a celebratory reception at Highgrove hosted by Prince Charles. The school adopted a web-site and the new parking area off the A29 came into use. When the whole school visited the Millennium Dome they saw former student Matthew Clark in his role as the leading acrobat.

Mr. May then pressed for a necessary new capital building programme. New teaching methods and technology demanded more generous and more specialised classroom spaces than the traditional 'chalk and talk' way of working. Science, Information Technology and Business Studies were particularly short of proper facilities. The Sixth Form had far outgrown the facility of 1974. Financially prospects were more promising. The school annual budget was just short of £4 M. Teachers salaries and conditions of service had improved. By 2002 two thirds of the Year 11 pupils entered the Sixth Form and many of those who left went into further education or training. Education had moved a long way from the anxieties about 'ROSLA to 16' back in 1972. Over 100 students each year were by now leaving the Sixth Form for university. The 'Trug', a battery-powered car built by Weald enthusiasts, was featuring in national newspapers for its success on the Goodwood circuit. These were winning days.

In 2003 a new burgundy school uniform was adopted and a fresh logo, the fourth symbolic oak tree in the school's history. A year of construction work lay ahead, valued at £3 M. This produced 7 new science labs and 5 lab makeovers, 8 classrooms, 3 business studies areas and a modern Sixth Form Centre to replace the 1974 structure, now totally inadequate for its purpose. The Weald main entrance had always been hidden from the highway and presented an unattractive architectural spectacle. The bold new buildings offered a striking modern aspect for passers-by on the A29. Internally the rooms showed high quality workmanship and a welcome spaciousness in contrast with the older school premises. Sixth

Burgundy uniforms

The Sixth Form Centre from Stane Street

Teachers were by this time relieved of much clerical and welfare work by a rapid expansion of non-teaching support staff. In 1956 they had been two in number. By 1990 they had risen to 32 and by 2007, including part-timers, the head count of ancillary staff had risen to 69. All classrooms were by now connected to the computer network and the Weald had become licensed to broadcast its own radio programme and showcased their work at two national conferences. A survey revealed that 94% of the pupils had access to a home computer! By 2005 400 computers were in use in the classrooms.

When in that year children invited their grandparents to a 'Generation Game' to show them how school work was being done it transpired that 50 of them had been pupils of the school themselves, underlining the fact that the school could no longer be regarded as a dubious experiment in social engineering but was a thoroughly respected local institution, widely admired for its excellent service to the community. It may not have produced as many cabinet ministers as Eton College, but for the vast majority of children, it had provided a sound liberal education and a springboard to fulfil their life chances. The ready sale of property in the neighbourhood and, regrettably, the enhanced price of it, bear eloquent witness to the satisfaction of incomers to the district.

The school continues to be thought of as a Community School but not with the same justifications that found favour in the late 20th century. The generous sporting provision of Jubilee Fields and the fine new Parish Hall, [lately designated The Community Centre], following major housing developments, removed the imperative need for the hiring of pitches, social gatherings, the Flower Show, conferences and civic meetings. Competition between schools discouraged the school management from offering generous access to Tom, Dick and Harry who might disturb the polish on the floors and interfere with the keeping up of appearances. National disquiet about deviants who might harm children led to anxiety about strangers and tight security measures to control access to the premises. Any dilution of resources on non-statutory causes was to be avoided in pursuit of more targeted objectives. The Youth Wing dwindled, its customers coming to regard a return to school in the evenings as unwelcome, a view which, strangely enough, had not troubled their older brothers and sisters. For a decade from 1978 the Governing body had entitled itself 'The Community Council' to reflect its wider responsibility, but the 1988 Education Act so prescribed the format of Governors' Meetings that it reverted to standard form. Finally responsibility for adult education was removed from the County Council and the funding for the Community Tutor discontinued. Adult education classes, once so valuable for socializing reasons and self-improvement, eventually disappeared altogether. Thankfully the Pool and Leisure Centre and the new Wakoos nursery have kept the Community School concept alive.

Wakoos – Billingshurst Family and Children's Centre

The school was now eligible to apply for another 'special status'. A bid was submitted to become a Sports College and this was awarded in 2006. The upshot was that the Weald became a district sports hub, the CSSSP [Central Sussex Schools Sports Partnership]. The catering work of the school was taken in-house rather than let to contractors, or as in the early days, run by the County Council. Planning was soon under way for the new 25 metre, 4 lane enclosed swimming pool and leisure centre at a cost of £5.7M to the County, District and Parish Councils. It was to be ready by 2008/9. Meantime Midhurst Grammar School was in difficulties as a result of unsatisfactory Ofsted reports and Mr. May was seconded to take charge there, jointly with the Weald.

Aerial view, 50th anniversary in 2006

There then began a remarkable new project. This was to build a school of 25 classrooms with a working party of 23 staff and students at Katale, north of Nairobi in Kenya, at a cost of £50,000 to be raised by the Weald. The Lions club contributed £6,000, the funds were raised and the project was successfully completed.

In 2007 the school celebrated its half century, entertaining many hundreds of visitors, including a small distinguished group of the original staff at the opening in September, 1956.

In December 2008 Mr. Peter may retired and Mr. Peter Woodman joined as Headmaster from Avon Vale High School. There were developments. The school is now organised once again on a House system, but with the difference that tutor groups are arranged so that each unit, with its permanent teacher-tutor, consists of pupils of all five ages from 11 to 16. The Tutor Group will belong to one of five Houses – Wilberforce, Elgar, Austen, Livingstone and Darwin, symbolising five branches of study. Tutors and House Heads care for the children's welfare and discipline and monitor their progress in studies. They are assisted by two Directors of Learning who monitor development through Key Stages 3 and 4. House competition for the House Cup is exercised in all aspects of school life, for example attendance, library use, sports achievements, and house points for good work and behaviour, calculated by computer.

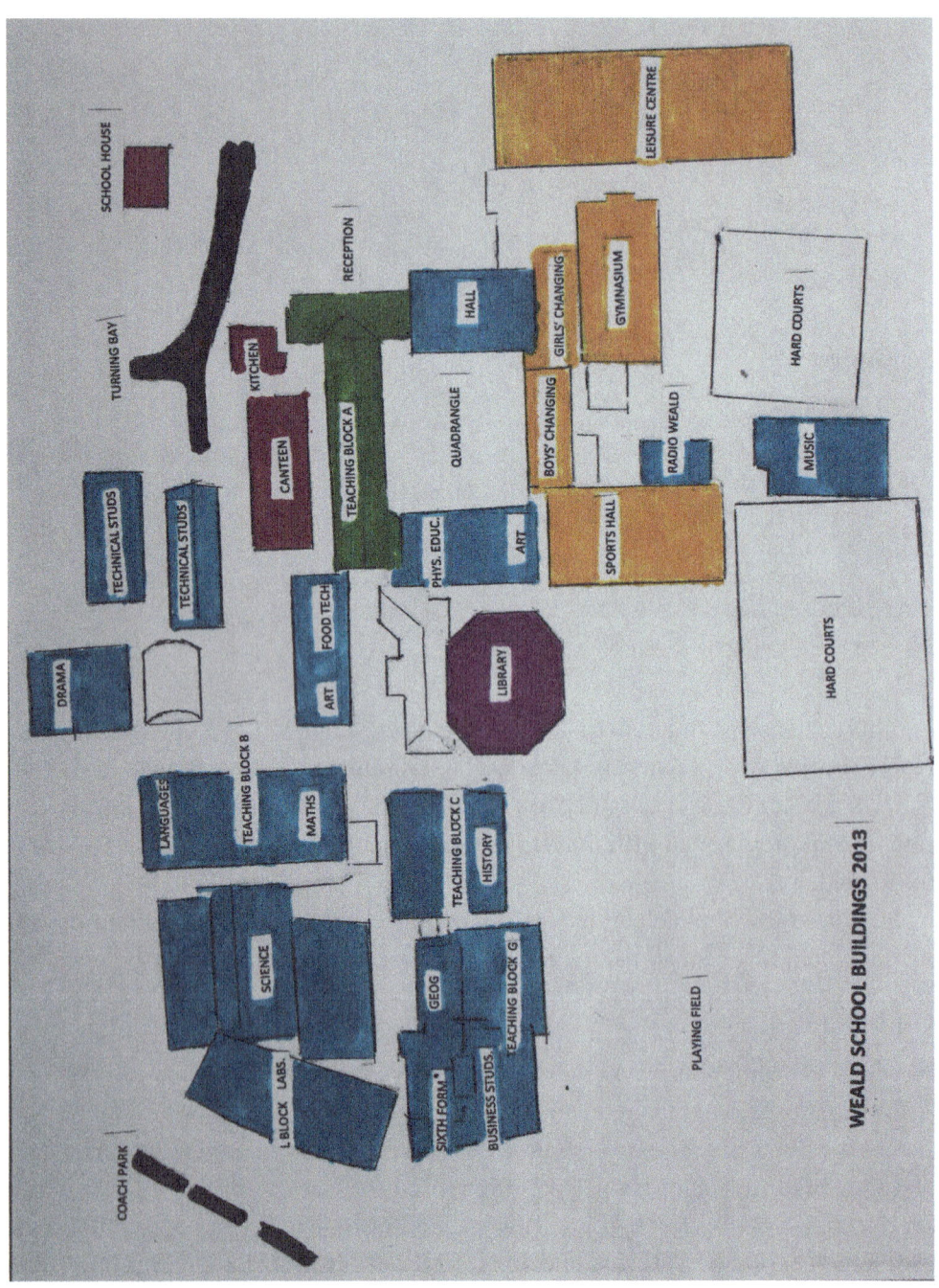

Weald School buildings

In 2011 and 12 the school had a £2M refurbishment and building programme. The former Youth Wing was reborn as a Drama Studio.

Since 2006 the school has raised £200,000 for Kenya schools enabling 50 classrooms to be built. Radio Weald broadcasts on 87.7 FM for a week in July and regularly in school. Since 2008 it has broadcast on the internet. In 2006 the 'Slippery Trug' battery-powered car was UK Champion in the National Greenpower Car Competition. Its successor, the 'Black Bullet' came second in 2010 and 11.

Communication with parents is enhanced by an excellent fortnightly Newsletter, e-mailed to them and available on the school website. In the past 12 years over 40 members of staff have sent their own children to the school. Examination results are highly commendable. In 2013 91% of the students gained A* to C passes at GCSE. 70% of them had both English and Maths passes. 99% of A level entries were successful, 7% with A* grading and 60% at A* to B. In November 2013 Ofsted, the National Office for Standards in Education, having recently inspected the school, graded the Weald as 'Outstanding in all areas and outstanding overall'.

Weald School Alumni include:

Billy Twelvetrees - England international rugby union footballer.
Hinda Hicks – popular singer
Tim Hincks - President of Endemol, TV company
Matthew Morrison – barrister
Lynsey nee Miller – JP
Mandy nee Miller – Hd of Dept. Universite de Meaux
Killa Kela - (Lee Potter) – beatbox musician
Michael Coupe – trading director for Messrs. J. Sainsbury
Piers Hernu – writer and editor of men's lifestyle magazines
Bryce Wolfe – Australian financier
Mark Hubbard – YMCA sports director, basketball USA
Dr. Paula Richards, Fellow of Royal College of Radiologists
Alison Garland – actress
Katie Blake (Beale) – actress
Laura Poot – President Oxford Union
Messrs. Crabbe, Hogan, Jones and Verheul all Doctors of Medicine
Roger Patterson – National authority on beecraft.

Billingshurst's Heritage No. 2

Oliver Reed and Josephine Burge

Just after Christmas, 1980 the Weald School was the unwelcome focus of a storm of tabloid journalism. Oliver Reed, a popular film actor of tough-guy characters, with a well-cultivated reputation for roistering pranks, arm wrestling and drunken exuberance, lived in Ellens Green with a pink rhinoceros at his gate. He is well-remembered for a male nude-wrestling scene with Alan Bates in 'Women in Love'. Jo Burge, a keen young horsewoman, was in the Lower Sixth Form. The press got hold of the story that she was absent with flu, but had been recovering in Barbados in company with Oliver Reed, a man 27 years her senior.

The paparazzi took up positions at the front gate of the school, where police Sergeant Dick Parrott and a colleague also took up camp. David Elling, Head of Sixth Form and Pat Bush, Deputy Head, smuggled Jo in and out of school under a blanket in the boot of a car, until Jo's mother wisely decided that Jo should leave school, in view of her social commitments. These resulted in marriage in 1985 and a partnership which endured until Oliver died in 1999 in Malta. He is buried at Churchtown, County Cork. Oliver claimed to have drunk 106 pints of beer on a two-day stag party binge. Mr. Elling described Jo as 'a smashing young girl, an elfin type, never a raving beauty, but a quiet sweet person'.

Billingshurst Primary School

The Station Road Primary School, under the Headship of Helen Williamson, MA caters for 500 pupils from the age of 4 until they leave for their Secondary education at 11 normally at the Weald School but elsewhere if parents so choose. She is supported by a staff of some 34 teachers and a large team of Teaching Assistants, Ancillary Staff, Lunchtime helpers and cleaners.

Volume 1 of *Billingshurst's Heritage* gave a general account of elementary schooling in Billingshurst and the history of the old schools in East Street which was the forerunner of the present modern and highly respected school for infants and juniors from reception classes to Year 6.

Billingshurst Primary School, Upper Station Road

Billingshurst's Heritage No. 2

The Hamlets – Five Oaks

The Norman Manors

The Normans from 1066 controlled law and order, collected rents and arranged for services and military forces by the feudal Manorial system. The King parcelled out his kingdom to his henchmen in return for Knight Service, in our case to Roger de Montgomery whose fiefdom was the Rape of Arundel. They in turn allocated 'Honours' to favoured parties, who were in charge of one or more Manors where rents were collected from tenants and courts of law held.

The most important Manor of the 20 or so with land in Billingshurst parish was Bassett's Fee, originally possessed by the Abbott of Fecamp, which also held lands in Rudgwick, Pulborough, West Chiltington, Slinfold and Kirdford. In Henry V's reign the ownership passed to the Abbess of Syon Nunnery in Middlesex. In the village centre it held property west of the High Street, Townland, Gingers and Taintland. Rosier and Okehurst were also part of the Manor but probably were acquired later. In the 15th century Manor House in the High Street was the residence of the Steward of Bassett's Fee. When Henry VIII dissolved the monasteries the Manor passed into lay hands and by the 19th century, a timber merchant, Mr. Clear was Lord of the Manor. He got into dispute with the Puttock's who lived where Austin's is now, over heriot, a sort of death duty. He sent two men to collect two animals but the mighty Billingshurst Puttocks rebuffed his demand.

At Five Oaks, lands east of Stane Street were in the Manor of Pinkhurst, with a Manor House at Slinfold, under Roger de Someri whose name is recalled at Summers Place. [In 1372 Richard Somer bought a house and garden in Billingshurst from William Newbrigge (Newbridge) paying 6s a year and one rose, to the Lord of the Manor.]

Lands west of the road were gifted to the Bishop of Fecamp in Normandy as part of the Manor of Wiggonholt. The Lords of the Manors' agents, the reeves and stewards, collected the Manorial dues. Billingshurst parish was parcelled out to a score of Manors since, in the earliest times, the woods were allocated for swine to forage in as outlying territories which belonged to the more southerly parent manorial headquarters. Other Billingshurst manorial lands included Pounds, Arundel, Ferring and Fure, W. Chiltington, Storrington, Marringdean and Guildenhurst and, of course, Bassett's Fee.

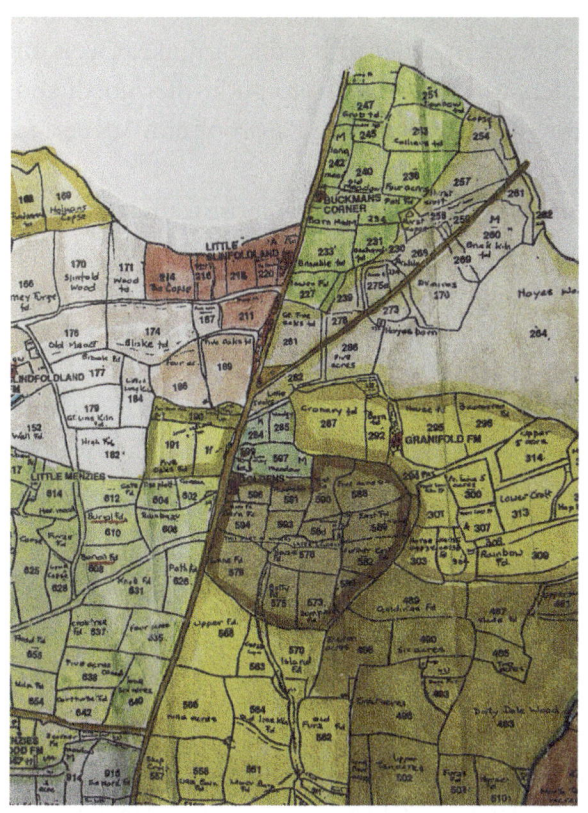

Tithe Map, 1841, of Five Oaks

Mediaeval Manors were grants of land to trusted Knights allocated in return for military service and rents to the feudal hierarchy, the Barons and Tenants-in-Chief, and ultimately the King. They had their own courts to control property rights and maintain law and order. Some lands were farmed 'in hand' but most were divided up among yeoman who paid rent, rendered labour services on demand and military service when called upon. They were effectively economic agricultural business units deliberately structured to entrench and defend the Norman body-politic. They were quite distinct from the ecclesiastical and civic institution which was the parish, expected to care for all the people, body and soul. This feudal format withered with time, particularly after the dissolution of the monasteries which had been major Lords of Manors, and when service and military obligations had been commuted to money payments.

Origins

The name of the cluster of houses and farmsteads where the A29 road to Guildford joins the road from Billingshurst to Horsham is first recorded on an estate plan in 1651 showing the whereabouts of trees. It is tempting to suppose that the road junction determined the growth of the settlement but as the Horsham road was not built until 1810, as a business venture in order to build a turnpike, this is an unlikely origin. Prior to that travellers to Horsham had to go further north and make their way via Hayes Lane through Slinfold. Unlike Parbrook and Adversane the area had no convenient streams either.

More probably the close conjunction of several thriving farmsteads straddling Stane Street led to an accumulation of dwellings which comprised the hamlet north of Billingshurst. The map of the Rape of Arundel (1819) names it Five Oaks Green. It also identifies 'E. Griningfold' on the way to Horsham and Buckman's Corner en route to Slinfold or Bucks Green and Rudgwick.

The name Buckman, incidentally, was substituted for the old name Buckmott in deference to a family of that name living nearby. Rev. Henry Beath, Vicar of Billingshurst lived at Buckmans Corner.

Grainingfold House was farmed by Joseph Dale in 1855 and ten years later by Thomas Chesman, followed by William Belcher and Haramand Scott by 1878. Later occupants were the Cullens who had aircraft landing there.

17th Century Five Oaks

In 1609 100 acres of land identified as Slinfoldland in the Manor of Wiggonholt was leased from Sir Thomas Palmer, the Elder, to Thomas Haylor.

The name Five Oaks occurs on a deed of 1622 where Jonathan Hayler sold 11 acres beside Stane Street 'where there stand five oaks'. We can conclude that the oaks stood near Slinfoldland west of Stane Street in Wiggonholt Manor. (The Manorial documents of 1832 contain a bill from John Allman, nurseryman of Billingshurst, for replacing a 30 foot oak which presumably some errant citizen had cut down against the custom of the Manor.)

Slinfoldland is now known as Fold Farm.

The 1622 deed reveals that Jonathan Haler, yeoman, leased the 11 acres known as Toms Field to William Clayton, husbandman, of Rudgwick. This stood west of Stane Street between Buckmotts Corner and Billingshurst on the north of Minstrells Wood, also known as Winstrills Wood or Menzies. He made up and sold another 17 acre landholding called Little Slinfoldland, now called Five Oaks Farm. On these grounds early cottages were built originating the hamlet. Present day 1 and 2 Fieldings Cottages are most likely on the site of the house that Clayton had built in the 17th century.

James Cooper and Thomas Penfold were witnesses to the 1622 deed. Gentlemen with those surnames were known to have had property at Kingsfold at that time before the Civil War.

Eight years later John Nye of 'Five Oaks House' (built on 'Five Oaks Land') is known to have paid Church Tax for bread and wine and the wages of the Parish Clerk. Possibly this was the house now known as Chequers. A subsequent farmer, Cornelius Voice, tenant of people called Sharp, renamed his holding The Chequer House and Land. A Checker House was a beer house so it may have been the predecessor of the Five Oaks Inn.

Mr. Voice went off to Canada in 1834 under the emigration scheme sponsored by Earl Egremont. Luke Wadey and wife Sarah, a carpenter and wheelwright, followed Mr. Voice in 1839 as a tenant and by 1861 had become a farmer with 60 acres, some of which may have been won in a wager! He had a big family, remarried a widow Sarah Jupp and employed eight men. His firm did the restoration work on St. Mary's Church. By 1871 he had 180 acres, a groom and a servant. Three of his sons were carpenters, James married to Jane, David married to Harriett and Isaac who was a wheelwright. Another son, Frank, was the blacksmith. All had big families. By 1890 we know that James' widow was in charge of 'Mrs. Jane Wadey & Sons, builders and contractors, plumbers and house decorators'. The farm bothy beside Chequers was renovated in 1979, now renamed Shire Cottage.

Later Buildings

Near Chequers was another farmhouse called Goldings or Goldens Farm in Pinkhurst Manor. It is now Oak House. Richard Bettesworth Denyer inherited it from his mother, together with Summers Farm in 1810. His great uncle, Thomas Bettesworth, a London merchant, had been the tenant at Summers in the 17th century and, in 1729, had permission from the Manor of Bassetts Fee, to which it belonged, to knock down a 12 roomed house and erect a stone building with a polished marble porch. (The Lord of the Manor House of Bassetts Fee was Maurice Ireland living at Billingshurst. ['Fee' is a short form of 'fiefdom', meaning a feudal grant of land]). Robert Goff of Poole bought the freehold of Summers in 1880 and commissioned John Norton to design the present edifice. It became a convent school in 1945 and Sotheby's sale rooms in 1984. It is now elaborately redeveloped as the main feature of an upmarket housing estate. As for Goldings, it was owned by Mrs' Louisa Maas at the end of the century, the land being farmed first by John Thorne and then Mrs. Mercy Penfold and her family. They delivered milk in Billingshurst.

Billingshurst's Heritage No. 2

The old Five Oaks Inn

The Five Oaks Inn as rebuilt before demolition

The actual Five Oaks hostelry is first recorded as a public house in 1838 with Peter Towse as the landlord. Previously a widow lady, Mary Seamar paid Land Tax in 1780 on her house on Mr. John Croucher's land. She left it and a shop to her daughter Mary. That Mary married Richard Hoad who held it till 1808. Then James Holden took it on, only to sell it on to Maurice Ireland, then the leading shopkeeper in Billingshurst. Mr. Towse took the tenancy in 1831 and by 1851 was described as a grocer and innkeeper.

19th Century – the new Horsham Road

John Croucher was a substantial land owner of Hayes House in Slinfold parish at the turn of the 19th century. He was a Dissenter and founder of the Congregational Chapel at Billingshurst. He organised a company to promote a new turnpike road in 1810 from Five Oaks to Horsham and profit from the tolls. The road also provided a prestigious new access to Hayes House. Tollgates were set up at Hayes with William Wilson as the gatekeeper and another at Lyons corner. One of Croucher's supporters was Richard Bettesworth Denyer who lived at Goldings in 1841. That gentleman's ancestor had had Summers Place built.

[The Bettesworths were linked by marriage to the Bartellots who had themselves gained possession of Okehurst by marriage. There is a memorial plate in Stopham Church commemorating 'Anne Bartellot, eldest daughter of Thomas Bettesworth, gentleman, cousin of Sir Peter Bettesworth, Knight, late the wife of Walter Bartellot, gentleman' (1690) Anne, nee Bettesworth, was herself descended from King Edward III.]

Well-to-do Incomers

In the late 19th century several rich men indulged themselves in country seats in and about Billingshurst. Land was relatively cheap from 1874 when the agricultural depression began, but several prosperous and nouveau-riche had enough money made in business elsewhere to set themselves up as country 'toffs' and enjoy the good life and sporting facilities available there. Improved rail and road access had made this practicable. The local farms were becoming unprofitable so the traditional farm owners were pleased to sell their lands at a mutually satisfactory price. Butlers, grooms and domestic help were readily available amongst the poorer villagers, eager for work. Perhaps the most egregious example nearby was the purchase, in 1908, of the enormous ancient Cowdray estate by Weetham Pearson, a Yorkshire-born Bradford contractor and Mexican oil tycoon. In Billingshurst Goff of Wooddale, Carnsew of Summers, Norris the brewer of Gratwicke and Hugh Fortescue Locke-King, doyen of Brooklands motor-racing circuit were just four of many such wealthy incomers. Their advent signalled the decline of the older yeoman social hierarchy of the district, the Greenfields, Streeters, Puttocks, Lakers, Irelands and Eversheds for example. The new circle of gentry enjoyed their mansions, their gardens, their servants, their country house weekend parties, their hunt meets, their pheasant rearing and shoots, all the pleasures of the fashionable glitterati who adorned the belle époque. Professor Asa Briggs describes it as 'the golden age of the country weekend...of the new business tycoon, of the Gaiety Girls, of the bustle and top hat, and above all of the golden sovereign'.

Their Legacy

The well-to-do brought in money for village improvements and stimulated the local economy through their building ventures and sophisticated needs for catering, transport and services. Eventually they were the later sponsors of local industry, as in the case of the American Ray Stiles and the Wyldes who ran the Thomas Keatings flea powder enterprise that came from London in 1927. The mode of living of the wealthy incomers made ordinary folk aware of the bountiful Victoriana newly available, the books, newspapers, magazines, the photographs, the finer clothing, the home furnishings, the exotic foods and drinks we read about in Mrs. Beeton, all the trappings of foreign trade and the industrial revolution that their parents and grandparents had known little of and had managed quite well without. The villagers now wanted bikes and bananas, greenhouses and a good time on holidays, pianos, photographs, china ornaments, proper football boots, fancy goods, table linen and finer foodstuffs. The 'toffs' introduced Cobbett's simple village folk to a new acquisitive society that placed value on the accumulation of 'things'. This material progress was to be brutally interrupted by the outbreak of the Great War in 1914.

Billingshurst's Heritage No. 2

Hugh Locke King c.1880s. Photograph taken in Vienna. (Brooklands

Hugh Locke-King inherited Slinfoldland and other major holdings which included Rowner, Okehurst and more land in Rudgwick. His Brooklands adventure, demanding bricks made from Okehurst clay and the employment of 2000 building workers, had depleted his fortune by the time the race track opened in 1907. Locke-King's father Peter, scion of many aristocratic families, by profession Barons, Bishops and Bankers, including the philosopher John Locke, and an MP for 26 years, was an astute land and property developer who amassed a fortune valued at well over £30M in today's money. The Five Oaks estate was a part of it. His son Hugh inherited most of Peter's fortune and by injudicious whims managed to spend most of it too.

He lost a small fortune on a food preservation scheme. He then bought and developed, in sumptuous style, like an oriental palace, an Egyptian hotel with 80 rooms in 1886 to ensure his own luxury accommodation. The great dining hall was an exact replica of a Cairo mosque but every effort was made to satisfy the English taste, with a golf course and a swimming pool, both the first in Egypt, tennis courts and magnificent riding stables. Mena House named after the earliest of the Egyptian Kings (4400 BC) stands still in the shadow of the Great Pyramid, early visitors including Sarah Bernhardt, Arthur Conan-Doyle and the Prince of Wales. The project cost him £35,000 equal to two and a half million pounds today and ran at a loss. It has enjoyed a remarkable subsequent history. Churchill,

Roosevelt and Chiang Kai Shek conferred there in 1943 to decide the future of war and peace in the Far-East. Today it has 500 rooms, 40 acres of gardens and has 850 employees for 1,050 guests.

Mrs. Locke-King at the Mena Hotel

Hugh and his rich wife Ethel were keen early motorists and, captivated by the early race track 'petrol-heads' with whom he mingled, rashly promised to finance the construction of the expensive Brooklands circuit at Weybridge on his late father's land. At the end of the construction period he was hard put to it, even with his wife and family's financial support, to pay off the contractors who threatened to foreclose on the Billingshurst property. He escaped ruin with help from his friends but sold the Five Oaks lands in Edwardian times to Robert Shepley-Shepley of New Gallowey, NB [Scotland] in 1908. Locke-King died still worth over a million pounds in today's money.

Shepley-Shepley, in turn, sold the estate to Sir Charles Fielding KBE in 1912. He was Chairman of Rio Tinto, a prosperous mining company originally founded in Spain in 1873. He designed and had built, Ingfield Manor as his home with a private road from the junction to serve it. It was first called Five Oaks Hall and was not properly named as a Manor. The eight roadside cottages of various ages and a new gatehouse provided tied dwellings for his staff. Descendants of the Fielding family still have Okehurst.

Other Properties

The 17 acres of Slinfoldland, which was separated off as Little Slinfoldland, has been farmed by the Morris family since 1825. They bought it from a Major St. John.

Another interesting property was built on the west side of Stane Street on waste land towards Billingshurst. About 1810, when the new road was opening, a Richard Voice who lived at Buckman's Corner successfully applied to the Steward of Wiggonholt Manor as follows:

'To Mr. Tyler, Petworth: Sir I have meashured the ground that I ask you for at 5 Oaks For to sett up a cottage for Euse of the Weeling business the lanth of the Ground is 7 rods wheath 1 1/2 Rod Witch makes 10 1/2 Rode of Ground that is as it Was stumpt out I should take it as a Favour if you will geat it For me please to Return a noat by post yours Resply Richd Voice Carpenter Buckmancorner. To pheasants withe the Baskeat if you please to Except of them'

The Billingshurst parish Officers bought the wheelwright's workshop in 1813 for £30, built a chimney and tiled the roof ready for use as two two-roomed tenements for poor relief. In 1840 these two cottages were the only buildings on the west of the street between the Inn and Okehurst Lane. [Fieldings Cottages 5, 6 and 6a now occupy the site.] One tenant, James Greenfield, a pin-cleaver, got behind with his shilling a week rent in 1844 and was ejected by law. Another tenant, Richard Allen, farm labourer, had five children but lost four of them at 15 weeks, 14 years, 7 and 9 respectively. Life was not easy for people 'on the parish' in Queen Victoria's time. By then the Petworth District Workhouse was functioning and the Parish Vestry deemed the cottages redundant and sold them off by auction. They were valued by Wiggonholt Manor in 1860, judged 'very old, low and damp', let for 1 shilling a week to Benjamin Knight by Peter Towse, who owned them, and deemed 'not fit for habitation'. The Towse family still owned them in 1887 when they housed Albert Knight and Sarah Pavey. Albert Towse the grocer eventually sold them to Locke-King as part of the estate bought by Sir Charles Fielding. They stood opposite Checkers and Pond Cottage.

Mr. Cliff Griffin renovated the Old Smithy. There were no openings in the south facing wall, probably in deference to the traditional belief that southerly winds brought the plague from the dreadful Continent of Europe.

20th Century developments

Numerous other changes have occurred in the 20th century. The little shop and Post Office, opened in 1926 by Mrs Scattergood and followed by Mesdames Conner, who had a private school, Williams and finally Henderson at 1 Elm Villas (now Willowbrook), has vanished. The Mission Hut, used for monthly communion services by the Vicar of St. Mary's and fortnightly whist drives and 'socials in the 30s, heated by an iron tortoise stove and lit by oil lamps, went in 1989. The old Five Oaks Inn was largely demolished and remodelled. Mr. Sam Van den Bergh ran it for many years but it was totally cleared away when Mr Harwood's new garage and salesroom needed a prominent forecourt. This business was an extension of the former Poplar Garage built up by the Griffin family on land north of the Inn. There was at first a shop, tea garden and garage alongside the Inn started by a Mr. Pole in 1926. Mr. Salt took it over. The garage caught fire in 1949. As the result of a fight he was sent to prison. His wife and family emigrated to Australia and Cliff Griffin started his enterprise in 1950. Cliff won third prize in the Bonfire Society juvenile section of the fancy dress competition in 1936 where the Skinner children also won a prize as 'The Bisto Kids'. Cliff has made his contribution to Billingshurst life ever since. During WW II he drove prisoners of war from Kingsfold to Cowdray Park golf course to pick up potatoes from the ploughed up fairways.

Ingfield Manor was sold to the Spastics Society in 1961 for residential conductive education for children with cerebral palsy, now renamed 'Scope' when the term 'spastic' was considered insensitive and hurtful. Dame Vera Lynn is the famous patron of the Charity which also has a School for Parents to help them care for their own children.

Along the road to Horsham is Furze View, an extraordinary ribbon development of houses built up over the years on a side lane in a fashion which runs counter to modern planning rules and would be deemed quite 'unsustainable' in current development lore. The residents of this little community would not agree!

Carnivals, Parades and Marches

In common with thousands of other English villages Billingshurst has long evinced an enthusiasm for taking to the streets in fancy dress and riding on bicycles, wagons and lorries to celebrate a wide variety of community activities. In this fashion the people loved to celebrate Royal Anniversaries or historical events, so demonstrating patriotism, loyalty and a warm sense of village neighbourliness and togetherness. Over the years this practice has taken various forms. The Bonfire Night torchlight procession was an annual festivity and the Jubilees and coronations of the monarchs often enough began with a parade and ended in a party such as that at Gratwicke House for George V in 1911. The Home Guard marched to celebrate the end of WW II and each year the High Street is closed for the Armistice Day memorial parade. In recent years the annual Billingshurst Show has begun with a themed parade processing from the new Village Hall to the Recreation Ground.

Bleriot flew the Channel in 1909 . George V's Coronation Parade

Before the coming of the National Health Service and other aspects of modern welfare village people relied for emergency help on their clubs and friendly societies which offered a form of community insurance for the common good. To further this cooperation there was an annual Hospital Parade and a Club Day Parade and in 1910 a morale boosting Floral Parade. After WW I the Billingshurst Band enlivened such civic occasions. Nowadays the tradition is maintained by an annual Carnival Parade as the opening feature of the Billingshurst Show, jointly organised by the Scouts and the Rotary Club. Bonfire Night is still celebrated on Jubilee Fields, but without the procession.

Mr. Joe Luxford lent the money to start the Billingshurst Band in 1919. George Skinner was the bass drummer for 60 years, George Messinger played the euphonium. Archie Stanton 'was a great bandmaster. He was the one who got us through so many competitions'. Fred, George, Ken and Wally Radbourne all played. When the band folded Mr. Wilding, Parish Clerk, stored the 17 instruments in his barn. They were handed over to Mr. Terry Wheeler, Head of Music at the Weald School. They were overhauled; the pitch lowered and formed the basis of the school wind concert band.

Clare Luckin wrote of the traditional celebrations, of how the children gathered on the cricket field at the Coronation of Queen Elizabeth II for games and competitions and a free tea, the field being decorated with red, white and blue bunting and Union Jacks. On Bonfire night the procession would visit the supposedly rich and elevated members of the village, the Manor House, and then Gratwicke. The last call was at Clevelands House, a Victorian house owned by Mrs. Puttock. She always had a Bonfire Night party at which the guests, fortified with mulled wine, waited on the terrace for the arrival of the procession. It was a scene reminiscent of the French Revolution when the huge procession armed with blazing torches swept across the lawn, rattling money boxes while the assembled guests fumbled for their money in the flickering light of the torches.

Another procession was on Rogation Day, albeit only concerning the church community. The Vicar, Choir and congregation would process from the Church, led by the Cross, to Cedars Farm, then a working farm. The farmer had been persuaded to collect as many animals as possible into the orchard. Rogation Day always coincided with apple blossom time and the orchard was a mass of pink and white, a perfect setting with the 16th century house in the background. At that time goats were part of the livestock, and they often caused consternation among the choir as they seemed specially keen to nibble the surplices, The geese pecked, the cockerels crowed, the horses kicked up their heels and galloped round the orchard while the cows continued their quiet ruminating, The Vicar then blessed the crops and livestock, exhorting them to increase and bring forth more. The Farmer's wife became pregnant with awesome regularity during the year following these services.

Billingshurst's Heritage No. 2

Clare 'The Reluctant Farmwife'

Clare Luckin was a notable feisty character with a liberal spirit. She wrote poems on natural themes. In her old age she joined a group of Billingshurst ladies in processing, via Piccadilly and ending at Hyde Park, to protest, unsuccessfully, about the war against Iraq. She wrote of the unsuccessful proposal to allow 'War Games', paintball etc in Rosier Wood. "There is no hope for civilization if people (presumably men) have the need to fantasize war in a way which must include pretending to kill each other". Clare was uncomfortable with what remained of Victorian class consciousness in the Billingshurst community. Some were evidently content with it. A friend of Mrs. Rogers of Parbrook wrote warmly of a holiday in Billingshurst in 1935:- "The people in Billingshurst are so very different from London people. Almost everyone you meet talks to you. They are very friendly and they all mix together, the workmen and their masters."

The account in Mr. Charles Tiler's newsletter in 1937 of the Coronation Games for George VI shows how the great and the good of Billingshurst, up to the Second World War, put themselves out to supervise community activities. Victorian class distinctions had become blurred by WWI but persisted in practice. People were well aware of their social position until the democratising effects of wartime comradeship after 1939 shattered the old class order. We can still witness its disintegration in the follies of *'Dads' Army'* and in the Labour landslide of the 1945 election. The pre-war well-to-do paid the serving working classes as little as the law of supply and demand allowed, but they felt an obligation to show some care for their welfare. It is doubtful if such a lengthy list of wealthy civic minded people could be made today in our more classless yet, curiously, less integrated village society.

Those who do still offer leadership in village affairs, the Parish Councillors, the Scout leaders, the Lions and Rotary members, the clergy, the Club and Society officers, the teachers and so forth, do so as private individuals rather than as 'toffs' or anyone's social superior. We no longer recognise the concept of 'workmen and their masters' even though there are still employers and employees. Before WWII no farm or middle class household could manage without a body of permanent and casual manual labour. This offered employment to 14 year old school leavers and to adults with limited educational qualifications but valuable hand skills. Nowadays farms and factories equipped with modern machinery such as combine harvesters, and homes with comparable labour-saving technology require little hand labour. Domestic servants, gardeners and farm labourers have given place to business contractors in those services, sophisticated machinery and domestic appliances. Maid-servants are now waitresses, nannies are au pairs or professionals with diplomas and butlers are as rare as 'top hats on Bradford Millionaires'. Consequently, for better or for worse, village society comprises people independent in character rather than necessarily interdependent. There are no longer employment opportunities for those with only their physical strength to offer as a source of income.

> **B**ILLINGSHURST was *en fête* last month. Coronation Festivities were celebrated on June 28th in grand style, and were well worthy of special and particular notice. My personal account will be given in narrative form, but in order to make it complete I have inserted in their proper places the *official* figures copied from "*Sussex Daily News.*" I will merely say a Committee was elected, and nearly £65 collected in the place by voluntary subscription. Now to proceed—
>
> *Chairman*, Mr. E. T. Norris; *Hon. Treasurer*, Mr. M. W. Ireland; *Hon. Secretary*, Mr. J. Luxford; *Collectors*, Messrs. W. Carter, Evans, Headland, J. Luxford, and W. Myram.
>
> FINANCE.—Rev. J. Stanley, Messrs. Cosway, Hubert, Holland, S. C. Halahan, Hardwick, Milward, Schwier, Wadey, and Webster.
>
> FLORAL PARADE.—Rev. J. Stanley, Messrs. Carter, Cosway, Milward, Shepherd, Ware, and C. Wadey.
>
> SPORTS.—Messrs. J. Argent, F. Black, R. Crisp, A. E. Clark, Craft, Frewen, Headland, Halahan, Hardwick, H. Hoadley, Isted, W. Joyes, C. Joyes, E. Lucas, H. Laker, R. Morris, W. H. Puttock, A. Sprinks, Schwier, W. Tribe, R. Voice, Wright, J. Wadey, and F. Woodcock.
>
> TEA.—Mrs. Alvis, Mrs. Brooks, Mrs. Blake, Miss Blake, Misses Beck, Misses Burtenshaw, Mrs. Carter, Mrs. Churchill, Mrs. Fielder, Mrs. Gosnall, Mrs. E. C. R. Goff, Misses Gosling, Mrs. Hubert, Mrs. A. Hubert, Mrs. Hardwick, Mrs. M. W. Ireland, Mrs. Morris, Miss Muskin, Mrs. W. H. Puttock, Mrs. A. Puttock, Mrs. Pearson, Mrs. Preston, Misses Puttock, Misses Schroeter, Miss Smyth, Miss Strong, Mrs. Thorburn, Misses Thorburn, Mrs. Wright, and Miss Woodhams.
>
> Kings' weather prevailed, and though fleecy clouds now and then veiled the blue sky—causing ... they finally passed away and left

Newsheet 1937 Coronation of George VI

The King comes to Five Oaks

Canadian troops were widely dispersed in camps in the whole district for training and to await embarkation to Normandy on D-day, 6th June 1944. They were at Wiggonholt, Ebernoe and Wisborough Green in great numbers, most often in tented camps in the woods. At Shillinglee they managed to set fire to the mansion of the Winterton family, and relics of their stay, ammunition, grenades and discarded equipment are still occasionally unearthed. At Wisborough Green they are proudly commemorated in St. Peter's Church.

Mrs. Dorothy Pullen, Granddaughter of James Wadey, writes:

"April, 1944 was an important month for the village. All round the district, at the time, were stationed the Canadian 2nd Division. Some of it was in a camp at Buckman's Corner [Five Oaks] and another big camp between Gleniffer House and Rookery Wood and down nearer Billingshurst, another big camp at Wooddale with the Headquarters at Rowfold Grange on the road from Billingshurst to Coolham.

Peter Newman remembers being told one day by the troops that the King [George VI] was coming to review them. There was great activity. The road was swept, grass cut and hedges trimmed all the way from Five Oaks to Billingshurst. The royal car was to park near the Old Forge, and though a red carpet was put down the King didn't walk on it. Now all the camps had their quota of stray dogs. On the day two of them decided to accompany the troops to be reviewed. The red carpet was just too much of an invitation. These two decided it provided a good playground. It took a lot of persuading by two very agitated officers to move them.

Much to the amusement of the local people the troops decided that the King might need to use the pub toilets which were outside on the end of what is now the Grill Room. Not only were they cleaned but repairs done and painted inside and out.

Peter remembers climbing a tree outside his home, No.1 Fieldings Cottages, to get a better view but the Military Police made him come down and so he had to watch from his bedroom window. I remember my father and uncle shutting the gates at the entrance to the yard and making a platform for the family and some friends to stand on. Again, like Peter, we were moved so we went inside one of the buildings that had a long window overlooking the road so we still had a good view.

All the children took the day off from school; after all the road was closed to traffic from 8 o'clock in the morning. When the King finally arrived he walked from Five Oaks to Hilland between Canadian troops 3 deep each side of the road. The royal car picked him up at Hilland to take him back to London. So ended Five Oaks Royal Review."

More Royal Celebrations

Billingshurst's Heritage No. 2

"One of my earliest memories was the celebrations of either King George V's Silver Jubilee or it could have been the Coronation of King George VI. We entered a float from Five Oaks to go in the parade at Billingshurst. The children of the village (there were about a dozen at the most) all wore red, white and blue caps and sat around the inside edge of a wagon-type trailer drawn by a tractor. Mr. Cullen, who lived where Mr. Stafford did [Grainingfold] lent the trailer and tractor and Mr. Overington drove it. He used to work for him at the time.

The Five Oaks Coronation Carnival Wagon, 1911

Mr. Bowring, the publican and helpers made a big boot and then he dressed up as The Old Woman who lived in a shoe. After parading through Billingshurst we were given tea and a celebration mug. Riding on that trailer-type wagon to Billingshurst was the best part of the day's events for us.

Five Oaks football club started in the 30s and played on three different fields. In 1939 they held the Horsham District 3rd Division Cup for a year after a tie with Horsham Council United. The Union Jack was waved by Mr. Pole and a crowd of locals to welcome the team home. The team reformed in 1946.

(Dorothy Pullen corrected and helped by Yvonne Wolzak.)

The Hamlets – Adversane

Two miles south of Billingshurst is the hamlet of Adversane, known as Hadfoldshern until the 1850s. In the middle ages lands there were owned by Tortington Priory. It is likely that the change of name came as a result of a mishearing of the name by a map-maker or official when pronounced in Sussex dialect. It is on Stane Street (A29) where the Roman road is crossed by the B2133, affording access to Petworth to the west and Ashington and Worthing to the east. The main business was always the pub and forge next door, naturally entitled The Blacksmiths' Arms. Gaius (George) Carley who lived at Griggs Cottages was the last smith, who wrote a book about his life. Eleanor Farjeon, the children's author, used the village as a setting for her 1921 novel 'Martin Pippin in the Apple Orchard'. This is an elaborate fairy tale where the children of the village are said to sing a ballad 'The Spring-Green Lady'. There was a post office and shop in the end house of Malt-house Cottages kept by Frank Sharville in the 1950s. Adversane has three notable ancient timber-framed houses, Old House, Southlands and the later Blacksmith's Arms. A former hotel called Newstead Hall run by Mr. And Mrs Cartner at the old Juppsland farm site was recently demolished and apartments erected in its stead.

Grigg's Cottages 2013

The Adversane cross roads is the most accident-prone junction in the parish. Originally the B2133 was a simple crossroads, the road crossing the green, but in an attempt to limit the danger it was decided to stagger the junction, so making matters a good deal worse. Strict speed controls currently curtail the number of accidents but the attractive Green would be seriously disfigured by building a roundabout.

'From Hadfoldshern...to Adversane'

Deborah Evershed's carefully researched account of late Victorian and early 20th century Adversane Hamlet and the four or more closely related families, the Miles, Taylors, Humphreys, Puttocks and Eversheds, who lived thereabouts goes some way to proving once again that truth can be quite as sensational as fiction. The general tenor of this study of an extended family is warm, romantic and engagingly comfortable with the busy, aspirational, neighbourly, harmonious bucolic lives the author presents to us.

But never long concealed are the inevitable blows of fate, the violence and tragic happenings that had to be stoically endured along with the delights of nostalgic reminiscence of flowery meadows, woodland walks and rides home by pony and trap under the stars. The childhood excitement of the annual fair is troubled by brutal boxing encounters and a gang murder, Adversane maltsters (the Allens) cheat the revenue by not paying malt tax and escape justice by flight to America, an alcoholic and debt-laden Alfred Taylor shoots himself, good women die in childbirth and young men fall ill and expire in their 20s. Amid the excitements such as the coming of the railway and the crystal wireless set and the comforting sights sound and smells of the rich countryside, the sweetshop and the toffee and aniseed balls, the feeding of lambs and the rearing of piglets, are mingled moments of sadness and pain such as Buzzy Wright's cane at Billingshurst School or a glimpse of disfigured soldiers at Billingshurst Station at the end of WW I and the lice in the army uniform of poor Uncle Jack.

The closing chapters give a warm account of the residents of the hamlet and the social life and film shows they enjoyed in the 1950s and 60s, focused on the pub, the blacksmith's forge, the Mission Hall with Social Club and the village shop, Lola Baxter, who kept a restaurant at Old House and gave ballet lessons and the teenagers who had their own Youth Club.

Lola Baxter, a divorcee, and her friend 'Noni' Frame had joined the Women's Voluntary Service in 1939 and organised theatrical revues for Wandsworth Borough Council. After the war they bought Old House combining the restaurant with an antiques business. Some 40 dealers were accommodated there. Lola ran her ballet classes and the Youth Club and held antique connoisseurs' soirees. After her death her collection of Staffordshire animal figures and ceramics, glassware and furniture in the Continental taste was sold by auction at Toovey's.

The maltings

Alfred Allen, maltster of Horsham, and Dennett, his brother of Colliers' Farm, Gay Street, West Chiltington where he had maltings, also owned malt businesses at Worthing and in buildings at Adversane, which are still there. The brothers flourished financially, becoming the equivalent of multi-millionaires today, but their success was based on fraud. They maintained a respectable business for the duty officers to inspect, duty properly paid, but at the same time they conducted a black market in duty-free malt, secretly prepared and stored in hidden rooms. They could pay farmers good prices for barley and sell malt cheaply, so undercutting their competitors. Their many workmen must have valued their well-paid jobs because they kept quiet about the tax evasion, just as people turned a blind eye on smugglers.

"Them that asks no questions, isn't told a lie, Watch the wall my darling while the gentlemen go by." [Rudyard Kipling]

They were rumbled in 1857 however, probably 'shopped' by legitimate maltsters whose profits were undermined by such illegal competition. Customs Officers raided the Worthing premises. Alfred swiftly organised wagons to clear out the illicit malt at Adversane and dump it into the River Arun at Newbridge. Local people salvaged what they could to feed their pigs and make some home-brew. The customs men confiscated £12,000 worth of malt which was sent to London by special train from Horsham.

Maltings Cottages, Adversane

The cunning brothers had a plan. They did not show up in the Court of the Exchequer where they were peremptorily found guilty and initially fined £375,000 on pain of imprisonment if the fine was not paid. This unrealistic figure was reduced by the Solicitor General to a feasible sum of £110,000. However the Allens outsmarted the law. They took a packet steamer to France, where pursuing officers searched in vain, as they had turned round at once on disembarking and returned to England. Then they took the trains to London and Liverpool and enjoyed their wealth in America until they judged it safe to return. They paid off their much reduced £10,000 fine and lived happily ever after! There are times when crime pays. The Allens 'had form'. During the Crimean war an extra duty was charged on malt to pay the military bill. The Allens fraudulently claimed £700 refund on duty they had never paid, claiming that they had lost stocks in their warehouses.

Public Houses in Billingshurst

Today there are 6 public houses, their signs here pictured. The Five Oaks Inn is the only recent closure at a time when, elsewhere, numerous inns have ceased trading and the sites been redeveloped. At earlier times there were several other pubs and beer outlets in the village. On the west side of the High Street stood the Rising Sun. To complicate matters there was an earlier King's Arms on the site of what is now Lloyds Bank. There was also an earlier King's Head which stood where Freemans, the undertakers, is. The pub 'crossed the road' to the present King's Head in the 18th century. The White Horse Inn nearby where Lloyds the Chemist stands has long since closed down.

On land called Lockyers along East Street another house was built which predated the later Gratwicke House. This building housed The Star Inn. There was also other beer house on the site of Southdown House named The Lyon House, and formerly The Bell or The Dog and Partridge. The Maltings and Gingers in the High Street, which stood where the entry to Jengers Mead is now, became polite tea rooms in the 20s, renowned for its home-made cakes, until demolished in 1964. ['Gingers' was built in 1370 and named after Oliver Gynguire. He was a Horsham man elected to Parliament in 1368].

Billingshurst's Heritage No. 2

THE RISING SUN was named as a beer house in 1862. In living memory it was converted to a private residence then demolished in the 1960s when the Malaya Garage was built. In the front wall of the Inn garden there were niches where drinkers could stand their pewter pots.

Though William Cobbett and J.B. Dashwood wrote handsomely about Billingshurst inns, one Arthur Becket, who was a journalist and founder of the Sussex County Magazine, wrote scathingly of one of them – "a certain evil spirit led us...to a certain roadside hostelry....but of the quality of that shelter and food I will say nothing, only praying that that self-same evil spirit that directed us to this inn, will direct thereto my greatest enemy when he comes upon that road".

Pauline Taylor wrote articles about the taverns. She tells of a travellers' guide by John Taylor, a Kings Waterman and the Egon Ronay of his day (1653). He wrote of John Agate the only listed licensee of the old KING'S ARMS. He praises the hospitality and refers to the destruction of the Inn sign some years previously by Parliamentarian troops, perhaps on the way to the siege of Arundel in 1643.

She presumes that when Cobbett visited Billingshurst James Fuller was the Licensee in 1820 of the present King's Arms. He was also the village butcher and in the 1831 Directory is listed as a basket maker. In the late 19th century the late 19th century the Arms provided the village Market room, was licensed to let horses and continued to be linked to the butchers' next door. The pub we know

Billingshurst's Heritage No. 2

now as the King's Arms was called The Carpenters Arms until about 1788. The Prince Regent was despised and when news came of the recovery of health of George III from his first illness William Greenfield renamed the Inn The King's Arms in celebration.

John Taylor wrote 'The travailles of an Uncertain Journey' in 1653 in the form of what can loosely be described as a poem with an undoubted debt to *The Prologue* to *The Canterbury Tales*:-

The year sixteen hundred fifty, with 3 added
Old Tib, my mare, and I a journey gadded.
August the tenth my bonny beast and I,
From Surrey travelled to South Saxony,
Now called Sussex, where at Billingshurst,
Six days I felt no longer cold or thirst.
'Twas the King's Arms, but shattering shot and flame
Did beat them down, as useless, of small stead,
For arms of no use without a head.
Mine host was mighty good, and great withal
And among hosts may be a general.
He's friendly, courteous, although big and burly,
Aright good fellow, no way proud or surly.
Six nights at Billingshurst I truly staid,
And all the charge for man and mare was paid
By a gentleman, to name whom I'll refrain,
Whose love my thankful mind still retain.
A Reverend preacher preached on Sunday twice
Directing souls to the Heavenly Paradise,
And, if we could but do as he did say,
His doctrine told us all the ready way.
Thus Billingshurst, thy bounty I extol,
Thou's feasted me in body and in soul.
There was rare music and sweet gentle airs.
For undeserved favours I am theirs.
My love to Mr. Fist and to mine host.
But love to T.H. deservest most.   John Taylor

Though hardly Chaucerian in quality, this doggerel is an entertaining narrative with a witty pun on the King's head which had been cut off from Charles I and it is a warm tribute to the people of Billingshurst. Fist suggests a Mr. Fiest, a local name. TH has been identified by John Hurd as Thomas Henshaw.

The King's Head had a poem under its 20th century advertisement:

Accommodation you will find
For travellers of every kind,
Most of whom who come from far
Appreciate a good cigar
Whilst wines and spirits are to hand
And served at anyone's command.
Bright sitting room and well-aired bed,
You'll always get at the 'King's Head'.

Pauline Taylor describes the present KING'S HEAD as an old timber framed building, some 400 years old, with a modernised frontage and the roof raised to give a third storey. The rear is 16th century, the front Georgian. It was used as a hostelry and dormitory together with the White Horse Inn. It was a staging post for the Comet coach which changed horses 'at a quarter before twelve every forenoon (except Sundays).' The archway and cobblestones of the stable yard survive. It was listed as a 'Commercial Inn'. On April Fool's Day 1839 the Tradesmen Club held their annual meeting there. "The dinner and attention of Mr. Aylward, the landlord met with acknowledged approbation'. In the 20th century (1903) it offered accommodation for cyclists. Earthenware footwarmers were found.

Of the SIX BELLS she writes of its varied history. Parts of the building have 14th century roots. It was once a yeoman farm, Taintland, a beer house, tannery, brewery and a '3d. Doss house'. Therein was the beginning of the modern pub, licensed since the beginning of the 19th century. Folk lore links it with smuggling. There is a 16th century fireback, a copy of one once used as a tombstone, in the saloon bar. The building is unusual among the old houses in the area having a continuous overhang storey or jetty along the whole first floor. The name was used before two more bells were added to St. Mary's to celebrate Queen Victoria's Silver Jubilee in 1897. It was called 'Ye Old Six Bells' until recently. 'Ye' was used by printers in place of the old disused letter 'thorn' (Þ), pronounced like 'th', as it most closely resembled a Y.

Mr. Bob Dames supplied additional information. In 1530 the building and land were known as Gillman, after its occupant William Gillman, whose kinsman, Thomas Gillman, was in residence at Great Gillmans. In 1563 the then owner and resident, William Tredcroft, a yeoman farmer, referred to it in his will as "Gylman otherwise named Tayntland". In 1673 it was known as Taintlands but by 1815 there was just a house and a yard, which in 1830 was referred to as a Tanyard. In 1851 the occupant, one Richard Mitchell was a carpenter and brewer – and the scene was set. In 1861 it was known as the Five Bells but by 1871 it was the Six Bells.

Aileen Walker commented that local tradition named the land between the Six Bells and the Post Office as Taintilands and there are 15th century documents using that name. The word, she suggests, may derive, as Tenterlands, from the word 'tenter', a machine for stretching out cloth on hooks round a frame, which relates to tainters or tenters who finished cloth, hence the expression 'on tenterhooks'. It is possible that the Six Bells once harboured a woollen cloth or linen finishing industry.

THE RAILWAY INN came with the railway and in 1862 was licensed as the Station Inn to William Harsant. The proprietors diversified their business. They were licensed to let horses, being convenient for arriving passengers and also ran a coal merchants business, being close to arriving coal trucks.

The other three village pubs, the BLACKSMITH'S ARMSs, the LIMEBURNERS and the demolished FIVE OAKS INN are described elsewhere in this book.

In Victorian times the most notable local brewer was Henry Michell. His immediate well-to-do ancestors owned Hermongers at Rudgwick. His father moved to Kithurst and Cootham Farms at Storrington where Henry was born, in 1809, the third of twelve children. He was schooled in Pulborough by a Mr. Billingshurst and then worked for his father brewing, malting and selling coal at Steyning. He had to earn his own living and became manager of a bank at Steyning and learnt the art of bookkeeping, so ensuring a shrewd and profitable business career. In 1834 he married, moved to Horsham and took on Mr. Allen's brewery on lease. He also had a malthouse in Gay Street but gave it up in favour of one in Billingshurst High Street. He expanded into the coal trade and made huge profits from brick-making. In 1838 he bought the Blacksmiths Arms at Adversane from Mr. R. Watkins for £750.

In 1841 he moved his brewery to West Street, Horsham on a dismantled site of a former brewery, let to him by Sir Timothy Shelley of Field Place, Warnham.

He could no longer do business with Mr. Allen 'on any fair terms' and gave up the lease, which included three pubs which he had to surrender, one of which was the Kings Head at Billingshurst. These Allens were the same infamous unscrupulous malt dealers.

We do not often think of the Victorians as growers of vines other than in greenhouses, especially the brewers. However there must have been a quantity in Billingshurst. In 1842, Michell records in his diary, 'we had 45 gallons of grapes brought home from the old malt house at Billingshurst and I trode them out in a tub and there were 27 gallons of juice which I put into a 36 Gn. cask and filled it up with sugar and a little water. This wine was like syrup at 20 years old.'

In 1845, in a masterly stroke of enterprise, he bought up the old Horsham County Gaol then sold off the materials, some land for building and some to the Waterworks Company. He built a new Malt house too, and 'made about ten million of bricks on the ground'. He cleared a £5000 profit on the deal, worth £5M today. Meantime he was brewing up to 1000 quarters of malt a year at some 60s a quarter. He became Chairman of the Gas Company and profited from the coming of the railway from Three Bridges to Horsham. He was able to buy cheap imported French barley from 1848 as 'the corn laws had been relaxed' making some £1000 a year profit. He could also send half a million bricks to the Crystal Palace at Sydenham. In 1850 he indulged his fancy to be a farmer and bought Stakers Farm, Southwater.

In 1852 the Gates Brewery at the Fountain Brewery collapsed and Michell bought it up together with five pubs, including the Kings Head, Billingshurst for £6000. He enlarged the Fountain Brewery rented from Sir Percy Shelley and 'at once gave up the old wretched Malthouse I had used for many years in Billingshurst'. He then gave up the coal trade.

Extra duty of 10s a quarter on malt at the outbreak of the Crimean War limited profit in 1854. By 1859 he had doubled his malt production to 2,500 quarters or so. Each year he bought more pubs, including The Rising Sun in Billingshurst for £260. In 1860 he bought Shiprods Farm, Itchingfield where he made bricks and drain pipes, built another malthouse and took over The Queens Head at Bucks Green. He was now getting his barley from Denmark and Scotland. His profits 1864 came to £5,000 when he built the Station Hotel, Arundel then he took on The King's Head, Slinfold. In 1868 'we did extensive repairs at Adversane, Billingshurst Station [hotel] and Billingshurst Street'.

Henry Michell died in 1874. His daughter Fanny was married to T.W. Cowan, an inventive engineer and famous as the Father of British Beekeeping. Fanny and Thomas inherited much of his fortune but his son Henry, 'a very weakly specimen' when born, carried on the business. It was taken over in 1911 by the

Rock Brewery of Brighton.

Henry Michell was the very model of a Victorian middle-class capitalist provincial entrepreneur. He loved travelling. He was a stout Protestant, but of radical Whig political sympathies, opposed to the landed squirearchy, High Church activists and those who wanted to protect English farmers by reintroducing the Corn Laws. His revealing diary is available in Kenneth Neale's book, *Victorian Horsham*.

Michell, brewer, at the Railway Hotel

Kelly's Post Office Directory 1867

In Volume I of 'Billingshurst's Heritage' directories for 1850 and 1888 were presented. The following is a summary of information for 1867, nearly 150 years ago, which read alongside the others will show changes in the village at the time when the new railway was altering the lives of the people.

'Billingshurst is part of the Petworth Union and the County Court District of Horsham, 6 and a half miles SW of it, 41 from London by road and 45 by rail – Mid-Sussex Railway. The Church is now (1866) undergoing a thorough restoration and the old galleries and pews have been cleared away to make way for the more suitable open seats designed to suit the style of the church; a new chancel aisle has been added, the plaster ceilings have been cleared away and the old open timber roofs restored and exposed to view, and the stonework and walls throughout cleaned of their whitewash; new east windows of stained glass have been put in the chancel and chapel, one of which is to be a memorial one; both have been given by H. Carnsew Esq. of Somers, to whose liberality the restoration of the church is mainly due. The work has been carried out by local builders, viz., Messrs. Luke Wadey and Sons and the stonework, ornamental etc., by Mr. Owen Voice, from the drawings of Robert W. Edis, Esq., MRIBA, architect, of London. The church will seat about 520. The Register dates from 1630. The living is a Vicarage, tithes commuted to £200 yearly, with 13 acres of Glebe and a neat residence, in the gift of Sir Charles Goring, Bart. and held by the Rev William Howie Bull, MA of St. John's College, Cambridge. There is a National School for boys and girls, supported by voluntary contributions, and a handsome new school room has lately been created. It is a simple Gothic building capable of accommodating 150 children with playgrounds and master's residence attached. The building, which is of red brick with stone dressings, has been built at the sole cost of Mr. Carnsew who also gave the site from the designs and under the superintendence of R.W.Edis Esq.'

A considerable business is carried on in the manufacture of wood hoops.... the corn market is held at the King's Arms every other Tuesday evening. The Station Inn adjoins the Station. William Bigwood, Station Master. Somers, the delightful residence of Henry Carnsew Esq., is an extensive mansion in the Domestic Gothic style, with mullioned windows. Area of the parish, 675 acres; the population in 1861 was 1,495.

Parish Clerk: Thomas Baker and Sen. Relieving Officer, Postmaster: Peter Laker: Receiver of Post at Five Oaks: Peter Towse: National School: Henry Wright, master: Academy: William Boorer: Sarah Potter: Ladies' Boarding

School: Rev. Joseph Harris: Independent Church.: Stephen Niblett MD physician at Brick House

Carriers: Charman from Pulborough every Saturday, Coombes from Wisborough Green and Kirdford, Mondays and Thursdays

Gentry and notable persons.

William Axworthy, Thomas Baker, Rev. Henry Beath, Andrews Hill; William Berrall Esq. Duncans; Richard Bescoby, Gratwick House; Rev. Bull, Vicarage; Henry Carnsew Esq. Somers; Cornelius Carter, Adversane; Peter Evershed Esq., Capt. Finch, John Ireland at High Seat; Thomas Puttock, Carlton House; Edward Robinson, Mrs. Rogers, Mr. William Smart, Stallkart Esq.; Capt Anthony Triscott of Manor House.

Farmers
Benjamin Boniface – Hook Farm
Francis Botting – Oakhurst Farm
William Botting – miller and farmer, Rowner's Mill
Henry Burchell
Thomas Chesman- Graningfold
John Dean – Fewhurst
Richard Denyer – farmer and landowner, Goldings at Five Oaks
? Dubbins – Combe land
George Duke – Duncans Farm
James Evershed – Ridge's Farm
John Dendy Evershed – Cobbed's Hall
Robert and James Evershed – props of steam threshing machines at Jeffries Farm
Thomas Evershed – Slatter
William Evershed – farmer and landowner, Tedfold
John Naldrett Farhall, jun. – Clark's land
Richard Greenfield – Lower Wood House
William Grinsted – Hadfold Farm
William Gumbrill – Parbrook
George Ireland – farmer and landowner, Highfure Farm
Walter Laker – Mintrell's Wood
Alfred Lloyd – farmer and landowner, Rowfold
Charles Peacock – Adversane
John Petter – Woodsdale
? Shilcock – Kingsfold
William Sprinks – miller and farmer, Hammonds
James Strudwick – Andrew's Hill

Elizabeth Turner (Mrs.) farmer and landowner, Rosa Farm

Commercial and Services

David Baker, watchmaker and builder
James Batchelor, farm bailiff to J.Farhall
George Botting, draper and grocer –Insurance Agent, Liverpool&London&Globe
Joseph Brown, shoemaker and glover
Edwd. Burchall, shopkeeper and beer retailer
William Durrant, builder and shopkeeper
John Etherton, blacksmith
Maurice Evershed, corn and seed merchant
Mrs. Sarah Evershed, Vetinary Surgeon
William Grinsted, butcher
George Hammond, plumber and painter
Maurice Harwood, shoemaker
Huggett and Son, grocer and draper, Insurance agent, Atlas Fire and Life
George Johns, King's Arms, licensed to let horses and butcher
George Jupp, blacksmith, Five Oaks
James King, maltster, living in Betchworth, Surrey
Alfred Laker, King's Head
Henry Laker, saddler and harness maker
Jesse Laker, currier
Peter Laker, tailor and postmaster
Frederick Peskett, shopkeeper
Charles Petar, brick and tile manufacturer
Mrs. Elizabeth Powell, shoe maker
Charles Puttock, Blacksmiths Arms and smith
Philip Puttock, nursery and seedsman
Mrs. Deborah Puttock, grocer and draper, Adversane
Thomas Puttock, timber, bark and wood hoop merchant, hoop manufacturer
Mrs. W. Redman, shopkeeper
Spencer Reed, baker and shopkeeper
Albert Sprinks, Station Inn, licensed to let horses and coal merchant
John Sprinks, wharfinger and collector
Peter Towse, Five Oaks Inn, grocer and Post Office
James Turner, tailor
Edward Voice, plumber, painter and stonemason
William Voice, shoe maker

Billingshurst's Heritage No. 2

Luke Wadey and Sons, builders, Five Oaks
Joseph Wadey, bookseller, stationer and shopkeeper
Walter Wadey, blacksmith
William Wadey, wheelwright
William Wood, beer retailer

Kelly's Directory - 1973

Appendix 7 of *Billingshurst's Heritage* gave a shortened account of Billingshurst's commerce in 1962. The 1973 publication contains valuable records of the village some forty years ago. The following selected information, extracted from the Directory, has High Street numbers shown in brackets. Items in square brackets [ ] are from the 1969 edition.

Officials:
Lord Lieutenant – Duke of Norfolk, Chairman of WSCC – Sir Peter Mursell MBE. DL. – Wisborough Green.

Justices of the Peace:
T.C.N. Flynn MC. Beke Place, Billingshurst
R.W Godden, Hilland Farm, Stane St. Billingshurst and 15 others

Registrar: -Miss R.E. Ogilvie (Thursday afternoons) Lindens, L Stat Rd.
Clergy: - Rev. R. Evan Hopkins, MA (St.Mary's), Rev Geo. A Nunn (Trinity), Rev Gerald J Candy (St Gabriels).
[Horsham Rural District Councillors, 1969: J.B. Sherlock of Renvyle, Okehurst Rd., H.J. Stafford of Grainingfold, Five Oaks and C.J. Wood, 2 Birch Drive. The Local Govt. Act 1972 had abolished the Rural Districts by 1974].

Doctors:
L.C. Bousfield, Evelyn Kilsby, T.A. Tillyard, 10 East St,

Dentist:
J. Symmons (114)

Vetinary Surgeon:
[Pasfield] Rhan & Luckhurst (96)

Library:
Trinity Congregational Hall, High St.

Post Office [A.W.Briden post master] (88)

Grocers:
R & J Ball (59), G. Edwards, L. Station Rd, [Fishers &PO L. Stat. Rd.,] E.Fiddler (41) [formerly G. Voice], International Tea Co's Stores (56), Mrs. P. Rogers & PO Five Oaks, Mrs. D.M.Rugg & PO Adversane,

Greengrocers:
R.A. Allen [formerly Mrs. Freeman] (47), A.E. Hearne (71), Orange Grove 3 Jengers Mead

Nurseries:
High Seat (1), J.H.Way, Little Platt, Marringdean

Butchers:
E.W. Cripps (82), S.A Wilson 12 Jengers Mead

Newsagents:
Humphries Stat. Rd., The Paper Shop (D. & M. Wakeling) (36/38)

Hairdressers and Barbers:
R. Brown (43), Burnelle (49), Helene (126), Yvette Hereford Hse. Stat. Rd.

Clothing and Outfitting:
Fabrics Galore, haberdashery, (32), Ninety-four fashions (94), Patswear A.E. Maynard L. Stat. Rd., Raggity Jane, children, (51), Mrs. M. Whitehead draper (58), [recently Family Fabrics 2 East St.]

Cafes, Restaurants:
Bistro Cafe (92), Jane's Tea Gardens Five Oaks, Shirley Cafe L. Stat Rd., Old Hse. Restaurant Adversane

Radio, TV, electrical services:
Aerial Fitters L. Stat Rd., B.L. Barnes, 13 Carpenters, L. Brown appliances (31), R. Crisp radio (43), R.G. Oulds photographs Coneyhurst.

Turf Accountants:
Partington Norman L Stat Rd., J. Pegley (116)

Garages, coaches, service stations:
Billingshurst Coaches (Williamson) (85), Everest Garages & White Hall Services (3), Hillview Garage, High St., H. Johnson car breakers Coneyhurst, Malaya Garage High St., Poplar Garage Five Oaks, Rice Bros. High St., Southern Counties Garage (82).Estate Agents:

Bridger & Sons (70) [formerly Keymarket, grocers], Churchman Burt & Sons (44/46), Johnston Pycraft (34), Whiteheads (35).

Builders:
E.W. Carley plumber Adversane, Daux Ltd. Rosier Gate, Raymond Voice Little East St., Charles Wadey & Sons Parbrook. [C..W. Norton Five Oaks]

Other Goods and Services:
Arun Travel (85), Card & Candy Box greetings cards (53), Convent School Summers Place, The Flower Box florists (45), Higgins ironmongers (52), Horsham Dry Cleaners High St., Horsham Travel 2 Jengers Mead, Raymond Jackson Lily Pools, 17 Daux Rd., Juppsland Country Club Adversane, H. Johnson car breaker Coneyhurst, T & D Kelland stationers (29), Alex Lockie chemist (54), Lyons Fish Bar 12 Jengers Mead, Marsh DIY 11 Jengers Mead, Reta Launderette 13 Jengers Mead, R. Rhodes & Son, boot repairers (112), St. Christopher's PNEU School Beechwood Hse. Daux Ave., Stanmore Guest Hse. (118/120), [There was also an hotel at Adversane], F.W.Watt & Sons seed merchants Stat. Rd., R.J. Witt confectioners (72)

Other listed businesses:
Askeys biscuit mfrs. Daux Rd., Beverley Chemical Engineering, Station Yard, C. Braby antiques Groomsland Farm, Braemar Construction civil engrs. Daux Rd., J.A. Burroughs plant hire & haulage Daux Rd., Frame & Baxter antiques Old Hse. Adversane, Thos.Keating tool makers Daux Rd., W.G Keyte & Sons precision engrs., Daux Rd., E.J.Lawrenson Haulage Natts Lane, Lorlins electrical components Stat. Rd., J.O. Lugg & Son agricultural engrs., East St., Mermaid Swimming Pools Daux Rd., SCATS agricultural engrs., Frenches Corner, Southern Fuels coal & coke Stat. Rd., Stane St Press printers Daux Rd.,[Mrs. Thurlow-Smith antiques (95), Toyland (55)], [unlisted – Lannards Art Gallery, Okehurst Rd.}

Farmers and farm houses:
Harold Arnold & Son Copped Hall Okehurst La, Mrs. Ayre Bridgewater Newbridge Rd., R.D. Barnes Little Daux East St., C.E. Barron and Rupert Dunham Denhams Andrews Hill, Leslie Bayfield Southlands Marringdean, Eileen Blanch St. Andrews Andrews Hill, Norman Blunden Jeffries Coneyhurst, Nigel Bower Fewhurst East St., Mrs. K Braun Kingslea Marringdean, J. Breecher Jackman's Adversane, Alan Bryant Fold Farm Hse. Five Oaks, D.D. Carr Sayers, Adversane, Donald French Willow Coneyhurst, Geoffrey Garbett Westland Adversane, Miss Gauk-Rodger Great Daux, R. Godden JP Hilland, David Grist Valelands Coneyhurst, Harold Jackson Lower Hook. W. Chiltington La., S. Hiscock High barns Coneyhurst, G.A. Hook Little Gilmans Marringdean, A.J.R. Izat Eastlands and Lower Woodhouse, J.Maslin Kingsfold Marringdean, P.D. Morey & A Merison, Pratts Barns Green, Paul Merison Hook, Clarence Morris Longmead Marringdean, Jn Morris Little Slinfoldland Five Oaks, Roderick Norris Wildens East St., Victor Nutter Kynance W. Chilt. La., A.B. Patterson Pear Tree, F. Pinches Woodlands Adversane, Jn Rogerson Guildenhurst, A. Rowlet

Billingshurst's Heritage No. 2

Upper Woodhouse, Patricia Sherlock Renvyle Okehurst Rd., G. Sims Menzies Wood Okehurst Rd., W.H. Smith Borough Five Oaks, H.J.Stafford Grainingfold Five Oaks, Stanley Stocker Kingslea Marringdean, Jn Tomlin Tisserane Stane St., J. Treen Sunwood Adversane, E.C. Van den Bergh Southouse Marringdean, Percy Voak Gess Gates Adversane, Bryan. D. Voice Southlands Adversane, A.D. Walker Stone Pits, Marringdean, Lionel Williams Home Farm at Summers.

A number of implications of social and economic change can be deduced from a comparison of the use of premises as recorded above with what exists today. In those days most people were demanding their own cars as rail and bus services declined. Business was booming in supply, service and maintenance of vehicles. Garage premises in the village High Street were profitable and not, as now, more valuable as building sites, often enough specifically to house the retired and elderly.

Supermarkets had not yet captured the business of independent grocers and other traders and there were no empty stores or charity shops. Shopkeepers could offer groceries and clothing to a local clientele as well as a wide range of niche goods and services. Several valuable enterprises such as sellers of books, cards, antiques, sports goods, videos, DIY, white goods and the like have not survived the passage of years though others catering for up-to-date technical advances have started up. The advent of an undertaker may be a reflection of the increasing accommodation built for the elderly! The growing demand for home ownership and steady expansion of the village by incomers in the 60s and 70s is reflected in the number of estate agents.

The taste for ethnic food was quite undeveloped in 1973; neither did people 'eat out' much. There were few restaurants or cafes and the only 'take away' was the fish and chip shop, in marked contrast to forty years later. Light industry was then mainly in Daux Road and near the Station. Other industrial estates were still undeveloped. Private education was then available in the parish at Summers Place and in Daux Avenue but has now ceased. There were no children's nurseries but now there are three. Civic buildings were just The Old Village Hall, now apartments, and the Women's Hall. The doctors' surgery is now a vetinarian's. Builders were busy at the Weald School expanding it for comprehensive schooling and a growing Sixth Form.

Billingshurst Roads and Estates

Volume 1 of 'Billingshurst's Heritage' gave as Appendix 1 a list of streets, their date, the developers and the origin of the name. Below is a revised list with some amendments and more recent additions prepared by Mr. Paul Smith.

\multicolumn{4}{c}{BILLINGSHURST ROADS AND ESTATES}			
Street Name/ Development	*Developer/Builder*	*Date Built & Notes*	*Named After*
Amberley Court, Brooker's Road	Bellway Homes	2002-03		After Amberley village
Anvil Close	Horsham DC	1976		After forge that stood on cnr of W & High Streets
Arun Court, Rosehill	Vinall	1988-89		River Arun
Arun Crescent	Saxon Weald	2009	6 Eco Houses	River Arun
Arun Road & Flats	Horsham RDC	E 1960's	Flats rebuilt	River Arun
Arundel Court, Brooker's Road	Bellway Homes	2002-03		After Arundel town
Barrow Close	Taywood Homes	2000-01	Penfold Grange Development Phase 3 & 4	Probable developer name
Belinus Drive	Sunley Homes	1974-76		After Roman surveyor of Stane Street
Berrall Way N	Taywood Homes	1999-2000	Penfold Grange Development Phase 1 & 2	Local family
Berrall Way S	Taywood Homes	2000-02	Penfold Grange Development Phase 3 & 4	Local family
Birch Drive - W end		L 1960's		Birch trees line much of the road
Birch Drive - E end	Sunley Homes	1970-71		name continued from W end, but few trees!
Bridgewater Close	Shared Ownership	1998-99		Although some distance away, maybe from Bridgewaters Farm
Brookers Road			On land called 'Brokers' (1476)	Named after William Brooker (1445)
Brookfield Way		c.1971		Plot adjoins Par Brook stream
Broomfield Drive	Sunley Homes	1970-71		After barn and cottage nearby
Caffyns Rise	Hillreed Homes (Sussex) Ltd	1998-99	Had a Marketing Name of Brook Rise - 15 homes	Wealthy local family. Jacob d. 1850, Matthew d. 1714 Baptist, and Matthew Victorian Surveyor

Billingshurst's Heritage No. 2

Carpenters	Croudace	1966-67	62 properties	Field name
Cedars Farm Close	Horsham DC	1976		From The Cedars (Farm)
Cherry Tree Close		M 1960's		Tree name
Chestnut Road - East End		1987-88		Tree name
Chestnut Road - West End		L C19 - E C20		Tree name
Cleve Way		E 1960's		After Clevelands House C19 nearby
Clevelands	Chichester Diocesan Housing Assoc	1978-79		After C19 house on site
Coombe Close		L 1980's		Uncertain
Coombe Hill	Horsham RDC	L 1940's - E 1950's		Uncertain
Cranham Avenue	Westbury & Westwood Estates Ltd	1998-99	Had a Marketing Name of Kings Meadow	Probable Developer Name - There is a Cranham in Gloucestershire
Daux Avenue	Various	1900's Onwards		After farm and nearby wood - William Daukes first recorded in 1369
Dauxwood Close	Charles Wadey & Sons	1981		Daux Wood lies behind road
Dell Lane	Fairclough Homes	1979-80		In a dip!
Downsview Cottages, West Street	Horsham RDC	L 1930's		Did have a view of the South Downs!
Easton Crescent	Gleeson Homes	L1990's - 2010		After Cllr Jack Easton, long time chairman of Parish Council
Farriers Close	Hilbery Chaplin	1982		Relating to the forge in the High Street
Forge Way - N end		L 1960's		After forge that stood on corner of W & High Streets
Forge Way - Middle Section	Horsham DC	1976		After forge that stood on corner of W & High Streets
Forge Way - E end	Sunley Homes	1974-76		After forge that stood on corner of W & High Streets
Forge Way - SW spur	Horsham DC	1983		After forge that stood on corner of W & High Streets
Forge House, West Street		E 1980's	Converted L 1990's from offices to flats	A blacksmith's forge stood on site
Freemans Close	Sunley Homes	1974-76		Possible local name
Frenches Mead	Horsham RDC	L 1940's - E 1950's		After farm that stood to the W

Freshlands	Bryant Homes/ Taylor Woodrow	2002-03	Penfold Grange Development Phase 5	Likely to be a developer name
Gorselands	Gleeson Homes	1978-80		Probable developer name
Gratwicke Close		L 1960's		After house the stood here called Gratwicke
Griffin Close	Sunninghill Construction/ Saxon Weald	2012	Architect - Kenn Scadden Associates	After 5 Oaks family, prominent in local affairs
Groomsland Drive	Horsham RDC	1939, 1950's - 60's		After Groomsland Farm that stood to the NW
Hayes Wood Road, Five Oaks	Horsham RDC	L 1950's		Hayes lies to the N in Slinfold Parish
High Seat Gardens		E 2000's		After High Seat, house nearby
High Street		C15 - 2000's	South end formerly South Street	The main and principal street in Billingshurst
Hillview Court	Taylor Wimpey	2010	14 Properties	After former Garage named Hillview that was on site
Holders Close	Bryant Homes/ Taylor Woodrow	2005-06	Newbridge Gardens Development	Formerly intended for over 55's and started, demolished and rebuilt on a new plan
Honeysuckle Drive	A2Dominion New Homes	2013	Marketing Name of Cereston	Off Marringdean Road
Hurstlands		1974		After house on site. 1st recorded 1296 after Adam ate Hurst
Ingfield Manor Drive, Five Oaks		L 2000's	Small development	Off drive to Ingfield Manor
Jengers Mead shops with flats above		L 1960's		Corruption of Gingers - C15 house that stood on site
Jengers Mead - NE Quadrant		1999-2000		Corruption of Gingers - C15 house that stood on site
Jubilee Court, High Street	McCarthy & Stone	2001	29 apartments with House Manager	Built during the HM Queen's Diamond Jubilee
Kenilworth Place, Natts Lane	David Wilson Homes	2004	Brooklands Place Development	After previous house on site built in 1930's
Kingsfold Close		1988-89		After nearby house of Kingsfold
Kingsley Mews, Brooker's Road		M 1990's		Probable developer name
Lakers Meadow		1988-89		After field on site used by slaughterhouse
Larks View	Bryant Homes/ Taylor Woodrow	2002-03		Skylarks could be heard here!

201

Laura House, Jengers Mead		L 1980's		Probable developer name
Laura's Garden, Behind 82a High Street		2011-12	4 Mews houses on site of Slaughterhouse	After florist shop that stands in front
Lordings Road			From Lordings Farm	Francis Lording (1602)
Luggs Close		L 1990's		After Lugg's Yard which formerly stood here
Luxford Way	Taywood Homes	1999-2000	Penfold Grange Development Phase 1	Local family. Member of 1st Parish Council
Manor Close	Cross Construction	2012	4 Eco homes sold before completion	After nearby Manor House
Maple Close		M 1960's		Tree Name
Maple Road	Sunley Homes	1970-71		Tree Name
Maplehurst Court, Brooker's Road	Bellway Homes	2002-03		After Maplehurst (Nuthurst Parish)
Marringdean Road			Originally (1288) Merehonedene	Means 'Woodland pasture near the boundary stone'
Mill Way	Horsham RDC	E 1960's		After nearby windmill
Morris Drive N	Bryant Homes/ Taylor Woodrow	2002-03	Penfold Grange Development Phase 5	Local family who lived at Five Oaks
Morris Drive S	Taywood Homes	1999-2000	Penfold Grange Development Phase 1	Local family who lived at Five Oaks
Myrtle Lane	Martin Grant Homes	2013	Marketing Name - Cobbett's Mews - 10 homes	Shrub Name
Newbridge Road				'la Nieubrugge' 1317
Newstead Hall, Adversane		2003	Development of 7 Mews Houses	On site of former hotel
Nightingale Walk	Gleeson Homes	1978-80		Probable developer name
Norman Close	Shared Ownership	M 1990's	Development of 59 homes	Uncertain
Oaklands		L 1950's		On site of part of garden of Broomfield Lodge/Knights
Okehurst Lane				Robert de Okehurst 1279
Osmund Court, Rowan Drive	Saxon Weald	2006	Flats For The Elderly	Probable developer name
Ostlers View	Hilbery Chaplin	1982		Faced Cedars Farm which had stabling
Pegasus Court, High Street	Pegasus Retirement Homes PLC	2002	Flats For The Elderly	From developer name
Petworth Court, Brooker's Road	Bellway Homes	2002-03		From Petworth town
Pine Close		M 1960's		Tree name

Platts Meadow	Shared ownership	1998-99		Probable Developer Name
Pond Close	Shared ownership	1998-99		There were small ponds in the vicinity
Renton Close	Sunley Homes	1974-76		Local family prominent in local affairs
Roman Way	Shared ownership	M 1990's		Inspired by the Roman Road Stane Street
Rosehill - South		c.1970		After house that stood on site
Rosehill - North		c.1987-88		After house that stood on site
Rosier Way		L 1950's	From the name Roserslond	After nearby wood - name first recorded in 1379
Rowan Court, Rowan Drive		L 1960's		Tree name
Rowan Drive		M 1960's		Tree name
Rowner Road			From the farm Ruwenore (1261)	Meaning 'at the rough bank'
St Gabriels Road	Gleeson Homes	1978-80		After Catholic church to the N
St Mary's Close		1988		After nearby Parish Church
Saddlers Close	Barratt Homes/ Saxon Weald	2008-09		Probable Developer Name
Saville Court, Station Road		1972		Built on site of house known as Saville House
Saville Gardens, Station Road		1972		Built on site of house known as Saville House
Saxon Close		M 1990's		Inspired by the Saxon origins of Billingshurst
Silver Lane (South End)		E 1960's		Silver Birches line the road
Silver Lane (North End)		M 1960's		Silver Birches line the road
Skylarks	Bryant Homes/ Taylor Woodrow	2002-03	Penfold Grange Development Phase 5	Skylarks could be heard here!!
Stemp Drive	Sunley Homes	1974-76		Local family name
Summers Place	Berkeley Homes	L 2000's	Mews houses around Summers Place	From Richard Somere first recorded in 1369
Sussex Court, Brooker's Road	Bellway Homes	2002-03		County Name
The Alders	Taylor Wimpey/ Saxon Weald	2011-12	Alders Edge Development (27 Properties)	Tree name
The Maltings, Jengers Mead	Barratt Homes	1999-2000	Marketing Name - Amberley Court - 18 units & shop	Named after the Malthouse that stood here

The Wadeys	Sunley Homes	1974-76		After local builder founded 1884
The Willows	Taywood Homes	2001-02	Penfold Grange Development Phase 4	Tree name
Treetops		L 2000's	Development of 16 homes	Named after house owned by the Wadey Family in East Street
Turner Avenue	Taywood Homes	2001-02	Penfold Grange Development Phase 4	Local family name – joint founder of Baptist Chapel
Weald Court, Station Road		1973		May have taken name from the school or the Weald as an area
Wicks Road	Sunley Homes	1974-76		Local family name
Willow Drive	Sunley Homes	1970-71		Tree name
Windmill Place	Devine Homes PLC	2012		Development name - road name not yet allocated
Woodlands Way		L 1950's		Adjoins woodland
Road Name Not Allocated	Charles Church	2013	Imperium Gate - Development of 14 homes	On site of Wadey's Builder's Yard
Daux Road - Station View	Thakeham Homes	2013	Station View - Development of 14 homes	On site of Thomas Keating's Factory

Acknowledgements and further reading

West Sussex within Living Memory – West Sussex Federation of Women's Institutes
The West Sussex Village Book – Tony Wales
London's Lost Route to the Sea – P.A.L. Vine
The Wey & Arun Junction Canal – P.A.L. Vine
Folklore of Sussex – Jacqueline Simpson
Trees, Woods & Man – H.L. Edlin
Stories of Old Horsham – Frank Holmes
My Animal Life – Maggie Gee
Crawley to Littlehampton – Mitchell and Smith
Bombers over Sussex, 1943-45 – Burgess and Saunders.
The Locke-Kings of Brooklands Weybridge – J.S.L. Pulford
Victorian Horsham, The Diary of Henry Michell – Kenneth Neale
The Unitarian Chapel, Billingshurst, A Celebration (2004)
Kelly's Post Office Directory of 1867, 1969 and 1973
The Billingshurst Society Newsletters, lent by Mrs. Jane Paton
Pauline Taylor – The Taverns of Billingshurst, Articles
Jane Robinson – A force to be Reckoned With, A History of the Women's Institute.
Billy Hoad – Diaries and Recollections
Madeleine Woods – about Tom Topper
Sussex Archaeological Collections
Mrs. G. Maria Ireland – a memoire WSRO
Tom Topper Remembers – WSRO
Peter Stockwood Remembers. Advice on Angling Society
The Development of Timber-framed Houses in the Sussex Weald – Diana Chatwin
From Hadfoldshern...to Adversane – Deborah Evershed
Going off the rails, The Country Railway in West Sussex – Gage, Harris and Sullivan
Highways and Byways in Sussex – E.V. Lucas
Social History of Edwardian Britain – James Bishop
The Village Parliaments – Valerie Porter
A History of Sussex – J.R. Armstrong
The Mena House Treasury – Andreas Augustin
Author – The Weald School - A History
The West Sussex Gazette July 1995
The West Sussex County Times

Mrs. Jane Paton – advice, records of Kingsfold, loan of maps and records
Mr. Paul Smith – advice and research, in particular 'roads and estates'.
Mrs. Wendy Lines – two books on Billingshurst, advice and research
Mr. John Hurd – advice and guidance from his authoritative original research which directly and indirectly has informed this book
Mrs Jackie Charman – advice on BDS
Mrs. Di Burroughs – advice on Tennis Club
Mrs. Gillian Yarham – advice on WI
Mrs. B.M.Barraclough – advice on Bowling Club
Mr Gordon New – advice on Football Club
Mr David Lowe - advice on Billingshurst Choral Society
Mr David Thompson - Lions Club
Mrs Jackie Bench – advice on Choral Society and Tennis Club
Mr. Myers, Roger Patterson, Roger Lusted and Jim Burroughs –
history of Billingshurst cricket
Mrs. Helen Abbott – advice and research on 5 Oaks, herself advised by Derek Sims, Roy Dumbril, John Morris, Yvonne Wolzak
Phyllis Adam - account of Tedfold Estate in Billingshurst Newsletter No. 82
Mrs. Sheila Van den Bergh – research materials, photographs and advice
Mrs. Wendy Holmes – records of Five Oaks
Mr. Julian Morgan – Hon Sec Wey & Arun Canal Trust. www.weyandarun.uk Contact – office@weyandarun.co.uk advice and photographs
English Heritage.
Mr. John Griffin - encouragement and proof-reading
My wife Gillian and daughter, Sarah Moloney, with grateful thanks for their patience and boundless support.

Index

Omissions: The Index does NOT include spelling variants and obsolete terminology nor names of people and places listed in Kelly's Directory, indicated on maps and illustrations or listed in 'Roads and Estates' and 'Weald Alumni' unless they occur elsewhere in the text.

Adversane, *passim*
Agate, 185
Aileen Walker, 16, 57, 188
Alick's Hill, 21, 80, 85, 86, 88, 142
Allen, 40, 43, 44, 170, 181, 188, 189, 196
Allman, 19, 164
Alman, 81
Almond, 121
Alwyn, 58
Andrew Hill, 136
Argent, 102
Arnold, 59, 197
Austin's, 19, 162
Aylward, 187
Ayre, 21, 197
Bank of England, 97
Baptist, 19, 53, 72, 81, 82, 94, 97, 140, 204
Barclays, 87
Barkhall, 42
Barralets, 79
Barry Barnes, 121
Bartelott, 50
Bassett's Fee, 50, 95, 162
Baxter, 180, 197
Beath, 164, 192
Beck, 9, 21, 22, 35, 59, 82
Beke, 38, 39, 195
Belcher, 164
Bench, 37, 121, 123, 206
Bettesworth, 165, 166
Betts, 117
Bignor, 50

Billingshurst Centre, 3
Birch Drive, 49, 195, 199
Blacksmith, 9, 127, 179
Blue Idol, 10, 59
Blundells, 139
Blunden, 89, 197
Bohm, 44
Bolden, 152
Bondwick, 137
Botting, 50, 68, 192, 193
Bousfield, 105, 195
Bowling Alley, 9, 19, 87, 88
Bowring, 178
Brereton, 23
Brian Barnes, 57
Brick House, 138, 192
Bridgeman, 31
Brier, 33
Brinsbury, 8
Brookers, 85, 199
Broomfield, 24, 79, 199, 202
Broomfield Lodge, 79, 202
Broomfields, 49, 81
Brown, 70, 193, 196
Buckmans, 50, 164
Budgen's, 48, 68, 91
Burge, 160
Burnt Row, 8, 73
Burntrough, 8
Burroughs, 36, 111, 121, 123, 148, 151, 197, 206
Bush, 160

Caffyn, 53
Campbell, 106
Carew-Gibson, 31, 44
Carley, 179, 196
Carnsew, 167, 191, 192
Carpenters, 26, 28, 48, 85, 116, 186, 196, 200
Carpenters Arms, 186
Carter, 68, 94, 192
Cartmell, 124
Cartner, 179
Causeway, 84, 97
Cedars, 137, 173, 200, 202
Champion, 34, 57, 126, 159
Chanctonbury, 2
Charman, 106, 192, 206
Cheeseman, 111
Chequer, 165
Cherryman, 45, 46
Chesman, 164, 192
Chime, 87
Chitty, 48
Church Path, 87, 99
Clark, 34, 46, 47, 137, 148, 154, 192
Clarksland, 29, 137
Clayton, 164
Clear, 95, 126, 162
Cleveland, 24, 85, 89
Clevelands, 46, 107, 173, 200
Clock Gallery, 49
Cobb's Wood, 34
Cobbett, 23, 60, 61, 64, 167, 185, 202
Community Gardens, 9
Congregational, 19, 84, 87, 166, 195
Conner, 171
Convent School, 94, 197
Coombe Hill, 87, 139, 200
Coombland, 52
Cooper, 28, 30, 95, 164

Copped Hall, 52, 197
Cornell, 35
Cosway, 39
Cowan, 23, 189
Coxbrook, 29, 48
Crawford, 119
Cripps, 21, 57, 90, 107, 139, 196
Crisp, 105, 106, 107, 196
Croft Villas, 19
Croucher, 166
Cullen, 178
Dalbiac, 109
Dale, 164
Darrow, 57
Dashwood, 66, 185
Daux, 11, 15, 29, 34, 50, 53, 77, 83, 87, 94, 116, 196, 197, 198, 200, 204
Daux Wood, 11, 34, 83, 87, 200
Davis, 33, 105
Deborah Evershed, 44, 59, 75, 180, 205
Dell Lane, 99, 132, 200
Denman, 129
Di Burroughs, 121, 123, 206
Domesday, 50, 68
Dors, 39, 57, 89
Drew, 88
Duckmore, 29, 88
Dudley-White, 91
Duffield, 33
Dugdale, 22, 23, 119
Duncans, 35, 52, 59, 192
Dutton, 85
East Street, *passim*
Easton, 38, 105, 120, 121, 200
Ede, 68
Edgar, 17, 97
Elling, 160
Elliott, 117
Enfield, 57, 90

Evershed, 34, 44, 53, 58, 59, 70, 71, 75, 94, 109, 180, 192, 193, 205
Falkner, 121
Family Church, 10
Farguhar, 31
Farhall, 43, 126, 192, 193
Farmer, 105, 106, 128, 173
Faulkner, 57
Ferring, 39, 43, 162
Fewhurst, 36, 39, 49, 192, 197
Fielding, 21, 50, 59, 169, 170
Fieldings Cottage, 164, 170, 177
Fiest, 187
Finlanger, 34
Firminger, 34
Five Oaks, *passim*
Flynn, 38, 195
Fold Farm, 164, 197
Forge Way, 116, 200
Fossbrooks, 51, 136
Foster, 145, 152
Four Seasons, 36
Fox, 15, 59
Frogshole, 50
Frye, 95
Fure, 29, 39, 43, 44, 94, 162
Furze View, 171
Garton, 21, 30, 68, 95, 137
Gatefield, 50
Gatwick, 78, 120
Gierth, 106
Gilmans, 37, 38, 48, 96, 116, 136, 137, 197
Gilmour, 57
Gingers, 26, 162, 183, 201
Glaysher, 116
Gleniffer, 120, 177
Goff, 20, 109, 165, 167
Goldings, 39, 102, 165, 166, 192
Gordon, 16, 56, 72, 206

Gore, 52, 87, 96
Goring, 50, 68, 191
Grainingfold, 52, 164, 178, 195, 198
Gratwicke, 24, 91, 119, 120, 167, 172, 173, 183, 201
Gravett, 93, 96
Gray, 46
Great Daux, 50, 53, 77, 94, 197
Great Grooms, 51, 86, 136
Greenfield, 28, 29, 30, 39, 41, 42, 43, 95, 141, 170, 186, 192
Griffin, 170, 171, 201
Groomsland, 85, 136, 137, 197, 201
Guildenhurst, 68, 162, 197
Gynguire, 26, 183
Hadfold, 48, 192
Hadfoldshern, 59, 179, 205
Halahan, 33, 34
Haler, 70, 164
Hammond, 23, 68, 193
Hard, 44, 90
Harries, 44
Harvey, 106
Harwood, 93, 171, 193
Hayes House, 166
Hayler, 164
Helsdon, 93
Henshaw, 95, 187
Herbert, 23
Hereford, 19, 84, 196
Hickford, 153
Hicks, 37, 159
Higgins, 107, 197
High Fure, 29, 39, 43, 44, 94
High Road, 26
High Seat, 19, 51, 89, 192, 196, 201
High Street, *passim*
Hilland, 5, 177, 195, 197
Hillview, 86, 88, 89, 142, 196, 201

Hoad, 140, 166, 205
Hobson, 89
Holden, 12, 31, 99, 166
Hole, 38, 66, 72, 73
Holly, 15, 151, 152, 153
Holmes, 85, 205, 206
Holy Well, 99
Hookers, 54
Horelands, 95
Horsham, *passim*
Howles, 39
Hubert, 92, 109
Humphries, 105, 106, 196
Hunt, 31, 139
Hurd, 70, 94, 100, 187, 206
Hurstlands, 136, 201
Imperium, 137, 204
Ingfield, 59, 169, 171, 201
International, 57, 128, 133, 139, 195
Ireland, 44, 76, 81, 109, 165, 166, 192, 205
Jabeena, 37
Jane's Tea Garden, 133, 196
Jeffery, 53
Jengers Mead, 84, 91, 116, 128, 183, 196, 197, 201, 202, 203
Jenny Wren, 51, 86, 136
Jestico, 116
Johnson, 44, 196, 197
Jones, 106, 123, 124, 139, 159
Joyce, 120
Joyes, 19
Jubilee Fields, 7, 8, 9, 103, 109, 111, 116, 121, 155, 172
Jubilee Meadow, 83, 87, 116
Julius, 31
Jupp, 165, 193
Juppsland, 179, 197
Keatings, 83, 167
Kerr, 120

King's Arms, 9, 53, 60, 81, 87, 89, 98, 127, 139, 142, 183, 185, 186, 191, 193
King's Head, 88, 119, 127, 183, 187, 189, 193
Kings Arms, 66, 141
Kingsbury, 31
Kingsfold Close, 18, 34, 201
Kingslea, 35, 46, 197, 198
Kingston, 22
Knight, 162, 166, 170
Knob's Crook, 51
Lake, 22, 103, 146
Laker, 82, 87, 89, 191, 192, 193
Lakers Meadow, 18, 90, 201
Lane, *passim*
Lathy, 126
Law, 57
Lawes, 148, 151
Lawrenson, 119, 197
Leaman, 38, 105
Lee, 29, 63, 102, 103, 159
Leisure Centre, 8, 116, 125, 130, 156
Leyhold, 72, 73
library, 53, 82, 128, 150, 152, 158
Limeburners, 65, 103
Lines, 21, 33, 94, 125, 126, 206
Little Daux, 83, 87, 94, 116, 197
Little East S, 19, 196
Lloyds Bank, 19, 183
Locke-King, 50, 59, 167, 168, 169, 170, 205
Lockyers, 29, 183
Longhurst, 8, 33
Lordings, 63, 65, 90, 119, 202
Lorlins, 79, 197
Loxwood, 20, 62, 66
Luckin, 19, 98, 172, 174
Lugg, 87, 197, 202
Lusted, 89, 107, 111, 206
Lutyens, 91

Wolzak, 178, 206
Women's Hall, 9, 53, 59, 82, 93, 105, 106, 143, 145, 198
Wooddale, 88, 167, 177
Woodhouse, 39, 197, 198
Woodman, 157
Woodworm, 113
World Stores, 139
Wright, 34, 110, 180, 191
Wyndham, 64
Wynstrode, 52, 59, 119, 123
Yarham, 58, 206

70, 106, 123, 124, 125, 165, 171, 187
St. Mary's Room, 9
Stafford, 164, 178, 195, 198
Stane Street, 12, 26, 31, 33, 35, 36, 97, 136, 154, 162, 164, 170, 179, 199, 203
Stanley, 44, 59, 92, 124, 198
Stanton, 172
Star Inn, 183
Steepwood, 33, 34, 44, 57
Steere, 141
Stiles, 79, 167
Stocker, 35, 44, 47, 108, 198
Stockwood, 89, 103, 205
Streele, 70, 71
Stroller, 57, 90
Stydolf, 28, 68
Summers, 20, 21, 29, 48, 94, 96, 109, 162, 165, 166, 197, 198, 203
Surgery, 9, 92, 93
Taintland, 162, 187
Tarrant, 62
Taylor, 45, 111, 180, 185, 186, 187, 201, 202, 203, 205
Tedfold, 8, 70, 71, 72, 73, 87, 116, 192, 206
The Ship, 138
Thorne, 165
Tiler, 80, 98, 174
Toat, 48
Tony Smith, 110
Topper, 84, 88, 119, 205
Town Hall, 61
Towner, 83
Townland, 19, 81, 162
Towse, 31, 34, 166, 170, 191, 193
Tredcroft, 188
Trees, 87, 205
Tribe, 139
Trinity Reformed Church, 9
Trower, 87, 127

Truelove, 97
Tucker, 33
Turner, 44, 53, 94, 193, 204
Twyford, 34
Unitarian Chapel, 10, 53, 205
Upton, 111
Van den Bergh, 44, 59, 171, 198, 206
Voice, 82, 83, 110, 138, 165, 170, 191, 193, 195, 196, 198
Wadey, 21, 44, 94, 99, 107, 109, 110, 136, 142, 165, 177, 191, 194, 196, 200, 204
Wakeford, 23
Wakoos, 8, 130, 149, 156
Wales, 70, 168, 205
Watts, 19, 21, 128
Weald School, 8, 10, 11, 22, 23, 37, 57, 78, 89, 103, 107, 111, 116, 121, 124, 125, 130, 136, 137, 144, 159, 160, 161, 164, 172, 198, 205
Weavers, 8, 97
Weavers Cottage, 8
Well, 17, 73, 99, 166
Wells, 126
West, *passim*
West Street, 8, 26, 90, 97, 188, 200
Western by-pass, 11, 18
Westminster, 138
Wey & Arun, 62, 64, 65, 66, 205, 206
Wheeler, 172
Whirlwind, 10, 79
White Horse Inn, 183, 187
Wicks, 21, 204
Wiggonholt, 66, 162, 164, 170, 177
Wildens, 84, 197
Wilding, 35, 57, 172
Williams, 97, 171, 198
Williamson, 161, 196
Willowbrook, 171
Wisborough, *passim*

213

Pocokes, 39
Pole, 171, 178
Pollard, 106
Pond Cottage, 170
Poplar, 171, 196
Portbury, 70
Post Office, 84, 87, 91, 139, 171, 188, 191, 193, 195, 205
Potbury, 36
Pound Cottage, 50
Pounds, 95, 162
Pratt, 48
Primary School, 10, 161
Pruess, 106
Pryor, 30, 31
Pullen, 177, 178
Puttock, 19, 21, 48, 81, 107, 109, 110, 126, 127, 152, 153, 162, 173, 192, 193
Quakers, 10, 30
Radbourne, 93, 142, 172
Railway Hotel, 119, 120, 190
Rape of Arundel, 39, 162, 164
Read, 57
Red Lane, 87
Reed, 160, 193
Renton, 20, 21, 59, 89, 145, 203
Rhodes, 87, 88, 89, 97, 139, 197
Ringwood, 73
Rising Sun, 81, 183, 189
Roberts, 57, 89
Roman Road, 19, 100, 203
Roman Way, 3, 9, 92, 203
Rose, 87, 89, 138, 140
Rose Hill, 89, 138
Rosier, 15, 83, 162, 174, 196, 203
Rowan Drive, 139, 202, 203
Rowe, 44
Rowfold, 20, 21, 59, 145, 177, 192
Rowfold Grange, 20, 59, 145, 177

Rowner, 28, 30, 50, 63, 65, 66, 68, 69, 87, 90, 168, 192, 203
Rudgwick, 5, 9, 76, 140, 162, 164, 168, 188
Sainsbury, 57, 111, 159
Salt, 171
Saunders, 117, 205
Saville, 79, 85, 203
Saxon Weald, 4, 199, 201, 202, 203
SCATS, 97, 133, 197
Scattergood, 171
Scolding, 35, 37
Scott, 164
Sendall, 53
Sharville, 179
Shepherd, 99, 148
Shepley-Shepley, 50, 169
Sheppard, 110
Sherlock, 21, 59, 119, 123, 195, 198
Shilcock, 31, 192
Shire Cottage, 165
Shirley Cafe, 133, 196
Short, 95
Sillett, 113
Silver Lane, 24, 203
Simkin, 16
Six Bells, 81, 87, 89, 97, 139, 187, 188
Skinner, 70, 116, 171, 172
Slaters, 40
Slinfoldland, 164, 168, 170, 197
Smart, 141, 192
Smith, 75, 97, 110, 197, 198, 199, 205, 206
Somer, 96, 162
Sonny Harrison, 117
Sopp, 44
South Eaton, 73
South House, 29, 30, 37, 38, 39, 40, 43, 44, 50, 52
St. Gabriel's, 8, 9, 10
St. Mary's, 9, 10, 30, 35, 43, 49, 50, 59, 68,

Luxford, 20, 21, 44, 92, 118, 172, 202
Maggie Gee, 57, 205
Maille, 91
Malaya, 185, 196
Malthouse, 79, 103, 189, 203
Maltings, 79, 101, 119, 138, 181, 183, 203
Manor Fields, 9, 19
Manor House, 50, 116, 142, 162, 165, 173, 192, 202
Marten, 83
Maslin, 37, 197
Maude, 2
May, 33, 44, 81, 99, 120, 141, 153, 154, 156, 204
McMurrugh, 111
McVeigh Parker, 36
Mears, 126
Meetens, 31
Mena, 168, 205
Merrikin, 86
Messinger, 172
Michell, 23, 188, 189, 190, 205
Miles, 59, 180
Mill Way, 10, 202
Millais, 111
Minstrells, 164
Mission Hut, 171
Mitchell, 188, 205
Molly Church, 105
Moreton, 105
Morris, 20, 21, 59, 93, 170, 197, 202, 206
Mothers' Garden, 9
Mursell, 98, 195
Myrtle Lane, 8, 82, 107, 202
Naldrett, 70, 192
Natts Lane, 8, 26, 31, 136, 197, 201
Nevin, 105, 106, 107
Newbridge, 9, 26, 44, 62, 63, 64, 66, 67, 69, 81, 89, 90, 97, 103, 119, 136, 162, 181, 197, 201, 202
Newcomb, 109, 116
Newman, 126, 177
Newstead Hall, 179, 202
Norris, 21, 91, 110, 167, 197
North Eaton, 72
North Heath, 136
Nye, 164
Oak House, 102, 165
Oakdene, 46
Okehurst, 49, 50, 52, 59, 95, 119, 162, 166, 168, 170, 195, 197, 198, 202
Old Cottage, 51
Old Hayes, 72
Old House, 179, 180
Old Smithy, 170
Oulds, 105, 106, 196
Overington, 178
Palmer, 28, 39, 46, 164
Parbrook, 26, 31, 33, 51, 86, 88, 100, 135, 136, 137, 139, 164, 174, 192, 196
Parish Council, 2, 3, 4, 5, 6, 11, 12, 19, 20, 33, 38, 57, 59, 89, 105, 111, 116, 119, 120, 121, 149, 156, 175, 200, 202
Parminter, 46
Parr, 154
Paton, 11, 37, 57, 152, 205, 206
Patterson, 54, 58, 111, 159, 197, 206
Pavey, 116, 170
Pear Tree, 54, 197
Penfold, 28, 30, 39, 48, 95, 164, 165, 199, 201, 202, 203, 204
Penn, 59, 60
Pennybrooks, 49
Petras, 111
Philips, 110
Pickering, 130
Pilchers, 139
Pinkhurst, 26, 48, 162, 165